Beyond One L

Beyond One L

*Stories About Finding Meaning and
Making a Difference in Law*

—

EDITED BY
NANCY LEVIT & ALLEN ROSTRON

Library of Congress Cataloging-in-Publication Data

Names: Levit, Nancy, editor. | Rostron, Allen, editor.
Title: Beyond One L : stories about finding meaning and making a difference
in law / edited by Nancy Levit, Allen Rostron.
Description: Durham, North Carolina : Carolina Academic Press, LLC, 2018.
Identifiers: LCCN 2018034485 | ISBN 9781531008352 (alk. paper)
Subjects: LCSH: Law students—United States—Handbooks, manuals, etc. |
Law schools—United States. | Law—Vocational guidance—United States.
Classification: LCC KF287 .B49 2018 | DDC 340.071/173—dc23
LC record available at https://lccn.loc.gov/2018034485

e-ISBN 978-1-5310-0836-9

Carolina Academic Press, LLC
700 Kent Street
Durham, North Carolina 27701
Telephone (919) 489-7486
Fax (919) 493-5668

We dedicate this book with love to:

Tim, Dylan, Aaron, Jon, Jess, Macs, Clara, Barb, Bob, and Bonnie
NEL

Cameron and Carter
AKR

and with gratitude to the thousands of students
who have enriched our lives.
NEL and *AKR*

Contents

Introduction

NANCY LEVIT & ALLEN ROSTRON

Scott Turow's *One L* is the classic account of the first year of law school. Every year, thousands of those about to enter law school, or just thinking about applying for admission, read Turow's riveting description of his experiences as a new student at Harvard Law School. The book has frightened, informed, and inspired a generation of lawyers-to-be.

Beyond One L is a collection of stories taking a further look at the often dramatic and sometimes traumatic experience of embarking on the study of law. The stories come from lawyers, law students, law professors, and judges, who attended a wide variety of law schools across the country. Several attended law school before Scott Turow, most in the years after. Two of the authors were in Turow's class at Harvard, but their experiences differed from his in intriguing ways. Many of the writers have taken their stories beyond just their first year in law school. They have written *Two L*, *Three L*, and *Bar Exam* for you. Some segue into their first years in practice. Others write about the game-changing events and decisions that altered the course of their practice or made them leave law altogether.

Much of what *One L* describes are universal truths about law school. Anyone who has run the gauntlet of legal education, no matter when or where, can relate to them. Trying to parse the dense verbiage of judicial opinions, being baffled by obscure legal terminology, relishing the atmosphere of intellectual excitement and competition, dreading the prospect of facing a decimating barrage of Socratic questioning in class. Admiring an eminently learned professor, or despising an exceedingly egotistical one. Disdaining the "gunner" students who obsequiously seek professors' attention, or dreading the possibility that you've become the "gunner" that all your classmates abhor. The fear of failure, the emotional roller coaster, the study groups, the nervous anticipation of grades, the camaraderie and bonding with fellow sufferers, the amount of focus that law school demands, the stress of having a course grade depend on a single exam at the end of the semester, the exhilaration of facing and surviving a momentous challenge. These and many other daunting and rewarding aspects of law school remain remarkably unchanged.

The diversity of law school experiences, and the way those experiences have changed over time, are equally striking. Turow arrived at the hallowed halls of Harvard in the fall of 1975, long before most of today's law students were born. During Turow's first few weeks of classes, Patty Hearst was arrested for armed robbery, former Teamsters' Union president Jimmy Hoffa disappeared, and one of Charles Manson's followers tried to assassinate President Gerald Ford. It was a time when disco music, mood rings, and pet rocks were the hot new fads. Law students did not have personal computers, the Internet, e-mail, or cell phones, let alone Westlaw, Lexis, Google, Facebook, Instagram, Snapchat, and Twitter.

The vast majority of Turow's classmates were male, white, and straight. Only about one in four of those who started law school in 1975 were women and less than one in ten were racial minorities. Today, nearly half of all law students are women and almost a quarter are minorities. Law schools now commonly have organizations for lesbian, gay, bisexual, and transgendered students.

And of course, most students entering one of the nation's 200 law schools are not entering an Ivy League institution. Many are not, as Turow was, coming to law school after a prior career or with a spouse. Many law students are single, some are parents, some are pregnant, some are working during the day and attending law school at night.

Law school may not be as frantic, stressful, or miserable as it was in 1975. The process of legal education has changed over time and it is different at different schools. Many law professors believe in "humanizing" legal education. While they may use the Socratic method, they employ it in a less terrorizing manner. Law school is still incredibly demanding, but technology enhances the efficiency of students' research, studying, outlining, and job searches. Law students in the new millennium can do a quick mass mail merge of their job search letters rather than typing each one individually on an Olivetti or a Selectric. Students now have access, for good or for ill, to blogs, discussion groups, and huge caches of outlines from prior semesters. They can readily call, text, e-mail, or Skype friends and family members for emotional support.

Most law schools today are kinder and gentler than Harvard was in 1975. The workload is somewhat less crushing, and most law schools have programs of academic support. The message is different. It used to be "Look to your left, look to your right, one of you won't be here next year." The message today at many schools is, "Look to your left, look to your right. These are the people who will be your colleagues, partners, or the judge in front of whom you will be practicing twenty years from now. Treat them well." Classes now available at law schools across the country include Environmental Law, Animal Law, Law and Economics, and Negotiation. A number of schools offer mindfulness and meditation classes, and one law school in the northwest provides therapy dogs during finals. During law school, more students are finding their own directions rather than stepping on the institutional glide path where the only brass rings are top grades, Law Review, and a job offer from a big law firm. Law review and moot court are still premier activities at most schools, but there are many more activities, organizations, and ways to fit in. The first year of law school is often no longer a harrowing ordeal.

What comes after the 1L year is the path toward lawyers' professional lives. The second and third years of law school are packed—with elective courses, internship or externship programs with judges or government agencies, live client clinics, moot court, and law journal experiences. Students are searching for jobs and studying for (and dreading) the bar exam, usually a two-day event with one day testing knowledge of multi-state law through 200 multiple choice questions and the other day devoted to a grueling series of essay questions. Law school grads faced a grim job market after the financial crisis of 2008, but the market began recovering in 2015 and the Bureau of Labor projects that over the next decade job growth for lawyers will be about average compared to other occupations. The median annual salary for lawyers in 2016 was $118,160. The structure of legal practice is changing, with an increase in the number of solo practitioners and small firms, globalization taking lawyers across the world, and the development of firm initiatives toward diversity, pro bono work, and community involvement.

The culture of legal practice is changing as well, with greater collaboration, teamwork, and mentoring. Law firms are becoming more nimble, recognizing both their clients' and lawyers' desires for something other than the billable hour model. As the Cleveland law firm of Tucker Ellis says, "Clients want to pay us for what we do, not how long it takes us to do it." Lawyers seek greater work-life balance and firms are beginning to accommodate them, with formal leave, flexible work schedules, and sabbatical policies. Truth be told, most law firms have not installed, as Google did in its Zurich office, a slide from an upper floor down to the lunchroom. But Bartlitt Beck offers a basketball court and a rock-climbing wall. A small firm in Kansas has a nice foosball table in the break room.

Most lawyers change jobs at least once—only 15 percent hold the same job at the end of their career that they had at graduation. The national average is to change jobs three times. Some lawyers who contributed stories for this book had real game-changers: a lawyer at a conference happens to wander into a session on judicial careers and winds up being inspired to become a judge; a college journalist becomes a lawyer and then ultimately goes back to writing and develops the largest legal tabloid blog in the country; a former state supreme court Chief Justice steps down from the bench and becomes a Buddhist monk. These stories are of people who found meaning in law or used their legal training as a springboard to another career. Some of the stories in *Beyond One L* offer, at least in some small part, an antidote to disillusionment with the legal profession.

Stories are a particularly fitting way to reflect on law school experiences and glimpse possible alternative futures. Storytelling is a fundamental part of legal practice, teaching, and thought. Telling stories as a method of practicing law reaches back to the days of the classical Greek orators who were lawyers. Before legal education became an academic matter, the apprenticeship system for training lawyers consisted of mentoring and telling "war stories."

Over the last few decades, storytelling has become a subject of enormous interest and controversy within the world of legal scholarship. Law review articles appeared in the form of stories. Law professors pointed out that legal decisions were really just stories that told a dominant narrative.

Critical theorists began to tell counterstories to challenge or critique the traditional canon. Some used fictional stories as a method of analytical critique; others told accounts of actual events in ways that gave voice to the experiences of outsiders.

Storytelling began to make its way into legal education in new ways. For instance, a major textbook publisher developed a new series of books that recount the stories behind landmark cases in specific subject areas, such as Torts or Employment Discrimination, to help students appreciate not only the players in major cases, but also the social context in which cases arise. Meanwhile, Scott Turow, John Grisham, and a legion of other lawyers invaded the realm of popular fiction and conquered the bestseller lists.

Legal theorists began to recognize what historians and practicing lawyers had long known and what cognitive psychologists were just discovering—the extraordinary power of stories. Stories are the way people, including judges and jurors, understand situations. People recall events in story form. Stories teach; they illuminate different perspectives and evoke empathy. Stories create bonds; their evocative details engage people in ways that sterile legal arguments do not.

The stories in *Beyond One L* reveal much about why the first year of law school leaves such intense and lasting impressions. Whether attending law school is in your future or your past, we hope you enjoy reading them.

Authors' Biographies

MELISSA ANDERSON graduated from St. Mary's School of Law in 2011. As a child, Melissa and her siblings suffered severe abuse at the hands of her parents, who beat, tortured, and starved their 16 children. At the age of 17 she escaped by joining the Army, where she met her husband. After leaving active duty, Melissa began her journey to law school at a community college, working her way from basic arithmetic to a bachelor's degree at the University of Arizona and then on to law school. Melissa managed to graduate at the top of her class despite juggling her coursework with her responsibilities as a mother of six with a husband on active duty in Iraq. Melissa's father is now serving two life sentences for abusing Melissa and her siblings, and Melissa devotes her career to practicing family law and representing the victims of child abuse. Melissa is also the author of a children's book, *The Big Fib*.

IAN AYRES graduated from Yale Law School in 1986. Two years later, he earned a Ph.D. in Economics from M.I.T. Ian's wide-ranging interests have led him into a number of fields, and he has enjoyed success in each of them. In 2006, his book with Greg Klass, *Insincere Promises: The Law of Misrepresented Intent,* won the Scribes book award for legal scholarship. Ian also writes a column for *Forbes* magazine, contributes to the Freakonomics blog, and has been a commentator on public radio's *Marketplace*. All told, he has published 11 books and written more than 100 professional articles on a wide array of topics. His best-selling books include: *Carrots and Sticks: Unlock the Power of Incentives to Get Things Done, Super Crunchers: Why Thinking-By-Numbers Is the New Way to Be Smart,* and *Why Not? How to Use Everyday Ingenuity to Solve Problems Big and Small* (with Barry Nalebuff). Ian is currently the William K. Townsend Professor of Law and an Anne Urowsky Professorial Fellow in Law at Yale Law School, and he also teaches at Yale's School of Management.

JOSH BLACKMAN graduated from the George Mason University School of Law in 2009. Later that year, while working as a federal district court law clerk, Josh launched FantasySCOTUS.net, a website hosting predictions and analysis of upcoming cases being decided by the U.S. Supreme Court. The site was an instant success, attracting the attention of national media outlets and prominent judges alike. Josh is a founder and currently the president of the Harlan Institute, a nonprofit dedicated to teaching high school students about the Constitution and American law through interactive online games. Following a Sixth Circuit federal appellate court clerkship and a Teaching Fellowship at the Pennsylvania State University Dickinson School of Law, he joined the South Texas College of Law faculty in the fall of 2012. He is the author of *Unprecedented: The Constitutional Challenge to Obamacare* and *Unraveled: Obamacare, Religious Liberty, and Executive Power.*

PAMELA BRIDGEWATER graduated from Florida State University College of Law. Much of her career was spent working as a lawyer, advocate, and activist for reproductive rights. She worked as a legal aid lawyer specializing in advanced directives for people living with HIV/AIDS and defended reproductive health care clinics and service providers. Her work in this area led to collaborations with scholars and policymakers, and Pamela served on the boards of Our Bodies Ourselves, *Wagadu: A Journal of Transnational Women's and Gender Studies,* and the Kopkind Project for Journalists and Activists. Pamela's professional articles have been published in prominent law reviews and journals, and she blogged at *www.hiphoplaw.blogspot.com.* She was the editor, with Donald Tibbs and andré douglas pond cummings, of *Hip Hop and the Law.* Pamela taught for many years at American University's Washington College of Law. She passed away in 2014.

ALAFAIR BURKE graduated from Stanford Law School in 1994. After clerking on the Ninth Circuit Court of Appeals, Alafair cut her teeth as a Deputy District Attorney with the Multnomah County District Attorney's office. Although she left the DA's office for private practice in the Buffalo, New York, office of Phillips Lytle LLP in 1999 before joining the faculty of Hofstra University School of Law in 2001, Alafair's experience as a prosecutor has continued to shape her career. She has published more than a dozen professional articles and presented at numerous conferences, many of them dealing with topics related to prosecution. She has also found an outlet for her experiences in the realm of fiction, having published two series of best-selling mystery novels, including *Judgment Calls, Missing Justice, Close Case, Dead Connection, Angel's Tip, 212*, and the standalones, *Long Gone, The Ex,* and *The Wife*.

STEPHEN L. CARTER graduated from Yale Law School in 1979. After clerking first on the U.S. Court of Appeals for the District of Columbia Circuit and then for U.S. Supreme Court Justice Thurgood Marshall, Stephen joined the faculty of Yale Law School in 1982. Over the past two decades, Stephen has published a dozen books, both fiction and nonfiction. On the academic side, he has written, among other books, *Reflections of an Affirmative Action Baby, The Confirmation Mess: Cleaning Up the Federal Appointments Process,* and *The Violence of Peace: America's Wars in the Age of Obama*. His first novel, *The Emperor of Ocean Park*, spent 11 weeks on the *New York Times* Bestseller List. In addition, Stephen writes a column for *Bloomberg View*, has contributed to *Newsweek, Christianity Today,* and *The Daily Beast*, and blogs on professional football for the *Washington Post*. Stephen is currently the William Nelson Cromwell Professor of Law at Yale Law School.

CAIT CLARKE graduated from Catholic University's Columbus School of Law in 1999, and then earned an S.J.D. from Harvard Law School. Cait served as the Director of Strategic Initiatives at the National Legal Aid & Defender Association, and then as the Director of Federal Programs at Equal Justice Works in Washington, D.C., a group whose mission is "to mobilize the next generation of public interest lawyers." Throughout all of these years, Cait has been a corporate and non-profit negotiation consultant with Watershed Associates, and is the author of two bestselling books on negotiation, *10 Minute Guide to Negotiating*, and *Dare to Ask: The Woman's Guidebook to Successful Negotiating* (co-authored with Neil Shister). Cait is presently the Chief of the Defender Services Office at the Administrative Office of the U.S. Courts in Washington, D.C.

HALA FURST graduated from the Roger Williams University School of Law in 2010. Prior to attending law school, Hala worked as an actress in Minnesota and California. Since graduating, Hala has been working as a Program Analyst and Presidential Management Fellow at the U.S. Department of Homeland Security.

JUDGE FERNANDO GAITAN graduated from the University of Missouri-Kansas City School of Law in 1974. He started his career as an attorney for the Southwestern Bell Telephone Company before joining the judiciary as a Missouri trial court judge in 1980. He was appointed to the state's court of appeals in 1986 and was nominated to the federal judiciary by President George H.W. Bush in 1991 as a judge on the U.S. District Court for the Western District of Missouri. He served as the Chief Judge of that court from 2007 to 2014, when he assumed senior status.

JUDGE DONN KESSLER graduated from Yale Law School in 1975. Immediately after law school, he served as a Deputy Attorney General for the State of Hawaii for two years, and then as an Assistant Attorney General for the Commonwealth of Virginia. In private practice, he was a trial and appellate attorney at Christian Barton Epps Brent & Chappell in Richmond, Virginia, Jennings Strouss & Salmon, and Ulrich, Kessler & Anger, and then Jones Skelton & Hochuli, all in Phoenix, Arizona. Before his appointment to the Arizona Court of Appeals in 2003, Judge Kessler served for four years as a pro tem judge for that court. He retired from the court in 2017. A strong believer in public service, Judge Kessler was the first chair of the State Bar Appellate Practice Section, as well as chair of the State Bar Antitrust Section, a member of the State Bar Civil Practice and Procedure Committee, and President of the Arizona Association of Healthcare Lawyers. He is the co-author of the *Arizona Healthcare Professional Liability Handbook* and of *Federal Appellate Practice: Ninth Circuit Second Edition*. An equally strong believer in mindfulness practices, Judge Kessler is willing to share his tips about searching for satisfaction and reacting with compassion.

DAVID LAT graduated from Yale Law School in 1999. After clerking on the Ninth Circuit Court of Appeals, a stint with the New York office of Wachtell Lipton Rosen & Katz, and working as a federal prosecutor in New Jersey, David left the practice of law for a career in publishing. David's foray into the media world began in 2004 when he started *Underneath Their Robes*, a cheeky blog about federal judges. When the blog's success created tension with his day job, David left the U.S. Attorney's Office and launched his second blog, *Above the Law*, a legal tabloid. David is currently the editor at large of the site, which enjoys massive popularity as a source of legal news, gossip, and commentary. He is also the author of *Supreme Ambitions: A Novel*.

MIKE LAUSSADE graduated from the University of Texas School of Law in 2006. While in law school, Mike managed to find time between classes and serving as the Editor in Chief of the *Texas Law Review* to write his wildly successful (and hilarious) blog, *Buffalo Wings & Vodka*. Mike is currently a partner in the Dallas office of Jackson Walker LLP and practices corporate and securities law. He has been recognized as one of the "Best Lawyers in Dallas" by *D Magazine* and named to the "Texas Super Lawyers-Rising Stars" list.

JONATHAN LITTLE graduated from the University of Missouri-Kansas City School of Law in 2007. During law school, Jon ran 120 to 140 miles per week, training for the Olympic Trials in the marathon. (He qualified for the Trials by running a 2:21:48 marathon.) After graduation, Jon worked in the county attorney's office in Flagstaff, Arizona. He developed a criminal defense practice, trying cases from cock-fighting to murder, and then moved to Indianapolis to pursue cases for athletes who had been molested by coaches in various U.S. Olympic Committee regulated sports (such as USA Swimming, USA Gymnastics, and USA Tae Kwon Do). Jon's work on behalf of sexual abuse victims has been featured in various media outlets from *20/20* to the *New York Times*. In 2010, due directly to Jon's advocacy, the U.S. Olympic Committee founded its first "Safe Sport Program." Now a partner at Saeed & Little, Jon centers his practice on athlete abuse cases and civil rights cases.

ANDREW JAY MCCLURG graduated from the University of Florida College of Law in 1980. After spending several years in private practice, Andrew began his career in academia in 1994. He has published dozens of law review articles, and his book *1L of a Ride: A Well-Traveled Professor's Roadmap to Success in the First Year of Law School*, now in its third edition, is assigned reading for first-year students at many law schools around the country. He also published *The "Companion Text" to Law School: Understanding and Surviving Life with a Law Student* to help law students' loved ones survive law school. Andrew is also well known for his humor. For four years, he wrote *Harmless Error*, a legal humor column published in the *American Bar Association Journal*. He has also published *The Law School Trip*, a parody of legal education, co-edited *Amicus Humoriae: An Anthology of Legal Humor*, and blogs at the popular site *lawhaha.com*. All jokes aside, Andrew has held a number of academic positions, including the

Herbert Herff Chair of Excellence in Law at the University of Memphis Cecil C. Humphreys School of Law, which he has held since 2006.

MARC POIRIER graduated from Harvard Law School in 1978. After law school, Marc spent 12 years with the Washington, D.C., firm Spiegel & McDiarmid LLP, practicing in the area of energy regulation. As a renowned scholar in the areas of hate crimes, same-sex marriage, and national resources management, Marc was twice the recipient of the Dukeminier Award honoring the best law review articles published each year. Marc was in demand as a speaker on the subject of same-sex marriage, and he also worked as an advocate on behalf of environmental and conservation interests. He served on the boards of the Coastal Society, the Society of American Law Teachers, and Diamond Metta Lesbian and Gay Buddhists of New York. Marc was the Martha Traylor Research Scholar at Seton Hall University School of Law for many years before his death in 2015.

DEBORAH WAIRE POST graduated from Harvard Law School in 1978. She began practice in the corporate section of a Houston law firm before embarking on her career in legal education at the University of Houston Law School. Deborah has published noteworthy works in the areas of business associations, legal education, and critical race theory, including the contracts casebook *Contracting Law* and *Cultivating Intelligence: Power, Law, and the Politics of Teaching*. Deborah was the Associate Dean for Academic Affairs and Faculty Development and Professor of Law at Touro College Jacob D. Fuchsberg Law Center, and she was a member of the Society of American Law Teachers Board of Governors for more than a decade and a co-President of the Society of American Law Teachers.

LISA PRUITT graduated from the University of Arkansas School of Law in 1989. In 1999, she joined the faculty at the UC Davis School of Law, a post she continues to hold. In the previous decade, Lisa's career spanned the globe. She worked as an associate for a private firm in London, lectured at the University of Amsterdam and Leiden University in the Netherlands, and served as a consultant to the International Criminal Tribunal in Kigali, Rwanda, investigating sexual assaults committed during the 1994 Rwandan genocide. As a scholar, Lisa's work on law draws on these diverse experiences to discuss the intersection between law and cultural conflicts and she has developed a specialty regarding the law of rural locations and an accompanying blog: http://legalruralism.blogspot.com/.

A multiple-time nominee for the Distinguished Teaching Award and a former Chair of the AALS Section on Women in Legal Education, Lisa has also served as a member of the Board of Governors of the Society of American Law Teachers.

SAIRA RAO graduated from New York University School of Law in 2002. Before going to law school, Saira worked as a journalist at WUSA TV in Washington, D.C., and WSVN TV in Miami. After graduating, Saira clerked on the Third Circuit Court of Appeals before practicing with Cleary Gottlieb Steen & Hamilton LLP. In 2007, Saira published her first novel, *Chambermaid*, which received enthusiastic reviews from national media outlets and the legal blogosphere.

JUSTICE MARILYN SKOGLUND did not graduate from, or even attend, law school. Her 1L experience was reading for the law. Marilyn graduated from Southern Illinois University in 1971. Several years later, after relocating to Vermont and as a working mother, she read for the law and passed the state's bar exam on her first try. With undergraduate degrees in sculpture and art history, she worked as a graphic designer for R. Buckminster Fuller, the architect and inventor best known for creating the geodesic dome. She spent more than a decade in various leadership positions with the state's Office of the Attorney General before being appointed as a trial court judge in 1994. Three years later, Marilyn became the second woman to serve as an Associate Justice of the Vermont Supreme Court, a post she continues to hold. As an Associate Justice, Marilyn has left her mark with the Art in the Supreme Court program, which hosts art exhibits in the bottom floor of the Supreme Court building.

GERRY SPENCE graduated from the University of Wyoming Law School in 1952. Gerry is an acclaimed trial lawyer, having tried numerous noteworthy cases, including the wrongful death lawsuit brought by the estate of Karen Silkwood on which the Academy Award-winning film *Silkwood* was based. He has famously never lost a criminal case—either as a prosecutor or defense attorney—and has not lost a civil case since 1969. In addition to his professional success, Gerry is the founder of the Trial Lawyers Academy, an advocacy school dedicated to training lawyers who represent individuals against large companies and the government. In that same vein, Gerry is the founder of Lawyers and Advocates for Wyoming, a pro bono law firm serving the legal needs of indigent clients. He is also the author of 16 books, including fiction, *Half-Moon and Empty Stars*, nonfiction, *Trial by Fire*, autobiography, *The Making of a Country Lawyer*, and photography, *Gerry Spence's Wyoming*.

CAMERON STRACHER graduated from Harvard Law School in 1987. He is also a graduate of the prestigious Iowa Writers Workshop at the University of Iowa, where he taught legal writing and helped found the law school's Writing Resource Center. Cameron specializes in media law, and he has taught the subject at New York Law School and served as litigation counsel for CBS. He is also a prolific writer: Cameron has written three works of fiction, and three works of nonfiction, including *Double-Billing: A Young Lawyer's Tale of Greed, Sex, Lies, and the Pursuit of a Swivel Chair* and *The Curve* (with Jeremy Blachman), and his work has appeared in the *New York Times*, the *Wall Street Journal*, and other national publications. Cameron is currently General Counsel-Media at American Media, Inc., and is of counsel to the law firm Levine Sullivan Koch & Schulz LLP in New York City.

WANDA M. TEMM is a law professor and the founder of the Bar Pass program at the University of Missouri-Kansas City School of Law, which has been ranked as one of the best schools in the nation for bar exam preparation. She is the former director of the school's legal writing program, and she has served as president of the Association of Legal Writing Directors. Wanda was a social worker for six years before attending law school, and she graduated from the University of Kansas School of Law in 1988. Prior to becoming a law professor, she did business and appellate litigation at the firm of Shook, Hardy & Bacon. Her publications include the books *Clearing the Last Hurdle: Mapping Success on the Bar Exam* and *Missouri Legal Research*.

SCOTT TUROW graduated from Harvard Law School in 1978. While still at Harvard, Scott wrote the instant classic *One L* about his experience as a first-year law student. After graduation, Scott worked as an Assistant United States Attorney in Chicago for nearly a decade before leaving for private practice. He is the author of 13 books, including *One L*, his first novel, *Presumed Innocent*, and its sequel, *Innocent*, which was published by Grand Central in 2010. His books have sold more than 30 million copies, and a number of these best-selling novels have been made into films, including *Presumed Innocent, The Burden of Proof, Reversible Errors,* and *Innocent.* Scott Turow is a partner at Dentons.

ROBERT R.M. VERCHICK graduated from Harvard Law School in 1989. Rob began his career practicing environmental law with a Seattle firm before taking the first in a series of academic teaching positions. His scholarly work has focused on environmental regulation and climate change, as well as feminist legal theory, and he has testified before Congress on several occasions, including in the aftermath of Hurricane Katrina. He recently published *Facing Catastrophe: Environmental Action for a Post-Katrina World* and the second edition of his co-authored *Disaster Law and Policy.* In 2009, Rob was appointed to serve in the Obama administration as the Deputy Associate Administrator for Policy at the U.S. Environmental Protection Agency. In that role, he helped shape U.S. policy on climate change and served on the President's Interagency Climate Change Adaptation Task Force. In 2010, Rob stepped down from that position and returned to his position as Director of the Center for Environmental Law and Land Use and holder of the Gauthier-St. Martin Chair in Environmental Law at Loyola University New Orleans College of Law, which he has held since 2004. He is the President of the Center for Progressive Reform.

ADRIEN KATHERINE WING graduated from Stanford Law School in 1982. Adrien practiced international law in New York City for five years, specializing in issues affecting Africa, the Middle East, and Latin America, before joining the faculty at the University of Iowa College of Law in 1987. Adrien's scholarly pursuits have spanned the globe. Her work has touched domestic topics such as race and gender discrimination, as well as international topics involving South Africa and the Muslim world. In addition, she has lectured all over the world and advised the drafters of the constitutions of South Africa, Palestine, and Rwanda. Among her books are *Critical Race Feminism: A Reader, Global Critical Race Feminism: An International Reader,* and *Democracy, Constitutionalism, and the Future State of Palestine.* Adrien is currently the Associate Dean for International and Comparative Law Programs and the Bessie Dutton Murray Professor of Law at the University of Iowa College of Law.

JUDGE/SENSEI MICHAEL ZIMMERMAN graduated from the University of Utah College of Law. He served as a law clerk for then–Chief Justice of the U.S. Supreme Court Warren Burger. He practiced with the Los Angeles law firm of O'Melveny & Myers, and then worked as special counsel to the governor of Utah. He served as a Justice on the Utah Supreme Court for 16 years, including four years as Chief Justice, stepping down when he began to feel that he was citing his own opinions as precedent too often. He was then a partner at Snell & Willmer for a decade. In 2011, he formed a boutique appellate litigation firm, Zimmerman Jones Booher. Michael Zimmerman's story in the past two decades is his journey into Zen meditation and his confirmation as a Buddhist monk.

Beyond One L

Part I
One L: The View in the Mirror

SCOTT TUROW

It is an honor, of course, for any writer to find that a book he wrote more than half a lifetime ago remains the touchstone for discussion, especially one as informed and heartfelt as that carried on in the following pages. I wrote *One L* on a kind of bet, not so much mine, as that of Ned Chase, now of blessed memory and then a senior editor at G.P. Putnam's Sons. Ned, whose best known child is the comedian Chevy, had another son who was a lawyer. In the spring of 1975, my literary agent at the time, Elizabeth McKee, showed Ned the letter I had written her announcing that I was abandoning academic life for law school, and mentioning that there seemed to be no non-fiction accounts of a law student's life. Ned commissioned the book on the spot. I was to receive $3,000 when I delivered an acceptable manuscript and another $1,000 on publication. By the time I sent in the book a year later, Ned had largely forgotten about it. "I need you to remind me of one thing," he told me, once he had read it, "Why did I ever want to buy this book?"

In response, I prophesized a booming American interest in the law as a result of Watergate, and backed it up with statistics showing that law school applications had quadrupled in the aftermath of the scandal. I had

3

no real idea what I was talking about, but Ned was convinced. The senior management at Putnam's was not and failed to order reprintings, even after the book drew favorable notices and seemed to be selling. Given *One L*'s precipitous start, it's amazing that it remains in print so many years later.

One L is not only the story of an education. It is also the diary of an unabashed neurotic. By turning to the law after five years at the Stanford Creative Writing Center—two as a fellow in the famous Stegner Program, and three as a lecturer in the English Department—and by returning to the cheap seats after my own stint at the head of the classroom, I had made a painful U-turn in my life. I had passion and intense curiosity about the law, but it seemed to come with a cost, since I thought I had put at risk the ambition I had clung to since childhood: becoming a novelist. To be clinical, I was enduring exactly what Erik Erikson meant when he coined the term "identity crisis." The law ultimately helped me solidify my sense of self. It let me enter a respected profession, and one with a smoother career trajectory than the arts, where it is all bust before the very rare boom, as it certainly had been for me. In the law you can be rewarded and appreciated when you are merely good for your age. But I had not reached even that point yet, and as a result I was questioning almost everything in my life, and often with a great deal of pain. That is not unusual for people in their mid-20s, and I suspect my frankness about the fact that there were moments when I really felt close to coming apart has helped the book endure.

Thus, despite its origins, the book that gathered itself as the product of the journal entries I wrote several times every week during my first year at Harvard Law School was not, for me, essentially a commercial enterprise. It was cathartic. I had been a writer, and, as it turned out, would never surrender that vocation. Keeping a journal was my refuge, a way to return to my former self and the values I knew. I wrote, as writers always do, for me, to be myself, and to join my very new identity as a would-be lawyer, with the person I had wanted to be before.

The fact that what I recorded has sometimes meant something to a generation and a half of law students, and a number of others, is one of those fortunate tricks of fate some writers are lucky enough to experience. I still regularly receive mail from readers of *One L*, usually a couple of messages every week. Those who write are grateful for the book's comfort or guidance, but I always wonder about the extent to which my personal turmoil has driven other people away from the profession.

One concrete contribution that *One L* indubitably made to legal culture is the term itself. When I started my book, "1L" was the computer code first-year students found accompanying their name at Harvard Law School ("HLS"). The term was well-established as an acronym at HLS, but only there. The success of the book made "1L" replace the more cumbersome "law school freshman" everywhere in the country. To be a "1L" now connotes to those inside the profession, and many outside, that the student in question is enduring a unique educational passage.

Reading the essays that appear in this volume, I'm struck by the degree to which every one of us insists on the primacy of our own experience. All of the authors, including me, basically maintain that what they experienced *really* was law school. And of course collectively we're all right. Yet despite the wide variety of experiences recorded, the first year of law school proved critical in forging the personal and professional identity of virtually all of these writers, and the sheer emotional intensity of the time rings through each of these essays. Something happens then, and that fact, more than any other, underpins *One L*'s continuing currency.

Many of these pieces struck personal notes for me, naturally. Those who attended Harvard write about professors I had—Duncan Kennedy, Lew Sargentich, and Arthur Miller—all of whom I recognize with fondness in other persons' remembrances and with continuing wonder at the extraordinary gifts all three displayed as teachers. I was also struck particularly by two of these pieces, those by my classmates, Deborah Post and Marc Poirier. Marc says he didn't know me. Well, ok. But I knew him, although it was an acquaintance in passing. I remember him as very funny. Since I was writing a book about my classmates and myself, I spent hours studying the 1L Facebook, so I would know who was who when I spoke to them in casual encounters. Given the sheer numbers, my class at Harvard Law School remains the most talented assemblage of human beings I've ever been privileged to be part of.

As for Deborah, I remember her, as she remembers herself, as slim and pretty. Deborah talks about what it meant to be a person of color at HLS, and the astonishing experience of being welcomed into an elite to which she had never felt she belonged. I'm pretty sure that nobody there felt he or she belonged. I had had what my mother described as "the education of a prince," at Amherst, Stanford, and Harvard, but I never forgot that one grandfather was a milkman and the other peddled ties and socks on the street.

I also want to take gentle issue with Deborah for asserting that I blamed Harvard for the competitive greed that overtook my classmates and me as the year headed toward a close. When I said, at the end of the book, "My enemy, that greedy little monster, will always be in there rattling his cage," I don't think I was pointing a finger at anybody but myself.

But my point in *One L*, and now, is that law school faculty members are not ignorant about the nature of the people who are drawn there—ambitious, competitive, aggressively intellectual—nor the fact that it remains a tender time in the development of virtually all students, a fact to which all of these essays, in fact, bear silent testimony. Law students should be treated as adults, but toughening them up for the combat of the courtroom or practice is not a good excuse for humiliating classroom interrogations. Court—or contract negotiations—are usually a few years off for all 1Ls, and, in any event, those activities will be undertaken only after each student has achieved a much more solid sense of professional membership. One of the keenest pleasures of teaching is the life-long impact of the lessons taught, but that is possible primarily because the personalities of students are not yet set in concrete; they are impressionable and professors must bear that in mind.

This point leads naturally to a question I am asked frequently, namely, how much law school has changed since I entered at Harvard in 1975. I have two answers: A great deal. And not enough. I watched my older daughter endure her own first year in law school at the University of Michigan, and thought she managed it with much more grace than I did. There was still considerable grade competition, but some of that was probably due to the fact that the legal economy had started to decline, meaning fewer jobs. But I don't recall her fearing class, or her classmates. Overall, it was an intense experience for her, but not soul-splitting, and part of that was due to the fact that she was in a less severe environment than I was, as I think is true at most top-tier law schools these days when the brute exertion of patriarchal authority has gotten a bad name.

At Harvard, the faculty schism that arose around Critical Legal Studies and promotion policies, especially of women and minorities, seems to be in the past. It truly seems to be a somewhat kinder and gentler place. For too many years, the feeling of being a Harvard law student remained too much like mine, feeling like you were playing King of the Hill, a tyro versus intellectual giants who were ready to take on all comers. When Elena Kagan became Dean, she seemed, to me, to bring about a sea change, largely by informing the faculty that the law school was first and foremost about its students, not its professors. Even the extraordinary intellectual contributions of the Harvard faculty do not hold a candle to what the HLS student body as a whole has done in the last century and a half to live and shape American law.

I continue to lament that many of the dour hallmarks of legal education that go all the way back to Dean Langdell—large classes and grading based on a single exam—continue to prevail in almost all U.S. law schools. Those features have a detrimental effect on both the pedagogical environment and the anxiety level of law students. Further, there is a fair chance that the educational model reinforces a culture of distance and competition, instead of collaboration.

Worse, Langdell's model continues to prevail for an ugly reason: money. In too many universities, law schools are profit centers, where a very small faculty teaches a very large student body, which pays a very high tuition. The eminent scholars who teach classes of eighty to one hundred and fifty students simply do not have the time to grade several papers every semester, nor to provide much one-on-one instruction. There are many inspired educators teaching in American law schools, but they are still battling a system whose fundamentals work against them and which encourage students to view those years as the road to an admission card, rather than an education that can shape their values throughout their years in practice.

Part II
Law School or Some Other Path?

America is home to 1.3 million lawyers. About three-fourths of them are in private practice, eight percent in government work and another eight percent in private industry, with five percent retired, three percent in the judiciary, and two percent in the legal academy or consulting.

People choose to become lawyers for many different reasons. Some people are influenced by a parent who is an attorney, or by a favorite teacher or a book. *To Kill a Mockingbird* is still one of the country's most widely read novels, almost 60 years after its publication. Students may have taken a Constitutional Law or Business Law class in high school or college or "majored" in debate. Some students may have political aspirations. They may have parents who encourage them to select a prestigious profession, but don't want to be a doctor because they don't like sick people and can't stand the sight of blood. At times, people come from other careers, and some of them later merge their prior passion with their legal knowledge. David Lat, whose story you will read in this chapter, was a journalist before law school; afterward, he founded and became managing editor of the innovative *Above the Law* blog. Sometimes popular or political events influence the decision to apply to law school. In 1989, the hit television show *L.A. Law* sparked a record-breaking increase in the number of law school applications. As Scott Turow noted, law school applications also burgeoned after the Watergate scandal. In 2017, the number of people taking the Law School Admissions Test (LSAT) was up dramatically compared to the previous year. Many called this "the Trump bump," attributing at least some of the hike to people who either applaud Trump's policies or want to use the rule of law to challenge them. Some students—misguidedly, we think—are attracted by the lure of competition or money. The best students want to use law to make a difference in their small corner of the world.

Law school applications have been mildly cyclical over the years, but experienced a sharp decline starting in 2010. A weak economy, bad press about law school debt loads, and a difficult job market together steered students away from law schools. After rising to a high of more than 100,000 in 2005, the number of law school applicants dropped precipitously, reaching a low of less than 55,000 applicants in 2015–2016 before starting to slowly rebound. For the most part, law school is no longer the default grad school for smart people.

The legal job market hit a low in 2011, but is making a comeback. Lawyer shortages exist in various subject matter and geographic areas. There is an undersupply of patent, immigration, and public interest lawyers, as well as lawyers in rural areas, such as smaller towns in Iowa. ("Is this heaven?" "No, it's Iowa.") Doctors may get incentives to practice in rural areas, but few such incentives are available for lawyers. Lisa Pruitt's story in this chapter talks about her rural beginnings and how she has circled back, as a law professor, to theorize about access to law and justice in small towns.

The *Wall Street Journal* reported a recent scarcity of entry-level solicitors in the United Kingdom and reminded readers that the recession of the 1990s led to a shortage of lawyers between 1995 and 1997. Industry-wide forecasts indicate a possible a shortage of lawyers as the Baby Boom generation begins to retire. In 2017, almost a quarter of all lawyers were 65 or older. Boomer retirements can create opportunities for younger lawyers to advance.

In so many different ways, law is a noble profession. Law is at the very foundation of American liberty and prosperity. Countries without democracy and a strong rule of law often have political unrest and faltering economies. Lawyers serve the public as prosecutors, public defenders, and in government agencies. People turn to lawyers to defend their liberties, put together deals, smooth out difficulties, and solve problems. It is personally and professionally rewarding to stand up for those who would otherwise lack a voice, find the missing piece of evidence that will allow the guilty to be convicted or the innocent to go free, assist an entrepreneur in changing a flourishing partnership into a publicly traded corporation, figure out how to secure intellectual property rights in an international marketplace, stand up to a bullying client who needs to hear that what he proposes is illegal and unjust, and craft a parenting plan that allows loving parents who cannot talk to each other to each remain involved in their children's lives. It is little wonder that 80 percent of lawyers are either moderately or extremely satisfied with their decisions to become lawyers, and equal percentages are proud of their jobs and find legal practice to be intellectually stimulating. And at the end of their careers, many lawyers have the sense of a well-lived life, the sort of reflective satisfaction of having made their corner of the world a better place. At the heart of a lawyer's job is protecting against injustice; at its soul is the hope for more peaceful coexistence among people.

Theodicy

—

IAN AYRES

After college, I bounced back and forth between MIT and Yale. First, I took a year of economics at MIT. Then I returned to Yale (where I had been an undergraduate) and started law school in the fall of 1982. Soon after law school classes started, I made my way over to Yale Hillel and asked if there were any Talmud classes that I could take. An undergraduate woman looked at me suspiciously and asked me why I was interested in taking the class. She surmised (correctly) that I was not Jewish. I deadpanned that I hoped to help destroy Judaism through intermarriage.

A less snarky response concerns my love of gearhead basketball. When I was at MIT, a large proportion of the econ grad students would meet on Friday mornings to play a fairly physical brand of basketball. I had the pleasure of exchanging elbows with some of the greatest economists in the world today. One day, I happened to see in the MIT newspaper an ad for "Torah and chocolates." I noticed that the meetings were on Friday, just after basketball was over, and the MIT Hillel was on my path back to the department, so I thought I'd give it a try. I was raised (and confirmed) as an Episcopalian. But even though I was an agnostic graduate student, I wanted to deepen my Biblical literacy. And I thought a close reading of text would stand me in good stead for law school the next year.

When I started law school, it was natural to take the next step and try to find a Talmud class. Yale Hillel had just what I was looking for. Rabbi Jim Ponet taught a course in English that collected an eclectic group that was diverse academically and spiritually. Some of the students were observant

Orthodox Jews who began and ended each session by kissing the text; others, like me, approached the meetings much more as a theoretical exercise. Ponet's class seemed to pull students from all fields of study. We had philosophy students, med students, divinity students, and more than one law student. Together, we spent hours parsing a different kind of legal text. I loved the disputatious tone of inquiry—where we were asked to join the sages in constantly questioning any claim with "why should that be true?"

But my attitude toward the class abruptly changed in the spring of my first year when my mother was struck by an unrelenting series of multiple sclerosis attacks. My mom had been suffering from MS for more than a decade. Three or four times a year, she would experience attacks of numbness in her arms or legs that would normally last for two or three weeks. But this time instead of numbness, my mom's body started to cramp. Thirty or forty times a day, my mom's entire left side would severely seize, bending her hand, arm, and leg up and down her left side into painful contortions. I remember standing next to her bed in the hospital, holding her hand during one of these attacks, and feeling like this frail, bed-ridden woman might break the bones in my fingers as the cramping vise that had been her hand tightened involuntarily.

Even today, my heart aches at the memory of her pain, coupled with the tortuous knowledge that another cramp was just a few minutes away. After several days of this repeated cramping, the muscles on her left side were shred into constant agony. And there was very little that my dad, sister, or I could do to help.

[I came up with a small palliative that put me at loggerheads with the hospital. I brought in a couple of heating pads to wrap around her cramping arm and leg. The number of cramps immediately subsided—from thirty or forty a day, to ten to fifteen per day. But when I came in on the third day, I was enraged to find the heating pads were gone and my mom's more frequent attacks were once again back. The hospital said that electric heating pads were dangerous and after twelve hours finally installed incredibly cumbersome and less effective pads which circulated warm water around my mother's arms and legs. But then again, maybe I was looking for someone or something to lash out against.]

The big surprise is what happened when I returned to school and tried going back to Talmud class. While many people in the class analyzed the text as literature or, sociologically, as the word of humans searching for meaning in life, I had preferred to treat the text as the word of God. For me, it was more interesting to try to find the meaning of God's message and to struggle to reconcile seeming contradictions and ambiguities. But after seeing my mom's tribulations, I couldn't bring myself to play this interpretative game anymore. I remember feeling the overwhelming desire to end each of my comments with the caveat "but of course this is all bullshit." I suppressed this urge. But I didn't go back to the class after that first attempt. (And I never explained to Rabbi Ponet my sudden absence).

I couldn't understand why a just, all-powerful God would subject my mother to this pain. This philosophical difficulty was not new to me. I had read and reread the Grand Inquisitor chapter in *The Brothers Karamazov* long before I had taken Torah or Talmud. But living it, seeing it, feeling it as my mother's hand tightened around my own left an impression that changed my view of what I thought was largely an intellectual exercise. It is often said that adversity drives us toward God—that there are no atheists in foxholes. But for me, seeing my mother's undeserved and needless pain drove me away from a belief in a just, all-powerful God.[1]

At the time, I remember thinking if God does exist, we are truly made in His image in that our capacity to do evil may resemble that same capacity in our Heavenly Father. I did not consider the possibility that we are made in God's image in a different way: perhaps God's powers are limited just as ours are.[2] God might exist and be both good and just, but not able to prevent evil in the ways we desire. The same empathetic pain I felt as I helplessly watched my mother suffer might also be shared by God.

My mom died in 2004. Her massive seizures during my first year were the last truly painful attacks she ever had. From that point on, she remained bed-ridden and slowly lost feeling and motor control of her limbs. But she was largely pain-free and mentally sharp as a tack. She retired the undefeated crossword puzzle champion of our family. My law professor bride, Jennifer Brown, and I were legally married at her bedside in 1993.

---

1. My reaction might also suggest a role for secular chaplains, who can counsel the grief stricken from a shared belief that God may not exist. The mere possibility that professional psychologists or grief counsels may believe in God could limit their ability to counsel those with little faith. Adelphi, Columbia, and Harvard have appointed secular or humanist chaplains in part to provide just this service.

2. *See* Gregg Easterbrook, Beside Still Waters: Searching for Meaning in an Age of Doubt (1999).

During law school, I would have told you that none of this impact-ed my view of law—that I successfully compartmentalized my personal and intellectual lives. But as I look back across the decades, I am now not so sure. Indeed, the center of the story is a failure to compartmentalize my mother's pain and my Talmud discussion. I now wonder whether my turning from God was also a turning toward law as a bulwark against evil. As a world weary fifty-year-old, I'm amazed that a young Ian Ayres could be so exorcised by a classroom discussion. Notwithstanding this history, I find myself today teaching Sunday school at an Episcopalian church, with my son as a co-teacher and my daughter as one of the "Teen Bible Study" students. And yes, when we weekly read the chapter and verse, my dominant interpretive approach is still to try to understand the text as the word of God.

Mistakes Were Made:
Lessons Drawn from My One L Experience

DAVID LAT

"Read and brief Contracts reading!"

"Study Bluebook!"

"Pick up dry cleaning!"

As I turn the pages of my appointment book for 1996, my heart beats faster and more forcefully. I'm taken back to the anxiety and ambition felt by my 21-year-old self, a first-year law student. Urgency permeates the pages, sandwiched between black pebbled leatherette covers and filled with tight penciled scribbling. An exclamation point follows almost every appointment or task: "Do Procedure homework!" "Copy Con Law outline!" "Start preparing and sending out letters and résumés!" Question marks accompany enjoyable activities of dubious productive value: "Watch Melrose Place?"

I am impressed by my sense of duty and my diligence (and my superb handwriting, the letters tiny but wonderfully legible after all these years). To me as a 1L, everything was a crisis, everything was high priority, everything required immediate and intense attention. Disasters lurked around every corner: public embarrassment in Owen Fiss's (highly Socratic) Procedure class, due to neglected reading; a poor performance on Akhil Amar's exam in Constitutional Law, caused by a missing outline; or unemployment for the summer, resulting from insufficient diligence in submitting applications. And this was at Yale Law School, where the first semester goes ungraded, there is an institutional ethos against appearing to exert excessive effort, and employment opportunities tend to be plentiful. I can only imagine how I would have fared in the Harvard Law School described by Scott Turow in *One L*.

Yale Law School in the late 1990s wasn't nearly as brutal as Harvard Law School in the late 1970s.[3] But my time as a 1L, while perhaps less dramatic and challenging than Turow's first year at HLS, fell far short of perfection. I experienced a huge amount of unnecessary stress, I didn't enjoy the experience as much as I could (or should) have, and I could have gotten even more out of the year than I did.

If I were to do it all over again, I can think of many things that I would do differently. For the benefit of current and future law students, here are three recommendations, derived from my 1L experience, as well as the experiences of the many lawyers I have met as a journalist covering the legal profession.

1. LOOK BEFORE YOU LEAP: MAKE AN INFORMED DECISION ABOUT GOING TO LAW SCHOOL
(and don't go directly from college to law school, if you can help it).

Like so many others both before and after me, I went to law school because I didn't know what else to do with myself. As then-Dean Anthony Kronman told me at some point during my 1L year—after he asked what brought me to law school, and I confessed that I wasn't really sure—law school is "the great American default option," for smart and motivated young people "who can't stand the sight of blood."

As an undergraduate at Harvard, I majored in English—not a terribly marketable degree. I enjoyed writing and arguing; I penned a column for the *Crimson* and I competed on the debate team. In my senior year, I applied to a few law schools and a handful of fellowships. When none of the fellowships came through, law school was the obvious option. Everyone else I knew was doing it, so how bad could it be?

---

3. Harvard Law School seems to have mellowed too. *See* Scott Turow, One L: The Turbulent True Story of a First Year at Harvard Law School 277 (Penguin Books ed. 2010) (1977) (describing Harvard Law in 2010 as "a kinder and gentler place, especially in the wake of the deanship of Elena Kagan, who worked a sea change by emphasizing that the students, not the faculty, deserved to be the first concern of the institution").

Looking back now, I don't regret going to law school, but I do wish I hadn't gone directly from college to law school. As a straight-from-under-grad 1L, I found myself studying with (and competing against) former Navy SEALs, McKinsey consultants, magazine editors, and Rhodes and Marshall Scholars. My lack of life experience, compared to their life-changing experiences, gave me a crisis of confidence; it made me anxious and insecure. Partly as a result of this insecurity, I became what law students today call a "gunner," sitting in the front row of classes and participating in classroom discussion overzealously, sometimes to the point of obnox-iousness—just to prove, to myself and to others, that I could hold my own against my peers. Had I arrived at law school more secure in myself, more comfortable in my own skin, I probably would have had a different, and better, first year (and so would my classmates).

I advise prospective law students to do something different between college and law school if they can. People who have some other experience prior to law school, whether working or traveling or pursuing other grad-uate study, seem to enjoy and get more out of the law school experience than those of us who came straight from undergraduate studies. They of-ten exhibit greater maturity and grace under stress, and they often have a better sense of how a legal education fits into their broader professional plans, due to greater self-knowledge. If you've worked on a billion-dollar merger as an analyst at Goldman Sachs, conducted a foot patrol in an Iraqi village, or maintained order in an inner-city classroom as a Teach for America corps member, you will probably develop various qualities— self-confidence, self-awareness, a sense of perspective—that will stand you in good stead during law school.

Going to law school ultimately worked out for me. After graduation, I practiced for several years, which I enjoyed, before entering legal journal-ism, which also draws upon my knowledge of law and the legal profession. But I consider myself very fortunate. My parents generously paid for my legal education, so I emerged from law school debt-free, and I had ample employment lined up at the time of my graduation—a clerkship with a federal appeals court judge, and an offer to return to the firm where I had spent my 2L summer. And the legal economy was so strong back then: the profession's most lucrative years still lay ahead of it, almost a decade of record expansion and profitability for the nation's largest law firms.

In the intervening years, much has changed—for the worse, in many respects. The Great Recession did not spare the legal profession. As chronicled on *Above the Law*, the blog that I founded in 2006, legal employers were forced to resort to layoffs of attorneys and staff, deferrals of incoming lawyers, and salary freezes or cuts, just in order to survive the economic downturn (and some firms, sadly, did not survive). Meanwhile, as many legal employment opportunities vanished, law schools continued to raise their tuition, generally at a pace significantly outstripping inflation.

As a result of these changes, many people who have followed in my footsteps, going to law school "by default," have come to regret that decision. Numerous law school graduates, after taking out six figures' worth of student loans, find themselves unemployed or underemployed after graduation. The plight of these individuals has received coverage not just in legal publications and websites, but in national and even international newspapers and magazines.[4]

For the record, I am not a law school naysayer.[5] Pursuing a law degree remains a good decision for many, and the legal profession still offers a wide range of deeply fulfilling career opportunities. But becoming a 1L is not a decision to be made lightly—especially since the benefits of a J.D. degree have arguably decreased, and the costs of obtaining one have most definitely increased in recent years. Prospective law students should carefully consider whether they should go to law school, ideally with the benefit of some post-undergraduate experience to help them make the choice.

2. MAKE FRIENDS AS WELL AS GOOD GRADES.

If you do decide to go to law school, remember that you are paying not just for classroom instruction and casebooks, but for the privilege of rubbing shoulders with future leaders of the legal profession (and beyond).

---

4. *See, e.g.*, Annie Lowrey, *A Case of Supply v. Demand*, SLATE (Oct. 27, 2010), http://www.slate.com/articles/business/moneybox/2010/10/a_case_of_supply_v_demand.html; David Segal, *Is Law School a Losing Game?*, N.Y. TIMES, Jan. 9, 2011, at BU1; *Trouble with the Law*, ECONOMIST (Nov. 11, 2010), http://www.economist.com/node/17461573; Alex Williams, *No Longer Their Golden Ticket*, N.Y. TIMES, Jan. 17, 2010, at ST1; *see also* Elie Mystal, *Debt: The Silent Killer*, ABOVE THE LAW (Jan. 6, 2010), http://abovethelaw.com/2010/01/debt-the-silent-killer/.

5. *See, e.g.*, David Lat, *In Defense of Going to Law School*, ABOVE THE LAW (July 13, 2010), http://abovethelaw.com/2010/07/in-defense-of-going-to-law-school/.

Get to know your classmates—not just because some of them are wonderful people, or because you might enjoy it, but also because, from the most crassly instrumentalist point of view, some of them will someday be in a position to help you. What Scott Turow observed about Harvard Law School could be said of law school in general: it is "cheerfully assumed to be the training ground for the power elite."[6]

Even though we're not yet fifteen years out of law school, many of my classmates have already achieved remarkable success, both within and beyond the legal world. They are partners at leading law firms, law school professors (and even deans), successful businesspeople, and rising stars in the political world. People a few classes ahead of us are already becoming judges (which is, by the way, one sign that you're getting old). I'm proud of the achievements of my law school friends and classmates, and I expect this pride will only grow over the coming years.

I just wish I had gotten to know my classmates better, back when we were still in school together. As I think back on my first year in law school, I am struck by how little socializing I did. My appointment book contains entries for the occasional lunch with a friend or birthday party for a classmate, but not much more; like so many 1L students, I spent much of the year in the company of my books. A typical dinner involved reading from a casebook while devouring chicken and broccoli from a Chinese take-out joint on Chapel Street.

Much of the socializing I did do was with people outside of the law school, such as an old high school friend of mine, who recently graduated from Yale College and was working at a research laboratory in New Haven, and one of my roommates from college, who was a grad student in political science at Yale. Hanging out with these non-law-school friends offered an escape from stress-inducing gossip about outline groups, the Yale Law Journal selection process, and summer job searches.[7] But structuring my

---

6. Turow, *supra* note 1, at 230 (noting that "it is simply assumed at HLS that a Harvard J.D. is a stepping stone to big things," and that professors viewed their students as future judges, law professors, and political leaders).

7. Scott Turow and his wife Annette may have had a similar experience at Harvard Law School. *See id.* at 120 ("The law school has not provided a community with which we're eager to get involved. It's not a social place. On the weekends we're all just as happy not to see each other. And with good reason. On the few evenings we've had law-school friends here, as we did last night, the conversation has centered obsessively on HLS.").

social life in this way, while understandable, caused me to miss out on many opportunities to get to know my fellow classmates. (My decision not to live in the law school dorms—YLS had dorms back then—exacerbated the problem.)

In the years since graduation, I have belatedly discovered how many wonderful classmates I had at Yale. I have become close friends with people who were just friends in law school, and I have become friends with people who were just acquaintances. With law school over a decade behind us, and with our professional paths diverging in so many different directions, we're secure enough in ourselves to no longer feel threatened by each other's success. Instead, we can just enjoy each other's company and friendship.

But I still regret that I didn't make more friends while in law school— perhaps due to fearing my classmates, to seeing them as competitors rather than allies. Don't make the same mistake that I did. Law school can be fearful, and brutal, and grueling, but going through the ordeal with friends will make it much easier to endure.

3. CALM DOWN.

This last piece of advice is much easier to give than to follow—especially for law students, who tend to be anxious and hyper-competitive,[8] and especially in this economy, where academic performance as a 1L can play a major role in determining employment opportunities. But if you have a tendency to get nervous and overwrought—which I did, as a law student, and still do, years later—you really should try and relax.

A certain amount of stress can be helpful, even necessary, for success in law school. It motivates law students to excel, both inside and outside the classroom. At a certain point, however, the stress becomes counterproductive. Try to figure out, while you're still a law student, where that tipping point lies for you; it's a skill that you'll be able to draw upon for years (or at least when you're studying for the bar exam).

In the end—thanks in part to my neurosis and paranoia, my appointment book filled with exclamation points—I survived, and even thrived during, my first year as a law student. I earned good grades, I made it on

---

8. *See id.* at *287* (describing the "personality types drawn to the law" as "articulate, assertive, frequently competitive—who will inevitably make one another nervous").

to the Law Journal, I developed good relationships with my professors, and I forged friendships that I maintain to this day. I learned a staggering amount, and I enjoyed the experience overall (despite occasional periods of stress and loneliness, handled through self-medication with Chinese takeout).

I survived my first year of law school, Scott Turow survived his, and you will survive yours too, probably.[9] You might think that your particular challenges as a 1L are unique: maybe you're the first in your family or from your community to go to law school, maybe you're in a particular minority group that doesn't enter the law in large numbers, or maybe you're juggling law school with other work or family responsibilities. But given that tens of thousands of people graduate from law school in the United States each year, it is likely that someone has confronted, and overcome, obstacles similar to the ones you're facing.

To reassure you about the 1L experience, I could leave you with the words of Nietzsche: "What does not kill me, makes me stronger." Or perhaps the old proverb: "This too shall pass." But I prefer the immortal words of Sven—I don't actually know if that's his name, it's just my guess—the deep-voiced narrator of Maelstrom, the Viking boat ride at Epcot Center's Norway pavilion:

"You are not the first to pass this way. Nor shall you be the last."

---

9. Just kidding! Of course you'll make it.

Neurotic, Paranoid Wimps—
Nothing Has Changed

ANDREW JAY MCCLURG

I first read Scott Turow's classic *One L* in 1978. The book had just been published and I was about to start law school at the University of Florida (UF). I remember being enthralled by it. It read like a thriller, due in large part to Turow's writing skill, of course, but also because that's exactly what the first year of law school is: a wild adventure, filled with thrills, chills, and spills.

These days, when I hear or read about *One L*, it's often in the context of assertions that the book is an outdated, overly dramatized, and inaccurate portrayal of the modern law school experience. This perspective can be found, for example, in Amazon.com customer reviews of the book, which include statements like: "totally divorced from the real world, but does so in a ridiculously dramatized manner"; "people should realize it's not a description of what most students experience in law school"; "law school is not like it was portrayed in *One L*"; and "I enjoyed reading this novel, and would recommend it to others as long as it was understood that law school has changed."

But in recently re-turning the pages of *One L*, I had exactly the opposite reaction. I was struck primarily by the book's currency, especially the impact of the first year on student psyches. Chapter after chapter, episode after episode, I kept thinking: "It's exactly the same today."

Certainly, some changes have occurred in U.S. legal education. Law schools are much more diverse, experiential learning opportunities are expanding, and law professors are kinder and gentler than in the 1970s, although, as discussed below, the perception that Turow's professors were a bunch of sadistic ogres is simply not true. But most of the core aspects of the first year—the ones that wreak the most emotional havoc on 1Ls— have stayed the same. First-year classes remain large, the first-year curriculum and heavy workload are substantially unchanged, most first-year courses are still taught using the Socratic method, most 1Ls still compete hard for grades, and the fate of most students still rests on a single make-it-or-break-it exam at the end of the semester.

I closed the book convinced that Turow's experience not only mirrored my own 1L journey, but captured the archetypal reactions of students everywhere to law school's harrowing first year—in his time, today, perhaps for all time. In large part, this is attributable to the remarkable uniformity in and glacially slow evolution of U.S. legal education. As noted, with disapproval, by the authors of the 2007 *Best Practices for Legal Education* report, "[t]ypical classroom instruction at most law schools today would be familiar to any lawyer who attended law school during the past hundred thirty years." In teaching at several law schools in different parts of the country, I've always been struck by the essential likeness of law students and the similarity of their responses to the first-year experience. At law schools great and small, students struggle to master the same material under the same teaching and evaluation methodologies.

Turow identified a variety of still-valid first-year themes: the competitive atmosphere; the deep bonding that occurs among 1Ls; the mental and physical exhaustion that accompany the burdensome workload; the detachment from personal values caused by law school's emphasis on objective analysis; the manner in which law school, by altering the way students think and view the world around them, fundamentally changes who they are; the toll law school takes on outside relationships; and the exhilaration and pride that come with conquering the mysteries of the law.

The book's dominant theme, however, seemed to be one of negative affect. I counted specific references by Turow to fear, anxiety, stress, panic, vulnerability, self-doubt, shame and grief, wounded self-esteem, unhappiness, paranoia, embarrassment, oppression, and insanity. These feelings pretty much summed up my 1L experience, particularly the first trimester, in a nutshell. Most of the more than one hundred Amazon.com customer reviews of *One L* are glowing, but among the accolades one can find criticism of Turow for being "neurotic" and a "paranoid wimp."

If those are fair descriptors for anxious, overwhelmed, and bewildered first-year law students, they applied to me too, as well as to most of my classmates and large numbers of students I have taught. Numerous studies show that law students suffer higher rates of depression, anxiety, and other types of psychological dysfunction than the general population and other graduate student populations, including medical students.

This narrative explores the neurotic, paranoid wimpiness of 1Ls, both from my own perspective and from the experiences of some of my students. For several years, since writing the first edition of my law school prep book, *1L of a Ride: A Well-Traveled Professor's Roadmap to Success in the First Year of Law School*, I have surveyed law students about their emotions and reactions to law school. Some of their responses inform this story.

* * *

The feeling aroused by all of that was something near to panic, a ferocious, grasping sense of uncertainty, and it held me, and I believe most of my classmates, often during that first week and for a long while after.

—Turow, *One L*

I spent much of the first year in a state of panic. In fact, I didn't even wait until arriving at law school. I decided to get an early jump on the competition and become a basket case at the LSAT. For some reason, I didn't stress at all before the test. I suppose I didn't know what I was getting into. No prep courses, no working through practice questions. I went out drinking with my buddies the Friday night before the exam at Café Gardens, a favorite Gainesville haunt. But come Saturday morning, I freaked out. Two embarrassing incidents remain indelibly imprinted in memory.

The first occurred before the test even started. The LSAT was held in an auditorium on the UF campus. About ten minutes before the 8:30 a.m. start time, I decided I needed to use a restroom. The doors to the test auditorium were still locked. All the LSAT-takers, a couple hundred of us, were gathered outside. I started strolling, then race-walking, and finally frantically sprinting around the UF campus in search of an open restroom, but all the buildings were locked. With 8:30 quickly approaching, I decided to just hold it and rushed back to the auditorium. A person at the door was hustling everyone inside. My bladder suddenly balked at the idea of trying to hold it for three-and-a-half hours. Five seconds of panic later found me urinating on a bush not far from the entrance as the other future legal leaders of America pushed into the auditorium.

Why didn't I simply ask one of the administrators if there was a restroom inside? I have no idea. Perhaps I had read an instruction similar to this one found in the current LSAT rules:

> If you find it necessary to leave the room during the test, raise your hand and obtain permission from the supervisor. Your test materials will be collected and held until your return. You will not be permitted to make up the time. Use the restroom before entering the testing room; once checked in, you will not be permitted to leave until after the start of Section I.

Fast forward to my first year: I'm sitting at an outdoor picnic table at the law school having lunch with some 1L classmates when one of them starts telling a story about one of the wildest things he'd ever seen: "You wouldn't believe it. As we were walking into the auditorium to take the LSAT, I look over and—in plain view—some dude is peeing on a bush!" Everyone laughed. I studied my shoes.

The other incident, just as embarrassing, occurred at the end of the test as I was turning it in. As the test slid from my fingers into the waiting hands of one of the proctors, I glanced down and saw something horrifying.

"Um, excuse me," I said to the woman holding my test. "Could I look at my answer sheet for a second?"

"No. Once you've turned it in, you're not permitted to retrieve it."

"I just need to look at it. I think I just saw that one of my sections had forty-one answers. Do any of the sections have forty-one questions? It seems like they wouldn't have odd numbers like that."

"I don't know." She turned away.

"Wait! I think I must have skipped an answer space. I just want to look at it to see. I don't want to change anything."

"I'm sorry, that's not permitted. Once it's turned in, it's turned in."

"Could you look to see if any of the sections have forty-one questions?"

"I'm sorry, no."

"Pleeeease!"

A supervisor came over to confirm her position in that smug, case-closed way one might expect.

I ranted about their arbitrariness and may have even mentioned due process. My legal knowledge and argumentation skills were not highly developed, however, and my pitiful pleas fell on deaf ears. I stormed out of the auditorium feeling miserable, convinced it was impossible there were forty-one questions in a section and that my fate was sealed. I did much better than I thought I would, scoring in the 95th percentile, but have always wondered if I would have done better but for my error. But who knows, maybe filling in the wrong bubbles benefitted me. Or maybe there really were forty-one questions in that section.

Things got much worse when I got to law school. I spent my first year tied so tightly in knots that I had to seek medical help for gastrointestinal issues. My mother was a newspaper reporter. For many years, she wrote a weekly column for whichever newspaper she happened to be working at the time in which she often used her kids' lives for material. In a box in the attic, I found a yellowed photocopy (it would have been called a "xerox" when it was made) of the column excerpted below. Published in 1978, the column adds credence to my distant memories:

> This tall, blond, young lad is too thin, I noted, as I stuffed . . . [him] with turkey and steaks. It's just that law school produces queasy stomachs and nerves, he said, at least in the first year. . . . A grinding nervous stomach a few weeks ago sent him to the school clinic, he said. He lost about 10 pounds on that tall frame but "if I stuff my pockets with change, the wind won't blow me over," he said with a grin. . . . Law school, he explained, is full of exceptionally bright people, the cream of the nation's crop. It is a place where for the first time in his life, everyone in class is as bright as the rest. . . . Many students are older than he. Many have master's degrees in accounting and engineering and whatever. But all have the same goal this freshman year—survival. . . . It's ulcer alley, mother, he said, no matter that his grades are high. Every day, the stomach cramps begin. . . .
>
> —Helen T. Rohloff, *Pride, Joy in a Maturing Son*,
> Stuart News, Sept. 3, 1978

A gastroenterologist put me on a medication for irritable bowel syndrome. My older brother, Doug, who graduated from UF law school the year before I started, later told me he didn't think I was going to make it. Neurotic, paranoid wimp.

*   *   *

For the next five days I will assume that I am somewhat less intelligent than anyone around me. At most moments I'll suspect that the privilege I enjoy was conferred as some kind of peculiar hoax. I will be certain that no matter what I do, I will not do it well enough; and when I fail, I know I will burn with shame.

—Turow, One L

Much of my fear and anxiety came from self-doubt. Law school is the undisputed world champion for causing accomplished, talented people to doubt their abilities. In an instant, all of life's prior accomplishments become irrelevant. Consider these comments from some of my recent students:

* Law school is where smart people go to feel dumb.
* I feel like I came here being a really good public speaker and writer. I've won awards for both. Somehow, law school has managed to turn that on its head. I'm apparently a bad public speaker and a mediocre writer at best.
* My biggest change in personality is a complete loss of self-confidence and feeling of self-worth.

Like Turow, I struggled to find meaning in the difficult cases. Like Turow, I was baffled by the professors' questions. Forget left field. Law professor questions seemed to come from a much more distant place. Like Turow, I sat through classes listening to my brilliant classmates volunteer answers I never would have thought of.

Whatever I did, it wasn't good enough. In law school, even when you win, you lose. There's no such thing as a perfect answer or work product. The best affirmation a student can hope for is a "Not bad, *but . . . ,*" with the "but" quickly overtaking and consuming the "Not bad." "You write well," my legal writing instructor scribbled on the last page of my first memorandum assignment. Fantastic! My very first law school feedback. "But," he continued, "you made a substantive error of malpractice dimensions." Oh well.

My lack of confidence ran so deeply that even though I landed in the top five percent of the class after the first trimester, it took until halfway through the first year before I voluntarily raised my hand for the first time. Our Property professor, D.T. Smith, was everyone's favorite, a true "teacher" with a great sense of humor. One day he asked a simple question. "What is the legal relationship of bank to bank depositor?" Several hands went up. "Bailor-bailee?" "Wrong." "Assignor-assignee?" "Wrong." "Mortagor-mortagee?" "Wrong." This kept going until the class had tossed out every possible combination of two words ending with "or" and "ee." All but one. I thought I knew the answer.

This was it. My moment of glory. I took a deep breath and stabbed my hand in the air.

"Mr. McClurg?"

"Lendor-lendee?"

"Wrong!"

Damn! The correct answer was debtor-creditor. Double "-or" words. Who would have thought? Another law school trick on the mind. O for 1. In *One L*, Turow described a similar experience and crisis of confidence when he gave a wrong answer in Criminal Law. He said it made him feel "horribly embarrassed—worse than that, corrosively ashamed."

That I so clearly recall such an insignificant event decades later is itself a statement about the blunt trauma of law school on the raw, tender brains of new recruits. I wish had I had known then what I know now: that the professor and other students remembered my wrong answer, if it registered at all, for less than three seconds, 0.0000003 percent of the time it has occupied emotional space in my brain.

After teaching a Torts class, I encountered a student waiting for me at the bottom of the stairs. She said she was embarrassed by and wanted to apologize for her classroom performance. She rapidly reeled off three perceived failings: "I said 'I don't know' to one question, but I did know. I had it in my notes. I just wasn't thinking right about it. Then I said 'I'm not sure' to another question. Finally, I was going to give the right answer on one question, but you corrected me before I had time to finish." Bless her neurotic, paranoid heart. I barely remembered calling on her.

Another student explained the whacks to self-efficacy dished out by the first year of law school:

> It's hard to have this image of yourself as a Top Student crumble. I hear that from many other students, and I think that if one doesn't realize that EVERYONE is feeling this, it may seem that everyone else has it all together and you're the only one struggling. Most people who come to law school have probably heard all their lives, from first grade onward, that they are "smarter." In college, scholarships get thrown your way, you win special fellowships or work for your professors on special projects. You have this feeling of being "good" at this school thing and feeling competent.
>
> I think the Socratic method (hearing someone give an answer that seems so much more intelligent than whatever you were thinking), and the evaluation method (not having feedback through assignments and midterm tests and what not) can really mess with you. I received an e-mail from a fellow student. She's a student I think people assume "has it all together," and she said, "I feel like I'm hanging on by my fingernails." My personal metaphor for law school is one of a mouse running on a wheel. You've seen mice running too fast and the next thing, they're spinning around with the wheel. I feel that if I stumble, the wheel will fling me off.

Neurotic, paranoid wimp.

*   *   *

> [T]he peculiar privilege which Socraticism grants a teacher to invade the security of every student in the room means that in the wrong hands it can become an instrument of terror.
>
> —Turow, *One L*

More than any other aspect of law school, the Socratic method scared the hell out of me. Professor Thomas Hurst, a likeable young professor, called on me disproportionately in Contracts, at least it seemed that way to me. Each time, I practically had a stroke. But it wasn't because of him. "Tommy Hurst," as we called him, was a nice guy. I was simply afraid of being exposed as dimwitted or, just as bad, average.

When people say law school has changed since Turow's days, they're often referring to the professors he described. The very mention of *One L* conjures images of abusive, intimidating professors. But in rereading the book, I was confused. Most of the professors Turow described were quite benign. Some even let unprepared students "pass" on a question, something I don't do even today. Only one of Turow's professors even arguably fit the model of the imperious professor who intentionally humiliates or otherwise abuses students: Professor Perini, his Contracts prof. And even he wasn't that bad.

Turow describes "the Incident," a classroom episode involving mistreatment of a student by Perini so outrageous it caused the class to organize a protest and circulate a petition. What did Perini do that was so terrible? He got mad at a student who wasn't prepared for Contracts class because he had been working on his legal writing paper instead. Perini told the student in a threatening manner that he hoped he would be "*very* well prepared on Monday." Then he told the class, "I had hoped to get further, but the level of preparation was so *poor*." When the class ended, he stomped out of the room.

That's it? That was the most horrible classroom incident of the year? What happened to the evil, abusive professors I recalled reading about back in 1978? Had they been edited out in subsequent editions? What about the students who got jolted with electric shocks and clubbed with batons when they gave wrong answers? Isn't that the way it went down? That's the way I remembered it.

Geez, what law professor hasn't got ticked off at unprepared students, especially those who blow off class because of legal writing assignments? And Perini didn't even leave until the class was over. I know plenty of professors who have walked out in the middle of classes because of poor preparation. (I did it once myself, but felt bad about it and came back before the students had a chance to leave.) Sure, Perini was rude, but I've seen judges treat lawyers much worse. As I tell my students, the real world of practicing law makes law school look like summer camp.

Turow acknowledged that the Incident might seem "trifling" to an outsider. But, as he noted, in that pebble-sized world of first-year law school, "there [is] so much wrapped up in . . . the pressures, and the uncertainty, and the personal humblings." In 1978, as an anxious kid about to start law school, the Incident no doubt resonated with me as it did with Turow and his classmates: as a scary, humiliating ordeal, much worse than an electric shock and clubbing.

Rereading *One L* reinforced what I have long known as a professor, but never realized as a student. It's not the professors who cause all the angst in 1Ls. It's the students. The pressure pumped into classrooms by the Socratic turbine comes from within. Looking back, I was more afraid of what I would do to myself than what my professors would do to me. It was bad enough feeling inadequate privately. I didn't want to display it to everyone else. The Socratic method can deliver a left-right combination punch to self-esteem: first, by reminding students how intelligent their classmates are when they volunteer articulate, responsive answers; and second, by reminding students how unintelligent they are (or think they are) when they can't come up with their own articulate, responsive answers. With everything occurring in a public arena, it can feel like finishing in third place and in the minus category on *Jeopardy* day after day.

Imagine you are sitting in class one day minding your own business. The professor is talking a hundred miles an hour when all of a sudden your name rings out:

> *Mr. Smith!* A shoots at B, but misses and hits C, who loses control of her car and crashes into D, driving a school bus full of children—H, I, J, K, L, M, N, O and P—down a winding mountain road. The school bus hits a gas pump at the same moment lightning strikes the pump. In the explosion, E, a piece of glass, hits F, walking his dog, G, which gets loose and bites Q, a law student formerly known as R, carrying casebooks up a staircase. The books fall on S, causing a head injury. S is rushed to the ER by EMTs, gets CPR from an RN and an IV from an MD, but it's too late. He's DOA. Who wins? [Three second pause.] Quick, quick, Mr. Smith! We don't have all day.

Perini-style Socratic traditionalists are dwindling in U.S. legal education, but anxiety about getting called on still runs rampant in first-year classes, which should be no surprise. Being cold-called on and expected to give an intelligent answer to a question one has never thought about is inherently intimidating no matter how nicely the professor poses the question.

I asked a group of new students what their biggest stressors or causes of anxiety were after two weeks of law school. These were the first three responses I came across:

* Waiting to be called on creates a lot of stress for me. It's like you're sitting in every class knowing that it could be your name that comes up at any time and you're not completely confident in what you will say. It's like waiting on the other shoe to drop!

* I have noticed in class that when questions are left open for students to answer, I find myself going blank in my head because I am fearful that the professor will revert to the seating chart and go directly to the clueless Mr. ———. However, when the question is directed at a specific student (not me), the pressure is off and I seem to be able to come up with the right answer. I think it is a confidence issue.

* My biggest stressor is that I will be called on in class, and will not have the slightest clue of the answer, or make a really off-the-wall statement. That hasn't changed because I haven't been called on just yet. Please don't call on me now that I've told you that.

Neurotic, paranoid wimps. Welcome to the club!

*   *   *

At one-thirty, wild now with drugs and frustration, I rolled out and began to flail at the mattress: I was *trying* to destroy myself, I shouted; I was *insuring* failure.

—Turow, *One L*

Drug rehab gone bad? Nah. Just another 1L—Turow, in this case—freaking out the night before his first exam. Nothing like that first set of law school exams to push a person over the edge. Grades, especially early grades, are important in law school. A 1984 national study of stress in undergraduate, graduate, law, and medical students concluded that "in no other university setting do grades have the importance at such an early point in one's education."

But simply making grades important was not enough to satisfy the architects of legal education. More stress and suffering were required, so legal educators came up with the single-exam format. Buried in the bowels of the Harvard Law School library, I discovered this one hundred percent authentically fake transcript of the origins of this diabolical device:

LAW DEAN:	I have an idea. We'll require the students to learn hundreds of rules—
LAW PROFESSOR 1:	No, make it thousands.
LAW DEAN:	Okay, good. Thousands of rules in a single semester and then give them only one test at the end.
LAW PROFESSOR 1:	Loving it, loving it.
LAW PROFESSOR 2:	How long should the test be?
LAW DEAN:	Three hours.
LAW PROFESSOR 2:	But how can we test thousands of rules in three hours?
LAW DEAN:	[*cackling*] We can't! Don't you see? That's the beauty of it.
LAW PROFESSOR 1:	So we'll just pick a handful of the thousands of rules and make their entire fate rest on that. Brilliant!
LAW PROFESSOR 2:	Okay, I think I'm getting it now. How about this? We'll also make loud animal noises while they're taking the exam.
LAW DEAN:	Too obvious, but I like the way you're thinking. Now, an important key to driving them completely over the edge—to guarantee they lose their minds—is we cannot give them *any feedback* on their progress during the semester until that single exam smacks them in the face.
LAW PROFESSOR 1:	I agree. Keeping them in the dark makes perfect pedagogical sense. Also, the best professors will test them with cockamamie fact patterns that bear no resemblance to real life.
LAW DEAN:	That goes without saying. And for the final touch, the last thing a professor will do when the exam starts is to write the ending time on the board. They'll obsess about that the entire time.
LAW PROFESSOR 2	Ooh, no wonder you're the dean.

My first law school exam was Criminal Law. The professor didn't teach us much actual law. He talked a lot about theory. My notes for the entire course were just a few pages. Fortunately, an upper-level student gave me an excellent piece of advice at the beginning of the year:

"Buy the *Gilberts* outline for Crim Law. Professor _____ won't teach you any blackletter law, but he'll expect you to know it all on the exam. Just buy the *Gilberts* and memorize it. Trust me."

Blind faith. I'm not sure why but I pinned all my hopes and effort on this insider tip. While many of my classmates spent their time in study groups trying to unravel the professor's theoretical ramblings, I immersed myself in the *Gilbert* study aid for Criminal Law. (Turow had a similar experience with Perini, the Contracts professor. He got a tip that Perini's course was straight out of his hornbook, but was reticent to believe it.)

The instant I laid eyes on it, my Criminal Law exam became forever associated with "Holy ——!" and other excited utterances that commonly greet surprising news. The exam was a classic blackletter law issue-spotter, with A, B, C and friends robbing, murdering, and committing other felonies against each other. Not a trace of the criminological theories of punishment and blame we spent the entire term beating to death in class. The exam went great . . . until I walked out of it and made that eternal law student mistake:

"What did you think?" classmate Ken said.

"I thought it was okay," I said. "Thank God someone told me to expect blackletter law questions."

"Yeah, I heard that too. But that conspiracy issue was tricky."

"Conspiracy issue? What conspiracy issue?"

Ken proceeded to explain an elaborate issue that I had missed. *Completely.* If it had been only Ken, I might have dismissed it, but then another classmate chimed in about the same issue. I stood there feeling like I had just wasted the three hardest months of my life, convinced I was about to flunk out of law school.

Naturally, I obsessed about this for the remainder of the exam period. As it turned out, I got my first *A* in law school on that exam. As usual, neurotic, paranoid wimpiness shows its limitations as a lifestyle. I never again stayed to autopsy an exam. I advise my students to do the same, but, of course, they don't listen.

*　　*　　*

"It's over!" I shouted when I got in the car. I've been repeating that to myself for the past few hours. It will probably take a couple of days for me to believe it. The first year of law school. It seemed sheer myth when my friends lived through it. Now I have, too. It is over. It is over. —Turow, *One L*

Students not only experience the lows of law school similarly, but the highs as well. My reaction to the end of the first year was the same mixture of relief and disbelief as Turow's. In the epilogue to *1L of a Ride*, I recount attending a party on the day of my last first-year exam:

I was the only law student there. I doubt if I mentioned law school the entire night, probably because I'd learned that non-law students could not care less about it. I did think about it though. I have a distinct memory of sitting in a chair watching the hubbub around me, sipping punch, and feeling blissfully happy, thinking: "I'm done! I can't believe I'm actually done!"

That's the best news about the first year of law school. It only lasts one year. My stress, fear, and anxiety diminished considerably after that first year, but that's not necessarily the case with everyone. In fact, studies show that the psychological dysfunction of law students continues through graduation and afterwards into their careers. In surveying a class of Torts students who were wrapping up their 1L odyssey, one wrote:

Dear God! I have two more years of this? It's kind of like being sent to war and then getting wounded in battle. You start to think you are finally going to get sent home after you heal only to find out you're being sent back to the front line, with even less chance of survival because now you're wounded.

Once a neurotic, paranoid wimp, always a neurotic, paranoid wimp. Nothing has changed.

How You Gonna Keep Her Down on the Farm . . .

LISA R. PRUITT

Too bad Mom wasn't there on the first day of law school to take a photo of me—a photo like the one she took the day I started first grade, a photo to document a milestone. The first-grade photo shows me in a Sears & Roebuck calico dress with a lace-trimmed bodice, red tights, pageboy hair cut, little red satchel. Maybe if I had a photo from the day I began law school, the random batches of memories I have been able to conjure up about my 1L year would be more complete, seem more reliable. Maybe I would have a clearer recollection of who I was when I became a law student at the University of Arkansas in the fall of 1986—and of how the experience changed me.

But a quarter of a century is a long time for impressions to morph and mutate, leaving my current memories of what "it" was like—what I was like—a little hazy. The tendency to see the past—perhaps particularly one-self—in the light of one's current consciousness strikes me as a powerful and distorting lens through which to reminisce. Even as the intervening decades of life-shaping events lend perspective and clarity to the here and now, the filter of those decades obscures my 1L experience. As it is, then, the only recollections from that year which feel very trustworthy are a couple of vignettes, a personality sketch or two (including a partial one of myself), and a few professorial quotes that I've appropriated in my own decade of teaching.

My skepticism of many of my memories stems in part from my early contemplation of what my very own 1L essay—this essay—might say. As I put fingers to keyboard for an initial draft, I recalled a rube-like person. No, not one with straw between her teeth in overalls or a Daisy Mae[10] outfit, though my rural roots might suggest those images. I had by then spent four years at the state's land grant, flagship public institution of higher education, and despite what outsiders may think—especially in light of all the hog calling that goes on at Razorback sporting events—it's a very civilized place. But when I initially recalled who I was intellectually and emotionally when I began law school, someone naïve and uninitiated came to mind. Someone who "just fell off the Grapette truck," to borrow one of my father's expressions.[11]

My preliminary recollections suggested that I had no idea what I was getting into—substantively or procedurally, as we law profs might say. Surely "tort" was a foreign word to me, I thought, as I must have been unfamiliar with both civil liability and epicurean variations. Certainly I had little sense of what lawyers did other than a vague belief that they "righted wrongs" or "did justice." I had heard of the ACLU and thought that would be a cool place to work some day. But I knew little else of law or lawyers. How could I have known more? The first episode of *L.A. Law* was still a few weeks away.

Further reflection, however—informed by a review of my college-era resume—led me to realize I could not have been as clueless a 1L as I initially imagined. As an undergraduate, I had taken the course on law for journalists and become quite fascinated with defamation law. My journalism advisor (also the supervisor for my weekly work-study hours, both during my later undergrad years and when I was a first-year law student) had introduced me to a law professor who specialized in this and other media law issues. That law professor (later my Torts professor) had supervised my undergraduate honors thesis: "A Survey of State Court Decisions Determining a Post-*Gertz* Standard of Liability for Private Plaintiff Libel Cases." It doesn't sound very scintillating now, but I was completely captivated then. The project had not only introduced me to the wonderful

---

10. The reference here is to a central character in Al Capp's comic strip, Li'l Abner. Daisy Mae was the buxom, scantily clad, blonde wife of Li'l Abner. For an academic exposition about Daisy Mae, see Sally W. Maggard, *Will the Real Daisy Mae Please Stand Up? A Methodological Essay on Gender Analysis in Appalachian Research*, 21 APPALACHIAN J. 136 (1994).

11. Another variation on this southern idiom involves falling from a turnip truck.

intricacies of a narrow slice of the law, it had taken me into the law library on a regular basis the year before I started law school. I was consequently familiar with the physical facility, and I had seriously grappled with one core legal concept (summary judgment) and some marginal and arcane ones (such as libel per se and libel per quod).

As a 1L, then, I knew a little about law after all. I nevertheless tend to think that my familiarity with law and legal institutions paled in comparison to that of most of my classmates. There were no lawyers in my family. Indeed, there was only one in my home county—Newton County, Arkansas, population about 8,000—but I had never met him.[12]

It is actually hard to say with any certainty why I was drawn to law school. My mother's long-time nickname for me, "last-word Lisa," suggests I was a tenacious talker and skilled hair-splitter from an early age. But law was a force largely absent from my life, consistent with one myth of rurality.[13] The only law enforcement officers in Newton County when I was growing up were a sheriff and a couple of deputies. The town where I went to school, Jasper, was still a decade or so away from having its first police officer. A circuit judge who resided in a neighboring county visited the Newton County courthouse only on a need-to basis. Otherwise, the building's courtroom was used for community events; as a teenager, I had occasionally participated in 4-H programs there.

Yet even as law and legal actors were absent from my life, the specter of law—its potential as a disciplining authority—loomed over my family. You see, my father was a scofflaw, and he was the type who liked to talk about his lawless exploits. Among other infractions, he frequently purchased beer from a local bootlegger (Newton County was and is a "dry" county, as are most contiguous counties), evaded various federal regulations of the trucking industry (in which he labored for virtually all of his working life), and bought votes on behalf of Democratic candidates in

---

12. This strikes me now as somewhat remarkable given the lack of anonymity that characterizes rural places, a feature I've made much of in my own scholarship. *See, e.g.,* Lisa R. Pruitt, *Place Matters: Domestic Violence and Rural Difference,* 23 Wis. J.L. Gender & Soc'y 347, 363–65 (2008). But even small towns have social hierarchies: he was the county's sole professional; I was a local teenager.

13. *See* Lisa R. Pruitt, *Rural Rhetoric,* 39 Conn. L. Rev. 159, 199–206 & n.240 (2006) (citing Robert C. Ellickson, Order Without Law: How Neighbors Settle Disputes (1991)).

local elections as far back as I can recall (quite a common practice by both parties in Newton County).[14] I remember being a nervous wreck every time I became aware of one of his crimes—once I realized that's what they were. I expected the awesome, punitive power of the law to come crashing down on us at any moment.

I didn't know then, of course, about rurality's association with an effective absence of law, and I doubt I would have been much comforted by such an academic notion had I been so informed. As it happened, I was well into my teens before I began to appreciate the inefficacy—never mind apparent disinterest—of the county's few law enforcement officers when it came to actually enforcing the law. Except in the run up to local elections, when the sheriff busted bootleggers, moonshiners and pot growers in a (usually temporary) law-and-order show, producers and purveyors of illicit substances—and certainly their customers—had little to fear.[15] As for the vote buying, a sheriff had no incentive to work with federal authorities to investigate those engaged in the practice when he was as likely as not a beneficiary of it.

I see those realities now, but I was fearful then. For some reason (probably the Christian upbringing my mother gave me), I took the law very seriously and respected its authority—in spite of its agents' relative inaction. Maybe, then, I was drawn to the law as a reaction against my father's disregard for it. My decision to pursue a legal education may have been a classic case of the child rebelling against the parent. I was simply joining the other team.

Whatever role my father's behavior played in my career choice, I recall practical, economic considerations also influencing me. My degree in journalism had set me up to earn about $8,000 a year, insufficient to cover both living expenses and student loan payments. Plus, I didn't think I was assertive enough to be a particularly good journalist, though I must have seen that as a shortcoming for a lawyer, too.

---

14. *See* United States v. Campbell, 845 F.2d 782 (8th Cir. 1988) (reporting the conviction of Newton County's chief administrative officer, the "county judge," for paying or offering to pay voters for voting, in violation of 42 U.S.C. § 1973i(c)).

15. For a wide-ranging discussion of the challenges and realities of rural law enforcement, see RALPH A. WEISHEIT, DAVID N. FALCONE & L. EDWARDS WELLS, CRIME AND POLICING IN RURAL AND SMALL-TOWN AMERICA 51 (3d ed. 2006).

I had held no internships or jobs at all related to law—let alone the high falutin' ones like those of many of the first-year students I teach. No, I had instead spent the summer before law school working in a shoe store, having spent the prior summer running a concession stand at a little league park, and the six summers before that working at a theme park near my hometown. Those six seasons at Dogpatch USA, a park based on the Al Capp comic strip Li'l Abner, and my other minimum wage (or less) jobs had equipped me with bookkeeping and people greeting skills, but little else really.

Further, my life experiences—at least as they might be obviously relevant to law—were very limited. My only personal encounter with the law had been a single speeding ticket. My lack of exposure to law was, I think, similar to that of a young lawyer whom I interviewed about a decade ago for a study of post-apartheid integration of the South African legal profession. The man of color said:

> I knew how to spell "stock exchange," but I didn't know what it was. Whites, on the other hand . . . many had inherited trust portfolios, were managing these by the time they were in their teens. This stuff was discussed at the dinner table, was second nature to [them].[16]

Apartheid's legacy for him was surely a very tough row to hoe. But it struck me during the interview that I had something in common with him: I, too, felt very much like an ill-equipped "other" in the context of law school, if only on the basis of class.

Of course, I might have better informed myself regarding what to expect in law school. But no one at my undergraduate institution, the J. William Fulbright College of Arts and Sciences at the University of Arkansas, had counseled me about law school—not about selecting one, nor about what to expect. I had taken the LSAT, of course, but not a prep course for it. I applied only to the University of Arkansas, hoping to be awarded the sole Robert A. Leflar Scholarship to pay my tuition and provide a stipend. The law school's dean of students advised me that I was unlikely to get it, in spite of my 4.00 undergrad GPA. This was apparently due to a lackluster

---

16. Lisa R. Pruitt, *No Black Names on the Letterhead? Efficient Discrimination and the South African Legal Profession*, 23 MICH. J. INT'L L. 545, 641 (2002).

LSAT, but I've mentally blocked the degree of the score's inferiority and kept no record of it. In the end, I got the Leflar scholarship, presumably because better applicants picked other law schools.

My failure to learn more about the law school scene in advance of becoming part of it is not, mind you, because I wasn't ambitious. I was, of a sort. But I didn't know enough to know what I didn't know. I didn't know what to ask, and I didn't have ready sources. This was well before the internet age, when any self-respecting, would-be law student Googles "1L" and finds out more than she ever wanted about the undertaking.

I have a vague recollection of watching an episode of *The Paper Chase* during the summer before law school. I must not have found it that interesting or I would surely have watched more. Perhaps I didn't view additional episodes because the show seemed irrelevant to me. I, after all, was at the University of Arkansas—not Harvard. I would not be walking the hallowed and historic halls of an Ivy League law school. The building in which I was to get my legal education looked rather less salubrious and pretentious—part vintage '60s, part '80s. I saw myself as training to be a Little Rock lawyer or some such, not—as a Yale-educated colleague once described his alumni network's sense of themselves—destined to be a leader of the free world.

Certainly I had not read *One L* by the time I started law school. I don't believe I even knew about it. I recall learning of the book near the end of my first semester. A classmate in my small section had read it, and she often referenced it—somewhat obnoxiously, I might add—as if it were the final word on all things law school. Maybe her slightly hoity-toity, I-know-something-you-don't-know attitude is what did it in.[17] As if Scott Turow knew everything because he went to Haaaaavard. Perhaps, as with *The Paper Chase*, I assumed Turow's Harvard experience was surely irrelevant—at least largely so—to my Arkansas one. Maybe that's why I never got around to reading the book. Maybe there just wasn't any time left once

---

17. Her superior attitude may have stemmed from the fact she was from the big city—Little Rock. I recall another classmate—this one from the great metropolis of Tulsa—commenting once on how all the people from small towns were always talking about how wonderful and distinctive their hometowns were. Why, she pondered, did they feel they had so much to prove? Why did it matter that their hometowns were interesting, even distinctive?

I had read every assigned case three times, looked up each unfamiliar word in *Black's Law Dictionary*, and written a brief that was about seventy-five percent as the long as the case excerpt itself.

You see, one thing I am quite clear on is that succeeding by the numbers was extremely important to me. The same had been true in my undergraduate studies, and my discipline and hard work had paid off. Those earlier achievements might have endowed me with more confidence as I began law school, but "everyone" (who, exactly, I cannot say) seemed to warn that undergraduate achievement was not a particularly good predictor of law school success.

While the anxiety-driven focus with which I began law school is surely typical of many 1Ls then and now, it strikes me that the pressure I experienced made the need to succeed tantamount to a matter of life and death. What was behind my focus and ambition? Fear of failure or desire to succeed? Perhaps I most wanted to succeed for the sake of being a success—or to be perceived as successful, if there's a difference.

Or maybe I was really driven by the material consequences I anticipated from my performance. Perhaps I wanted to ensure I had options other than returning to "the farm"—the confines of Newton County, that is, to generate some competition (or business) for its sole attorney. Or perhaps I was acting on the fear of god regarding education that my mother had instilled in me from an early age. She had long been hell-bent on her daughters getting educated, seeing this as a path to a life different than hers, a life with choices. I think I understood that. I wanted choices, independence, and bargaining power.

Why else, I wonder, would I have invested upwards of eighty hours a week on my law school endeavor? My diligence in my daily class preparation, outlining, and exam-period review left nothing to chance. I must have had enormous energy to work so hard. (Ah, the forces of youth and good health!) But I also must have been quite engaged with law's substance, or I would surely have burned out sooner than I did, as a 3L.

Lest these recollections about my work ethic be met with skepticism invited by my earlier admission of hazy memories, let me attempt some substantiation. In my efforts to generate content for this essay, I looked for any law school memorabilia I might have saved. My mother found in her home a single, massive cardboard box holding fifty-five pounds of first-year notes, briefs and outlines.[18] I had set them all aside in neatly labeled Redweld expanding file folders, along with a handful of memos I wrote during my first law firm job, the summer after that initial year of law school. Why I saved these I cannot say. Maybe they represented too great an investment to discard. Whatever my thinking then, the papers now serve as some evidence of a certain over-the-top, by-the-book approach to law school.

∗　∗　∗

As I suggested at the outset, my reminiscences about my first year of law school are necessarily colored by my current perspective. From my vantage point as a scholar of rurality and—at least by implication—of class,[19] I find myself somewhat preoccupied with whether (and how) I played what I have elsewhere called "the rural card"[20] as I undertook this new endeavor, seeking assimilation into a new milieu, a new microcosm.

The title I gave this essay suggests agricultural roots, but the farm reference is a bit of a false advertising. I did not, in fact, grow up on a farm—at least not a working farm.[21] I grew up on land that had been in my father's family for five generations, but no one in my family had actively farmed it for many years. Next to the house in which I was raised was a pasture my paternal grandfather owned; someone from town rented it to keep cattle there.

My maternal grandparents lived on a subsistence farm about ten miles out of town. They raised a huge garden, chickens, and a few cows there, also keeping a mule to plow the garden and provide the brute strength needed for other farm tasks. Not only were my grandparents farmers, they were far

---

18. I know the box weighed fifty-five pounds because UPS told me so when they charged me $38 to ship it to California!

19. *See* Ezra Rosser, *On Becoming "Professor": A Semi-Serious Look in the Mirror*, 36 FLA. ST. U. L. REV. 215 (2009) (musing on the influence of the author's impoverished upbringing on his transition into the legal academy); *see also* Ruthann Robson, *A Couple of Questions Concerning Class Mobility*, 36 HARV. REV. 165, 172–74 (2009) (reflecting on the author's experiences as a law student from a working class background).

20. Lisa R. Pruitt, *Toward a Feminist Theory of the Rural*, 2007 UTAH L. REV. 421, 450.

21. The astute reader will have grasped that I do not consider "farm" and "rural" to be synonymous. Only 6.2% of people who live in rural places in the United States are engaged in agriculture. USDA Economic Research Service, Economic Information Bulletin No. 21, Rural Employment at a Glance 3 (2006).

more rural than I by many indicia: grade school educations, hand-rolled cigarettes from Prince Albert tobacco, overalls and home-sewn dresses—to name a few. They were also poorer, having gotten indoor plumbing—finally—about the time I started law school.[22] Before that, there were out-houses. Water was hand drawn, a bucket at a time, from a well on the front porch, where a wringer-type washing machine also sat.

I had been sustained by that farm's bounty my entire life. Certainly, I felt I had done my share of picking and canning. But I didn't see myself as a farm girl any more than I saw myself as Daisy Mae[23] or Elly May.[24]

I may nevertheless have self-identified as rural. I'd had sufficient experiences in cities to have observed firsthand aspects of the rural-urban binary, but I'd had few enough such encounters that cities still intrigued and intimidated me. If I acknowledged my rural home in the largely Arkansas context of the law school, it was probably as specifically hailing from Newton County. Both my mother's and father's families had lived there since shortly after the Civil War and, like many rural southerners, a significant component of my identity was (and is) grounded in place, based largely on the depth and breadth of my family's roots. And certainly Newton County is a rural place. It is the most rural county in Arkansas by several ecological measures, e.g., population size and density.[25] But it

---

22. Lisa R. Pruitt, A Rural Life (as distinct from "The Rural Life"), blog post to Legal Ruralism, http://legalruralism.blogspot.com/2007/12/rural-life-as-distinct-from-rural-life. html (Dec. 2, 2007).

23. I suspect I would not then have mentioned my farm-type experiences to my law school colleagues because they were not cool and would have made me seem (more) like a hick. Lisa Heldke has argued that our "metrocentric society" assumes that those with rural knowledge are unsophisticated, which has contributed to a loss of knowledge of rural life, especially among young people. *See* Lisa Heldke, *Farming Made Her Stupid*, 21 HYPATIA 151, 160–61 (2006). This may be changing now as the locavore and Slow Food phenomena are making farming trendy and hip, though these movements are not necessarily having that positive impact on attitudes toward rural life more broadly. *See* Legal Ruralism Blog, Agritourism label, http://legalruralism.blogspot.com/search/label/agritourism.

24. The reference here is to a character on the long-running and very popular television show, *The Beverly Hillbillies*. Elly May was a member of the unsophisticated Clampett family, who moved to Beverly Hills after they were enriched by the discovery of oil on their Ozarks property.

25. *See* Gerald W. Creed & Barbara Ching, *Introduction—Recognizing Rusticity: Identity and the Power of Place*, in KNOWING YOUR PLACE: RURAL IDENTITY AND CULTURAL HIERARCHY 1 (Barbara Ching & Gerald W. Creed eds., 1997) (discussing rurality as relative

is also culturally rural—the stuff of hillbilly lore even within Arkansas, which outsiders might see as an essentially or entirely hillbilly state.

Newton County is also known to other Arkansans as a place that produces a lot of marijuana and is home to the headwaters of and best floating on the Buffalo National River. I suspect that, upon learning of my provenance, my new colleagues made jokes about *Deliverance* and Dogpatch. Maybe a few mentioned that they had floated the Buffalo.

I don't think I had a clue back then about identity politics. Diversity was certainly a concern within the state's higher education system, but I recall its discussion only in relation to the state's persistent black-white divide. As an undergraduate student leader, I had become more aware of those concerns. Because I was white, though, it never occurred to me that I might have been seen as a more valuable or interesting member of the community had I "come out" as the product of a working class family.[26] Perhaps some would have seen me in a more positive light—rather than the negative one I anticipated and projected onto myself—had I disclosed that my mother was a teacher's aide, my father was a truck driver, and I was the first person in my family to go to graduate school, only the second after my sister to get a bachelor's degree.

As it was, I recall needing to keep secret those familial details. If I was asked about my family of origin, I probably referred to my father as the owner of a "small business." Which he was, of course; it's just that his office had eighteen wheels and he spent his days (and very often his nights) traversing the country in it.

---

concept culturally); Lisa R. Pruitt, *Gender, Geography & Rural Justice*, 23 BERKELEY J. GENDER L. & JUST. 338, 343–48 (2008).

26. On the other hand, first-generation college students who were white may have been seen as a dime a dozen at the University of Arkansas, and so not as a source of diversity at all. Even if our numbers were few, the University and School of Law might not have appreciated the diversity represented by working-class whites. Law faculties tend to be liberal, and they have become quite adept at facilitating difficult conversations about many characteristics associated with disadvantage—race, ethnicity, and sexual orientation among them. I have not, however, found law faculties very willing or able to discuss socioeconomic disadvantage in any meaningful way when it does not intersect with some quasi-immutable and/or more highly visible minority status. Perhaps liberal whites, who are typically middle class, avoid engaging with socioeconomic disadvantage as a stand-alone issue because they feel more vulnerable when they think about poor whites than when they think and talk about poor people of color. But I will stop here, as I am on the verge of a whole 'nother story.

I now know that my behavior is called "passing"—class passing, to be precise. And the photos I have from that year support my recollection that it was incredibly important to me to "clean up well," self-conscious as I was about my working class roots in the Ozarks plateau. An eye on an (improbable) future in state politics reinforced my concern about what others thought. For me, a desire to fit in meant never going out of the house without a full face of make-up, hair carefully styled. I often wore skirts and sweaters of the preppy variety—this was, after all, the South. Pretenses had to be kept up, appearances maintained.

Complicating this extreme concern about appearances was the fact that I drove a pick-up truck during much of my law school career. Not a beat up, farm-type of truck, but rather a fairly late model, short-wheel base, black and silver Chevy Silverado. I didn't choose the truck. It's what my parents supplied for me to drive, and I was grateful to have it. It wasn't consistent with the image I was trying to cultivate, but I nevertheless recall enjoying somewhat the attention the truck attracted. Preppy, smart "girl" in a pick-up truck. Even on the land grant campus, that stood out!

While I was no doubt prissy, I was not—I am confident—a frivolous, giggly girly girl. I am nevertheless quite sure I still thought of myself as a "girl"—such an unthreatening label. I had not by then had my feminist epiphany and surely thought "feminism" was a dirty word. No, I wasn't ready for feminism, in part because I thought it was unnecessary and passé, in part because it represented risk, non-conformity, and challenge to authority—all decidedly not for me. Indeed, those who know me now may find this hard to believe, but I am pretty sure "edgy" was not in my repertoire back in 1986. Ambitious, yes. Edgy, no. Being a self-styled "girl" was consistent with both—at least in the 1980s South.

Given my attention to appearance, it is not at all surprising that I had a boyfriend. Given my ambition, it is not at all surprising that he didn't last beyond that first year of law school. He had been a holdover from my undergraduate days and didn't weather the 1L storm. It was no fault of his; I'm sure he put up with a lot. A friend has reminded me that I'd go for dinner and a movie with him on the weekend, only to come home and be studying again by 10 p.m. One eye on *Saturday Night Live*, the other on a casebook.

But the more significant consequences of my ambition were—to quote a favorite proximate cause case—still "in the bosom of time, as yet unrevealed."[27] Events at the end of my second year gave that first year the glow of halcyon days. By then, more negative consequences of my ambition had come home to roost. Those events were my comeuppance for being an ambitious girl; they became the feminist epiphany that caused me to give up that girl thing and embrace my womanhood. But that is all another story.[28]

Which brings me to the ways in which my feminist identity and my own feminist scholarship influence my reflections on my 1L year. I have already admitted having been prissy and what I would now label "anti-feminist." I also recall taking "equality" for granted, though I'd not given much thought to what equality meant beyond the opportunity to compete with men to do what I wanted to do professionally. For me, equality was about the absence, by and large, of formal gender barriers; I was oblivious to the possibility of informal ones. When it came to gender awareness, I truly had just tumbled off the metaphorical Grapette truck.

Seeing gender as irrelevant to my career, I figure I expected ultimately to marry (of course!), but not until I was perhaps thirty—an advanced age in that time and place. I suspect that a strong identity as a self-reliant and independent person had already emerged and that I knew by then that I would always work outside the home. My evolving capacity to see myself as a lawyer surely enhanced these aspects of my identity.

I am also relatively sure that issues of work-life balance never crossed my mind.[29] Even apart from gender roles, balance, also, was not in my repertoire. I was a Maximizer—bent on having the proverbial "all." That ambition thing again.

While I was not switched on to gender issues as a 1L, my feminist leanings and scholarship now color my reflections on the 1L classroom experience. The *Becoming Gentlemen* study at the University of Pennsylvania includes this quote from a female law student: "Law school is the most bizarre place I have ever been. . . . [First year] was like a frightening out-of-body experience. Lots of women agree with me. I have no words to say what I feel. My voice from that year is gone."[30]

---

27. Marshall v. Nugent, 222 F.2d 604, 612 (1st Cir. 1955).

28. Lisa R. Pruitt, *Law Review Story*, 50 ARK. L. REV. 77 (1997).

29. *See* Joanne Lipman, Op-Ed, *The Mismeasure of Woman*, N.Y. TIMES, Oct. 24, 2009, at A21 (recounting some similar sentiments).

30. Lani Guinier et al., *Becoming Gentlemen: Women's Experiences at One Ivy League School*, 143 U. PA. L. REV. 1, 4 (1994).

Reading this and similar sentiments from female law students in a wide range of studies made me wonder if I, too, lost my voice during the first year of law school. Certainly, I did not experience the 1L classroom as an empowering place. I recall being petrified when called on—indeed, even at the prospect of it. Sadly, however, the answer to the loss-of-voice question may be that I had not by the time I started law school found a voice—at least not one that felt worth keeping, not one that was a significant part of my identity.

Don't get me wrong. I had some convictions. I know I felt strongly about right and wrong, about kindness, charity, industry. But I don't think I had yet developed a capacity for critical thinking, for considering how a particular legal rule worked an injustice for some populations. I took my whiteness for granted, and I wasn't identifying—perhaps even to myself—as working class or feminist, so for whom was I to go out on a limb? On whose behalf was I to get angry and indignant at the law? Certainly not my own.

I presumably approached law school as I had my prior educational experiences: taking in information, memorizing it, regurgitating it back out—prettily, of course, with proper grammar, in cogent sentences and neat paragraphs. But I probably did all of that without much critical thought. Could it be that I had spent so much energy ensuring report cards full of As, earning scholarship after scholarship to help finance my education, that development of my critical faculties had been completely overlooked?

Law was an ultimate sort of authority, and I have already admitted that I was not in the business of challenging authority. Indeed, I embraced it, rebelling against my father instead of the establishment. I saw my task as mastering law in substance, not questioning it. To the extent that I was encouraged to question and critique law, I suspect I didn't have much respect for my own opinions. I didn't have confidence in my voice, such as it was.

I regret that these comments may be interpreted to reflect poorly on the University of Arkansas, as some will also see them reflecting on me. My ruminations presumably fuel the school of thought which holds that graduates of third-tier law schools are unsuited for the scholarly life. One rationale for this, as a colleague once explained to me, is that you can't be sure that graduates of non-elite law schools have been exposed to all of the "important" and "big" ideas. This tempts a digression into the travails of a law professor with an inferior educational pedigree, but I'll resist. For that, clearly, is another story.

In any event, as often as I have been made to regret the impact of my Arkansas law degree on my academic career, I have also sought the proverbial silver lining. When I reflect on this admittedly incomplete picture of my 1L self, I can see how Arkansas was an appropriate place for me to study law, a good fit for who I was then. I might, after all, have been intellectually eaten alive at an elite law school. Perhaps I was better prepared for such an environment by the time I began my PhD, if only because my 3L feminist epiphany ultimately caused my critical faculties to surface. Those events endowed me with just enough edginess to move down that path.

*　　*　　*

Just as my scholarly endeavors have led me to reflect on aspects of my identity at the time, the teaching part of my role as a professor has caused me to reflect on how I was taught and who taught me. One initial observation is dismay at the low number of women on the University of Arkansas law faculty in 1986: four tenured or tenure-track women to be exact. One or two may have taught in the first-year curriculum, but none taught my small section. My only female professor that year was a legal writing instructor—not a great surprise given that this field is now well-documented as a pink ghetto.

While this dearth of women angers me now, I don't recall it as jarring then—no doubt another illustration of my undeveloped critical faculties. Shortly before I graduated, I had a conversation with one of the tenured women in which she asked me why I had not sought a mentor from among the women faculty. I recall telling her that I didn't know—it just hadn't happened. Further, my path had naturally not crossed with any of theirs because I was not particularly interested in their fields of expertise. If pressed to speculate now, though, I would say I lacked female mentors because none of the women professors reached out to me, and I did not have the courage to reach out to them. I also did not perceive a need for their mentorship, in part because male professors had filled the gap by initiating mentoring relationships with me.

My all-male line up of first-year professors for substantive courses ran the gamut from affable to cruel, from pedagogically effective to crushingly inept. As I reflect on them now, I see more clearly the power trips some were on. I believe my assessments were more generous then. That authority thing again.

My Criminal Law professor was one of those legendary types—legendary in his own mind, anyway. His most striking physical characteristic was surely his sun-bed tan. He had a well-worn script—admittedly a pretty effective one—from which he seemed never to deviate. It must have taken him decades to refine that script, yet he didn't have it memorized so he mostly stayed close to the lectern and his notes. The professor did not hesitate to issue a verbal slap down and was only begrudgingly positive when someone gave the correct answer. On those occasions he frequently commented, "you know it now, but will you know it under the presss-ss-sure coook-ker of the exam?"

I recall the scowl on my Property professor's face as he marched into class every day, books tucked under one arm. He would slam them on the table before proceeding to the board to scrawl a few illegible words. Behind his back, students called him Darth Vader, in part because of the dark circles beneath his eyes, in part because of his brooding demeanor. He delivered some fairly harsh lines. I remember specifically his "suggestion" to one student (who shall remain nameless here, although his name is a rare detail I do recall) that the young man consider an alternative career path. I don't recall ever being a target of his ire, armored no doubt by my thorough preparation and lengthy case briefs—even if my voice shook during their oral recitation.

My Torts professor was the avuncular type with lots of war stories. He's definitely the one I quote most often these days in my own classroom—perhaps because I, too, teach Torts. "It's his own damn fault" is very handy when discussing contributory negligence. "There's no such thing as good writing, only good re-writing," is equally useful when I'm trying to convince my seminar students to budget plenty of time for revision. Consider the virtually limitless uses (in both law and life) for "there's a broad and fuzzy line between_____ and _____."

My Contracts professor resembled a bulldog, mostly in physique, but also in manner. I recall him as phenomenally ineffective—without even a sense of humor to provide some slight redemption. In retrospect, I don't even recall a formidable intellect. I don't feel a bit bad saying this because he is now dead; I can neither hurt his feelings nor defame him.

The Contracts professor was the type who plodded from case to case with no effort to stitch any of the concepts together. That year in his classroom may have led to my dislike not only of him, but also of contract law as a subject. To this day, when a contracts principle is implicated in a torts case, I announce to my students that I'm "breaking out in hives" and that they, as budding contracts scholars, will have to come to my rescue.

In the interest of full disclosure, my estimation of this professor is surely influenced by the fact he gave me the lowest grade I got in my law school career—indeed, in my entire academic life. My grade for first-semester Contracts was a B-. That's right, a B-! All of my other grades were As of some sort. Even my second semester Contracts grade rose to a robust, fulsome A.

I recall the winter day, classes not yet back in session, when I schlepped over to the law school to check for grades. They were posted by Social Security number, behind a glass-covered case in a common area. I must have felt great disappointment at the B-, and presumably a sense of failure, too. Whatever the range and intensity of my emotional response, however, it was probably ultimately shaped by the fact that the Contracts grade was such an outlier.

On a less positive note, my response was surely also shaped by the fact that everyone seemed to know I had made a B-. Posting grades publicly, by small section and by SSN, ultimately permitted the ultra curious with time on their hands to decipher who had made what grades. My B- became a topic of law-school gossip.

I also recall other students knowing even before I did that I was at the top of the class after our first semester. I think I initially learned my class rank through the grapevine, though it was later confirmed by some member of the Dean's office staff. Is it possible that I didn't know class rankings were calculated until someone told me? Probably not. More likely, I was too afraid to ask—or maybe didn't know where or how to inquire.

I do know that I never investigated the Contracts grade—never visited the professor or sought to look at the Bluebooks. My current regret about this is surely influenced by my own students' eagerness to let me know if their grade in my class is anomalous. At the time, however, I wasn't interested in re-visiting what I saw as the scene of the crime. Mostly out of curiosity, I now wish I had sought his explanation of my shortcomings. What did his grading rubric look like? What issues had I missed?[31]

My regret about how I handled this matter is also surely related to my more global regret about having so little confidence and so little sense of entitlement about my education. I had not yet learned that there was a time for questioning authority—or at least making an inquiry—and that the two were not necessarily synonymous. I also had not yet learned that constructive criticism was a net gain, well worth the immediate discomfort of facing my fallibility.

Somewhat ironically in light of my then-recent journalism degree and my current career, my other low grade my first year of law school was in Legal Writing, an A-. The adjunct professor practiced law at one of the best firms in Fayetteville, a credential I respected. I don't recall knowing what writing habit or style of mine didn't sit well with her. As with my Contracts grade, I regrettably never sought to learn.

The law librarian taught Legal Research to all first-year students. He was widely viewed as a goof, so few took him seriously. His reputation for eccentricity was bolstered by the fact that he wore a toupee and by his enthusiasm for the law school party scene. Indeed, I am certain he was far more a fixture of that scene than I was.

*　　*　　*

I lived just a few blocks from the law school, in the same house I had rented during the last few years of undergrad. Partly as a consequence of that convenience—and partly because I saw myself as on the periphery of the law school scene—I didn't spend time at the law school building except to attend classes and do what work had to be done at the law library.

---

31. On the other hand, a professor whose office was next door to that of the Contracts professor tells this story, which makes me glad I did not investigate:

I once eavesdropped on a conversation he was having with a student.

STUDENT:　"I'm not sure why I got a D on the exam, Professor."

PROFESSOR:　"Well, let me explain. After reading your exam, I leaned back in this chair here and waited for a letter to coalesce in my mind. That letter was a D. Does that answer your question?"

STUDENT:　"Thanks for your time, Professor."

I was never what one of my professors called a "lounge lizard"; I never got distracted by the "law of the lounge" because I never exposed myself to it. It was thus only in the context of my small study group, which coalesced near the end of the first semester, that I realized what varied expectations students had about what we were supposed to be learning.

I don't recall any practice exams or other tutelage on how to take a law school exam. Only after I became a professor and began to grade Bluebooks could I see that not every law student intuitively knows how to take law school exams, how to argue by analogy. This is just something I somehow knew how to do. I didn't need the law broken into elements, and I certainly didn't need a *Gilbert*, an *Emanuel*, or a *Nutshell*.

Perhaps that is one way in which a characteristic often associated with women—attention to context—served me well as a law student. Doing law was fun for me because it was about stories, about context. Learning law by the case method alleviated the need to memorize abstract legal rules. All of the delicious detail associated with applying the law to the *facts* played to my strengths.

*   *   *

Reflecting on my first year of law school makes me wonder: Did I fall in love with the law that year? Probably. To some extent. For a while. At least I think I fell in love with the substance and the nuance—and, of course, with my own success at this new undertaking. I recall becoming enamored with the prospect of a career in appellate litigation or, better yet, as a law professor. Either, I thought, would permit me to wallow around in the finer points of doctrine and Supreme Court politics, matters far more interesting to me then than now.

As I finished my 1L year, I probably still assumed I would live out my life in Arkansas. Perhaps I had begun to think about larger cities in neighboring states, as I became aware that firms from Dallas, Kansas City, and Tulsa came for on-campus interviews of 2Ls and 3Ls. But one thing became clearer and clearer as that year progressed: I would not be returning to Newton County, to the (metaphorical) farm. I would instead be part of the rural brain drain.

At the end of that first year, the ambitious Maximizer in me was riding high. I would work on Law Review in the fall, and I'd been elected student body president for my 2L year. I secured a summer job at a large Little

Rock law firm—the very firm where then-Governor Bill Clinton had once worked. They paid summer associates a whopping $550 per week—more, I think, than either of my parents had ever earned. More importantly, they represented the prospect of making me one of them—a tall-building lawyer.

*　*　*

So, the lack of a photo from my first day of law school is perhaps not so great a loss after all. I can imagine myself as almost as sweet and cute—and surely as filled with a mix of anticipation and fear—as the day I started first grade. I can be pretty certain I wore a skirt, a little cotton sweater and—on what was surely a hot, humid August day—pantyhose, too. My hair was no doubt curled, make-up carefully applied—all in the hopes of making a good first impression.

Besides, who needs a photo when you've got fifty-five pounds of 1L class notes and outlines? In this case, a picture probably isn't worth those gazillions of words.

Take Two

SAIRA RAO

Room 207 was orderly and laundered-looking. I could see that right away, how glossy and scenic, all eggshell paint and vacuum tracks. Built-in seats and desks rose up in rows and columns, ascending towards expansive windows. And then I saw it. The United States Capitol! Sure, the dome was a bit out of focus, cocooned by an uncharacteristic fog. But it was there, no question about it.

Yes, I thought giddily, *this set would do.*

About ten rows up, I unloaded my equipment, a two-ton Compaq laptop, blue Jansport backpack, and plastic name card.

On cue, a stubborn cloud exited left stage, revealing the sun. Enter warmth, optimism, just the right light.

"Hey, I'm Rachel."

I spun around to find a petite woman, mid-twenties, unloading her own bag of tricks. We both wore glasses, wavy bobs, and Banana Republic.

"I'm Saira. I see you're a seltzer girl too."

"Yup," she said, sipping a Vintage raspberry. "So what brings you here?"

Yikes, I thought, *rehearsals were over.*

Quickly, I fumbled through my mental rolodex of scripts, each draft written and revised, the one for Law School tucked between Fox News and *The Heartbreak Kid*.

Two buff bucks on the top row shoved aside their Manhattan Portage messenger bags, parting like the Red Sea, to make room for a third. Tragically, it would be six years until the CW started casting *Gossip Girl*.

59

"So, law school?" Rachel politely asked again, smiling this time, her bottle half-empty.

I clutched my Jansport, as if it contained a teleprompter.

"You know. I was a TV news journalist, and then I went to this think tank. You know, my libertarian phase." (a beat and a chuckle) "And I just felt passive, like I wasn't doing anything. I wanted to help those that I reported about, you know? Like give a voice to those who've been silenced. To help, change, fix things."

My hasty, amateurish delivery didn't do justice to the snappy monologue I'd spent months tweaking, a montage of self-righteous platitudes cribbed from *The Pelican Brief, A Few Good Men* and websites ending with dot org.

"Cool." Rachel said it like she meant it. "Me too. Only print. I was at a magazine."

"Have you read any Grisham?"

She hadn't.

I stretched my ankles, circling the right one and then the left. My red toenail polish was peeling. Where was hair and makeup?

A middle-aged man with sad eyes, khaki pants, and an uneven gait pulled up on the other side of Rachel and me.

"Taken?" He asked.

"All yours," I motioned.

His name was Tony and he was a plastic surgeon. "I've had it up to here with medical malpractice," he sighed, saluting his left ear. "I'm done with the lawsuits, you know, tort run amok. I figured I'd bring down the master's house with the master's tools."

Nice line, I thought enviously. Was it *Jerry Maguire?*

A stellar ensemble cast of blondes, blacks, browns, two nose piercings, and an ascot marched inside, mostly one by one. I wondered what Michael was doing. Michael was my boyfriend. *Ex-boyfriend*, I reminded myself. He'd have liked this ascot, checkered and all.

The guy behind me kicked my chair. An accident, but nonetheless appreciated. He was waxing on about hypocrites and Harvard and ivy tower suits who were cross that he and other civic-minded students had gotten involved with bringing a "living wage" to the janitors there.

"It inspired me to come here, to gain a command of the law. You know," he winked, "so I'd be equipped in the future."

Good Will Hunting!

A dribble of sweat was making its way from his right temple to a reddish soul patch. *A permanent fixture or for character*, I wondered.

"Wow. That was you?" His neighbor, a sly brunette, cooed, "I went to Harvard and remember the whole thing. Amazing."

"Really?!" He pulled on his chin, attempting to reign in a smile that was currently crossing the Mississippi, like Manifest Destiny.

The cloud returned, casting long shadows, introducing a touch of macabre.

"Um, yeah? Helping the little guy? Squelching the man? I'd say that's pretty amazing."

There was something about the way she clutched her number two pencil that indicated the serious nature of her words. Upon closer inspection, he was no Matt Damon.

We weren't in rehearsals, that much was true. But this, the real deal, wasn't a feature film. It was Georgetown University Law Center.

I zipped up my signature gray hoodie in an effort to conceal my silliness, my fraud.

One of these things is not like the others.

My peers had arrived with purpose, impressed with the school's faculty and the promise of do-gooding. Me? Well, I'd arrived a shallow mess, impressed with the school's sweeping views and my peers' facial hair.

Pause. Rewind. Play.

What brings you here?

Adulthood wasn't exactly working out. In the three years since graduating from college, I'd switched jobs and cities three times, desperately attempting, and failing, to get it right. At least I had Michael, I'd thought. My love, my rock, the father of my unborn children. But then he decided I wasn't right.

Michael was a management consultant. I had no clue what he did specifically, only that it was glamorous and exciting generally. After all, his office was on Fifth Avenue.

I was a "program associate" at a midtown think tank with an unexceptional address. This is to say I distributed nametags to freedom-loving septuagenarians during policy luncheons at the Harvard Club. The fast track to a wall-to-wall carpeted nowhere.

Michael started traveling to Kansas City for work and fielding calls from a woman named Heather with an unfamiliar area code. I asked questions, developed a sweating problem and signed up for Kaplan's LSAT test prep. Contingency plans never went out of style.

Michael stopped writing me love letters. Soon after, I asked my college professors for letters of recommendation.

Michael dumped me. I clipped my ponytail, moved in with my sister, drank boxed rosé wine, and began fielding the same question: *So, Saira, why law school?*

Let's see, I needed a profession and a place to live. There was most definitely not a ring to that truth. So, I lied.

The chatter grew louder, charitably interrupting my struggle down memory lane.

"It just seemed so much cooler than the regular J.D. program." Rachel said, cracking open a new bottle of seltzer.

Tony nodded, in agreement.

They spoke of Section 3, our section, Room 207, the school's interdisciplinary program, a big reason students chose Georgetown over comparable schools.

"Saira, what about you?" Tony asked.

I picked Georgetown because N.Y.U. didn't pick me and I chose Section 3 because I saw the word "alternative." Seeing as I'd been squatting in a cheap-wine-induced stupor for months, an alternative sounded nice.

"Same." I glanced at the chalkboard. "So, what have you guys heard about Bargain, Exchange and Liability?"

"It's some sort of crazy mix of torts and contracts. Sounds wonderful." Tony's eyes sparkled. I bet he had a nice bedside manner.

The chatter suddenly stopped, a hush froze the room. The professor had arrived. I craned my neck, half expecting President Clinton or the Dalai Lama. It was neither. Just a middle-aged guy in jeans and a long sleeved T-shirt. He coolly tossed a book from under his arm onto the shiny desk in the front.

"We'll begin with the case of the hairy hand. *Hawkins versus McGee.*"

Click, click, click. At lightning speed, fingers hit letters, the space bar, is "versus" spelled out, a little v, a big V, is there a period? I peered over at Rachel's screen (little v.).

Before I could delete, backspace, he'd already mentioned another case—this too involved a hand. Then he laughed nervously.

"You must be wondering why this guy is so obsessed with messed up hands, right?"

You. [space] Must. [space] Be. [space] Wondering . . . .

Again he laughed. The clicking stopped. More than a hundred heads popped up, not wanting to miss the joke.

Our professor stood meekly before the chalkboard. He'd rolled up a sleeve, revealing a deformed hand. He laughed, awkwardly, conspicuously this time. But nobody else did.

"This, this is the reason this guy is obsessed with cases involving hands."

Standing there, in front of the chalkboard, wearing his Scarlet Letter, he seemed more like a shy, stuttering tween than a renowned Critical Legal Studies scholar.

I wondered what his story had been, if he'd even had one—*why law school?*—decades earlier in Cambridge, when he sat where I was sitting.

Months later, after sporadic Googling and frequent study breaks, a group of us would theorize that his condition was caused, in utero, by the drug Thalidomide—something prescribed to pregnant women decades earlier to combat morning sickness. Also, we'd learn that one of the pretty guys in the back had always wanted to work in film but didn't think he was talented enough, that the sly brunette came from a family of lawyers and that "law" was her first word, that others had been dumped by husbands and wives, that the blond guy in the front row came to law school because he was gay and was sick and tired of being treated like dirt and wanted to fight back. Then there was the guy who made a statement about rape victims "needing to just get over it," and the three girls who cried hysterically, leaving Room 207, unable to even look at him.

But all of that came later.

"So who wants to discuss the facts in *Hawkins*?" The professor had pulled his sleeve back down and was now confidently circling the table in search of volunteers.

A half dozen hands sprang to action, one of them knocking over Rachel's seltzer. A bubbly pool formed by my feet, hoarding bits of dirt, like a messy rainstorm.

That day, that year, 1L. Some were there just because. Some to change, to fix, to better the world. Others, like me, to fix that which you could not see with the naked eye. And then there were things you just couldn't fix.

I unzipped my hoodie and got to work.

Part III
One L Revisited

The first year of law school has a notorious reputation. It is widely regarded as a grueling and frightening ordeal. The professors are cruel tyrants who take delight in intimidating and berating students in the classroom. Students work themselves to the point of exhaustion, but many will nevertheless still flunk out. The competition is cut-throat, with every student willing to do whatever it takes to get the best grades. Someone will slice the crucial pages out of a book in the library to prevent classmates from being able to complete the necessary research for an assignment. In this nightmarish vision, the first-year experience is pure misery and students will feel fortunate just to survive it.

There is some truth in these stereotypes. The first year of law school is undeniably challenging. Students must learn a great deal of unfamiliar terminology and even new ways of thinking. They must develop the ability to read and understand various kinds of difficult materials like judicial opinions and statutes. The classroom experience can be daunting. While few law teachers today employ the chillingly stern style of Professor Kingsfield of *The Paper Chase* (or even Professor Stromwell of *Legally Blonde*), calling on students and using some milder form of the Socratic method to question them is still standard in law schools. No one wants to seem unprepared or dim-witted in front of a teacher and fellow students.

Competition and pressure certainly exist. People who go to law school have had success in their previous academic endeavors, and often in business, athletics, or other realms as well. Many are accustomed to being among the best and brightest in their classes. They are strivers who like to work hard and to be rewarded for it. The manner in which law schools typically assess students adds to the anxiety. A law student's grade in a course often will depend entirely on a final exam, with no scores from mid-term tests or homework assignments to offset the consequences of a poor exam performance. Grading curves in law schools have drifted upward over the years, but many remain tougher than what students faced at the high school or college level, so some students inevitably will be in for a disappointing shock when they receive their first set of law school grades.

But at the same time, first-year experiences are more varied and complex than the simple stereotypes would suggest. For many students, the first year is genuinely exciting. Law is a field filled with interesting and important issues. Once students get over their initial fears of embarrassment, many appreciate the more dynamic and participatory nature of the dialogue in law school classrooms. Most professors try to treat students in a humane, respectful way. While law schools a century ago generally had very lax admissions standards and weeded out their weaker students during the first year, most schools today are more careful about admissions and student attrition rates are lower. Far from looking to stab their classmates in the back to get ahead, most students form close friendships in law school that last for life. Indeed, after hearing all the hype about how terrifying and dismal the first year will be, some students even wind up being a little disappointed to find that law school is kinder and gentler than they had anticipated.

The stories in this section recount a wide range of experiences. Deborah Waire Post and Cameron Stracher describe how their first years at Harvard Law School compared to those in popular chronicles like *The Paper Chase* or Scott Turow's *One L*. Alafair Burke recounts a gripping moment in Criminal Law class that made her see the real stakes underlying abstract legal issues. Hala Furst recalls the toughest bumps in her 1L road, from the heartbreak of a low grade to the fear induced by a professor's tactics. Melissa Anderson describes the unusual challenges she faced when, midway through her 1L year and pregnant with her sixth child, she learned that her husband would be leaving for a military deployment in Iraq. Cumulatively, these stories begin to suggest the kaleidoscope of experiences that 1L students have.

Two Pink Lines

MELISSA N. ANDERSON

Two pink lines. That's how I started my first year of law school. I was pregnant. As I attempted to process the information my mental flow was interrupted by a loud knock on the bathroom door, "Mom! Maggie hit me in the face!" followed directly by my little defendant yelling back "It was an accident!" I did a quick calculation in my head and realized that I would be due to give birth to my sixth child one week before final exams in the spring of my 1L year. I promptly peed my pants.

My husband Jared and I had just moved our entire family, including five children ranging in age from six and a half years to nine months old, from Arizona to Texas. Jared was a non-commissioned officer in the Army and had requested to be sent to San Antonio for three years because it was one of only a handful of Army bases located in the same city as a law school. I had exactly three years to finish law school or my family would be separated. A pregnancy in my first year was not enough to make me take the year off given the sacrifices that my family had already made. Besides, I was firmly of the opinion that my husband and I could raise our little family while I attended graduate school at the same time, and do well at both.

That would have worked out fine had the military not had other plans.

My first class on my first day was Property I, taught by a professor with magnificent white hair that only a seasoned lawyer could have earned the right to wear in public. His pot-bellied stature and slow Southern drawl would have lulled me right to sleep with the rest of the class, except that I had a nasty case of morning sickness and needed to skip less-than-merrily from the room to avoid puking on his bundle of sticks. While I loomed over the toilet, trying to keep my hair out of my own vomit, I couldn't help but think, "Who cares? It's just a silly fox."

I learned early that my law school experience was vastly different from those of my classmates. While many had ample time to study late in the library or go drinking on the weekends, I spent my nights bathing children and my weekends studying on a park bench while my children played with daddy. I studied Contracts at my kitchen table while teaching my oldest how to subtract, my youngest to stop licking the window, and the three in between that high-heeled shoes are not for whacking each other in the spine. I stole precious study moments reading my children to sleep at night from *Learning Civil Procedure*. Old Dittfurth sure could write a bedtime story.

I must admit that I did have one breakdown. One solitary, all-out breakdown. My husband came home early, unusual for a soldier, and gave me the dreaded one liner, "We need to talk." The world, and law, stood still for a single moment. He had orders for Iraq and would be leaving the next semester. I put aside my studies for a moment, just a moment, to explain to five sets of wondering eyes what "war" is and why daddy was going there. Attempting to explain war to a child was more difficult than explaining the Rule Against Perpetuities to a law student. And both tend to cause a great amount of tears.

But if I thought my first semester was hectic, I was in for a shock for my second semester. The week before school started Jared packed up his boots and his duffle bag for pre-deployment training, kissed me on the forehead and headed out of state. He was gone and I was five months pregnant.

I lived in two worlds. During the day I dutifully studied, wrote briefs, outlined and attended every class. I answered to "Ms. Anderson." I bought bottles of water from vending machines and gulped down cucumbers before class. I watched classmates roaming the halls like caffeine-addicted zombies. I was a law student. My identity changed the moment I drove home and walked through the front door. I was greeted by five rambunctious children and one worn-out babysitter. Ms. Anderson disappeared and I answered only to mama. I was the PTA mother, the kitchen mother, the laundry and homework mother, the kissing and lullaby mother, stealing glimpses of my class notes over a pot of boiling pasta.

Evidently, my two sons decided that dad's departure to training presented the perfect opportunity for hospitalizations. My four-year-old, Sam, was bitten by a mosquito. Isn't everyone in Texas? But Sam, unfortunately, is allergic to mosquito bites, as I learned from this experience. His face swelling to the size of a large basketball was my first indication. By the time I rushed him to the hospital he couldn't see out of his left eye because it was swollen shut. I did have to miss class that day, but while we were sitting in the emergency room Sam learned all about constitutional law.

Within the next month my then fourteen-month-old, Timothy, came down with a bad case of bilateral pneumonia. I spent the week in the hospital with him, nasal canula and all. Luckily, Jared was home again and we were able to tag team. Jared stayed with Timothy while I rushed from the hospital to the classroom and back. While Timothy slept, I outlined.

Being incredibly pregnant in law school has its share of drawbacks. First, it's difficult to sit through a class and pay complete attention when there's a head sitting right on top of your bladder and your sweet, innocent, little pumpkin likes to kick it when it's full. In my opinion, the fact that the female bladder lies directly beneath the uterus is proof that the Good Lord does indeed have a sense of humor. Beyond that, the size of my stomach was difficult to fit behind a desk. I couldn't tell what weighed more, my backpack or my ever expanding belly and backside. The man in the seat next to me was more afraid that my water would break during Torts than he was of the Torts professor.

Not that I had time to think about that. In the middle of the semester my water broke. One month early. Jared circled the house nervously with my hospital bag in one hand and the car keys in the other, begging me to please get in the car. I made him wait while I e-mailed all of my professors to let them know that I would be out of class. I also grabbed my backpack. When we finally got to the hospital my darling husband almost had a heart attack when I pulled out a law book and a highlighter and studied in between contractions. The nurse thought I was insane.

This is where my sixth child and third son entered the picture. He wanted to make an entrance a little earlier than he should have. His lungs weren't fully developed. My little black-haired, blue-eyed baby boy went straight to the neonatal intensive care unit. I studied in the recovery room, studied while I ate, and even studied when I had to use the breast pump, but when I visited my baby, the law, once again, had to stand still for a moment. When he laid in my arms, or held my finger through the isolette, there was never a law book in my hand.

I had been told that anything that can happen will happen right before finals. I thought that was a little dramatic until I learned how true it really is. There is one organization in the world that doesn't care if you just had a baby who just got home from the hospital, or if you're just about to go into finals, or if your husband is about to get on a plane to Iraq, or if you now have six children under the age of seven to care for while you prepare for Moot Court. That organization is called the Internal Revenue Service. It was about this time that the IRS sent me a letter letting me know that they found discrepancies in the taxes I had filed two years back. Under these circumstances, final exams could not have been more welcome. I was perfectly ready to put my first year behind me. So was the rest of my first year class.

I noticed that during final exam period my classmates seemed to trade their vocal ability for dark bags under their eyes, commercial outlines and energy drinks. The word "hello" was replaced by a placid expression clearly communicating that we were all the undead, a large community of stress induced insomniacs trudging through the same hell, each openly hoping to do better than the next.

The worst part about final exams is the smell. I would gladly sniff a male locker room right after a football game than smell a room full of nervous, perspiring law students taking a final exam. First, football players probably shower on a daily basis. First-year law students in the middle of final exams try so hard to remember the risk/utility analysis of design defects that they seem to forget where the soap is located. The library passed out ear plugs. I wish they would have given away free deodorant. Or a scrub brush.

I am happy to report that despite one hellish year, I not only passed all my classes, I did very well. My second year was much calmer. Although my story is extreme, I was not alone. I was only a single member of a large underground community of parents in graduate school. These students have a highlighter in one hand and crayons and gummi snacks in the other. They balance catching the school bus with a commute and pack at least two backpacks every morning while attending parent-teacher conferences in the evening. They sit in the pediatrician's waiting room with a Criminal Law textbook instead of a magazine and plastic tabs instead of a cell phone. The margins of their textbooks contain shopping lists and tiny dirty fingerprints.

Sometimes we just barely survive. We wipe off the sweat, square our shoulders and set our minds to make it one more day. Other days we thrive. As parents in law school we come out learning one thing they couldn't teach us: How to have it all.

Classroom Storytelling

ALAFAIR S. BURKE

I remember the class. It was Criminal Law. We were studying defenses.

Like so many other students who were comfortable doing so, Mark Cooper raised his hand, and the professor acknowledged him. Before the days of laptops in classrooms, I placed my pen on the table, confident that one of only a handful of conversational variants was coming.

Sometimes a student with a raised hand would ask the professor to repeat the material. *Could you explain the difference between knowledge and recklessness again? What was the thing you just said about the degree of certainty for knowledge?* Or in another form, the question might request clarification through example. *So if the defendant is nearly certain that the girl's only fifteen, that's knowledge? But if he thinks she's probably eighteen, but might be fifteen, that's recklessness?* Some students begged for clear rules and firm lines to divide black from white where only gray existed. *What if there's a seventy percent chance she's only fifteen? Is that knowledge or recklessness?*

I was still a 1L, but I had been in law school long enough to know that student questions rarely elicited the kind of dense, methodical material warranting frenzied scribbles in my spiral notebook. It was better (for me, at least) to sit back, listen, and process the material internally. I used the time to work out the kinks in my right wrist.

But there's a reason I still remember this class nearly twenty years later.

"So is it true that if you shoot a person on your property, it's legal as long as the police find the body inside your house?"

To be honest, I don't remember the professor's initial response. My guess is he said something to the effect that the Model Penal Code and a majority of states do not allow an unqualified justification to use deadly force in defense of property. A jury would have to conclude that the defendant reasonably believed that his life, or the life of another, was in jeopardy. Maybe he went on to say something about the possibility that a legislature could certainly create such a defense if it wanted. Maybe this would have raised the subject (once again) of the differences between rules and standards.

But Cooper wasn't done with the topic. What was the law in California, he wanted to know. And, even without an automatic rule justifying self-defense within one's castle, wouldn't the defendant have a better chance of acquittal if the person he shot were physically on his property?

I don't remember how Cooper's comments transitioned from the hypothetical to the personal. Perhaps the professor finally responded the same way I probably would now as a professor, if faced with persistent student questioning about such a specific topic: *Why such curiosity about this issue, Mr. Cooper? Are you planning on shooting someone on your property?*

As it turned out. Cooper was not planning a shooting. At least, not anymore.

For the next ten minutes, the entire class—our professor included—sat attentive while a fellow student told us about the day he almost became a killer.

My girlfriend and I were living in Berkeley, and we both worked at night. The first time it happened, we weren't even sure there had been a break-in. Some items in the bedroom seemed out of place. Jenna was pretty sure she'd made the bed before she left the house, but the sheets were flipped back when we got home. The second time was a couple of weeks later, and this time we were sure. Jenna said her things had been moved in the dresser—you know, like her underwear and stuff.

As a few students quietly vocalized their disgust, I wondered whether the word "ewww" had just experienced its first utterance in a law school course.

We called our landlord to install better locks on our windows, but he didn't seem to be in any hurry. We called the police, but they told us that with nothing missing, it was only a misdemeanor and they'd never put in the kind of resources it would take to find the guy. Over the next few weeks, it kept hap-

pening. It got to the point where we almost expected to find signs he'd been there whenever we were both gone at night. Jenna hid her personal stuff, but he found them and laid a couple on the bed for display.

More ewww's.

So one night I decided I was going to catch him myself. I turned out all the lights and told Jenna to come with me, like we were leaving. We drove off in my car, but then I stopped two blocks away and parked on the street. We snuck back to the house through our neighbor's yard and climbed through our bedroom window. I had a gun I'd bought when I was living in Oakland. I sat there on the bed waiting for him to come.

Jenna eventually fell asleep, but I couldn't. I was too wired. I just lay there on the bed with the gun on my chest. I was finally thinking about giving up when I heard him at the window. I couldn't see his face, but I could see his form against the backlighting of the street lamp outside our house. I knew he was there. I saw him place one foot inside the window—the same one we'd climbed through ourselves. I had the gun pointed right at him. I remember watching his shape and waiting for him. I saw his shoulders tip toward me. Then all of the sudden, Jenna rolled over in her sleep. He must have heard her, because he hauled—he jumped backwards. The guy never came back again.

The professor asked Cooper what his intention was as he waited in the bedroom.

Honestly?

Yes, honestly.

I was going to kill him. I think Jenna thought I was trying to catch him for the cops. Or maybe scare him. But I was going to shoot him. As I watched him from the bed, I kept waiting for him to be far enough inside the house that, if I shot him, he'd fall forward into our bedroom instead of backwards outside the window. I was staring at him, trying to anticipate when the balance of his weight would shift. I was just about to pull the trigger when Jenna scared him off.

Other students might remember that single class for any one of several legal issues raised by Mark Cooper's surprising confession. The difference between intent and motive. The difference between justification and excuse. The difference between common law provocation and the more relaxed California standard based on the Model Penal Code's defense of extreme emotional disturbance. The difference between what really goes on in an actor's mind and the self-defense version a jury might be willing to believe.

The class might also be remembered for the debate it sparked among the students. Did Cooper have an understandable reaction to the legal system's inability to help him and his girlfriend? Or was he an unstable vigilante? Was he exaggerating his intentions or had we caught him in a moment of unfiltered candor? Had he added to the class discussion with his comments, or was the entire story just plain creepy?

The day was noteworthy on many levels. But I remember that discussion for a specific reason: It was the moment I realized I belonged in law school.

Unlike some of my classmates, I had come to law school with no clear reason for being there. Like most of my classmates, I'd seen law school as an escape from a job market that would have a liberal arts major only behind a Starbuck's counter, a safer (and shorter) alternative than graduate school. Maybe I'd follow my love of pop culture and become an entertainment lawyer. Maybe I'd go into politics. Maybe I'd work for my hero, Morris Dees, at the Southern Poverty Law Center. Maybe I'd be a professor. Whatever the case, I knew I could figure it out later. The first year was for learning.

But as I soaked in the material, I couldn't help but wonder what I would eventually do with it. As friends basked in the glory of landing on-campus interviews with top-tier firms, I knew I could never put in those kinds of hours fighting about other people's money. I checked out the public interest clinic for battered women, but walked out when I learned we weren't supposed to tell the clients to leave their batterers. Even at a meeting of the Entertainment Law Society, I knew I wasn't reading *Variety* with the same interest as the other members.

But when a fellow student spoke about sitting in a darkened room, forming the intention to kill while wondering if the law would allow him to do it, I knew I belonged in law school.

I grew up in Wichita, Kansas, when a killer who called himself BTK— Bind, Torture, Kill—terrorized an entire city by murdering seven people and then writing letters to reporters and police to gloat about his crimes. He eluded police for more than thirty years.

When I was in high school, two young girls and their father were found murdered in their home. Their contractor, a man named Bill Butterworth, was reported missing, along with the family car. When Butterworth turned up with the car in Florida, he claimed a four-day bout of amnesia. After undergoing hypnosis, he claimed to remember fleeing from the home after walking into the murder scene. A Wichita jury acquitted him.

For as long as I could remember, I had watched crime television shows, read mystery novels, and followed every major crime story to make headlines. But until that class, Criminal Law was just the study of *actus reus*, mens rea, and statutory interpretation. It wasn't about the human condition.

It is often said that the first year of law school is for learning how to think like a lawyer. As a 1L, I certainly experienced that cognitive evolution. But ideally students should see a connection between the law and real people. They should see how the story of the men who contracted for the purchase of a pregnant cow[32] might affect a first-time entrepreneur starting her own business. They should realize how the tale of Mrs. Palsgraf[33] might affect someone injured by the sale of a gun to a minor.[34] They should recognize how singer Connie Francis's lawsuit after her rape has made hotels safer for guests.[35] And, most ideally of all, they should have a moment when they recognize how they might as future lawyers help make those connections between the law in the abstract and the realities of human lives.

I had that moment when Mark Cooper told us about the night he almost killed a man.

---

32. I refer, of course, to *Sherwood v. Walker*, 33 N.W. 919 (Mich. 1887). Hiram Walker, a successful distiller and cattle rancher, agreed to sell a cow called "Rose 2d of Aberlone" to banker Theodore Sherwood for eighty dollars, with both men believing Rose to be sterile. When Walker discovered Rose was pregnant, he refused to honor the contract price. The appellate court sided with Walker, and the case is now a standard first-year contracts chestnut for the doctrine of mutual mistake.

33. Here I refer to *Palsgraf v. Long Island Railroad Co.*, 162 N.E. 99 (N.Y. 1928). Anyone reading this essay who is not familiar with Mrs. Palsgraf's most unfortunate luck and Judge Cardozo's dismissal of her complaint must have picked up this collection of stories by accident.

34. See the hypothetical raised by philosopher Andreas Teuber for his students at *Twenty-One Legal Puzzlers*, Phil 22B (Spring 2000), http://people.brandeis.edu/~teuber/puzz6.html.

35. *Garzilli v. Howard Johnson's Motor Lodges, Inc.*, 419 F. Supp. 1210 (E.D.N.Y. 1976) (rapist broke into plaintiff's motel room through sliding glass doors). I thank my colleague, Larry Kessler, for reminding me of this case.

One-L-ow Brick Road

HALA V. FURST

"I have a feeling we're not in Kansas anymore . . ."[36]

Whenever I tell people I'm from Kansas, their inevitable response is always, "Well, you're not in Kansas anymore, huh?" Or, "Where are your ruby slippers?" Or, "Did your farm ever get hit by a tornado?" I've found people don't know much about Kansas other than what they learned in *The Wizard of Oz*. But it seems the movie had a profound effect on me, too, because when I was twenty-five years old I ran away from home, just like Dorothy. Truth be told, I'd been running since I left Wichita for college in Minneapolis; in fact, I'd been running since before that, as eager as I was to leave the windswept prairie. But it wasn't until I left the Central Standard Time zone, until I moved from the safe distance of a long day's drive, that I really left Kansas behind. Something loomed just over the horizon; my future was just beyond the vanishing point. Over the rainbow, if you will.

As a product of great public schools and a good state university, I had romanticized the idea of attending law school on the east coast. An eastern legal education seemed to me to be my entrée into a world of power and prestige that I had forgone by going to college on a nearly full scholarship. It didn't matter if I went to an Ivy or not; going to school in the Northeast,

---

36. In case you, gentle reader, have no powers of deductive reasoning or comprehension of popular culture, the italicized quotes that begin each section of this story are from THE WIZARD OF OZ (Metro-Goldwyn-Mayer 1939).

home of prep schools and old money, was a wish I'd had since childhood. Rhode Island held the promise of weekends on Cape Cod, yachting off the coast of Newport, hobnobbing at polo matches, and of course, learning from professors with elbow patches on their tweed jackets. I picked my school for a variety of reasons: location, price, scholarship of faculty, and the financial package they offered me. But if I'm honest with myself, a fantasy of New England living was a large part of it. It was my Emerald City, the place where all my dreams could come true.

So eastward I headed, driving along the coast with my father on a three-day odyssey. We arrived on a beautiful August morning in the scenic, even picturesque, seaside town I was to call home for the next three years. I bounded up the three flights of stairs to the apartment I'd only seen pictures of on Craigslist, to find a stuffy, cramped attic with dormered ceilings and the stale odor of garbage. The lovely water view I'd been promised was visible only through skylights, which I, at five foot tall, could look out of only with the help of a stepladder. Returning in defeat to my car, my father's expectant face crumbled as he watched me burst into tears.

"Who moves to *Rhode Island*??? Who does that? Who picks up their life and moves here? No one's even heard of this state!" I sobbed, by now sitting in a pile of my belongings on the street. The enormity, the insanity of picking up and moving half-way across the country to a place completely bereft of friends and family to begin one of the hardest years of my life finally sunk in. For the first time in years, I wanted to go back to Kansas. But my ruby slippers were packed under eight pounds of cooking utensils and sweaters. I had no choice but to unpack.

"If I only had a brain"

Things did get better, as they have a tendency to do. By the time my father left the next week, I was settled into my apartment, I had purchased my books for class, and I was ready to begin my adventure.

Going to law school had been pretty much a whim for me. I was an actress by trade. My degree was in theatre, and really all I'd ever done up until this point was perform, write, direct, or generally emote. I went to law school because I considered myself an activist, and was frustrated with the limited way in which art was able to foster social change. I decided to get more directly involved in the process, and law school seemed like the place to do it. So I applied, I was accepted, I went. I didn't read

AbovetheLaw.com, I didn't read *One L*, I didn't read *Getting to Maybe*,[37] I didn't really prepare in any way. I went into law school under a complete veil of willful ignorance.

Law school is hard.[38] Everyone knows this. Everyone tells you this. My mother, a lawyer, told me this. Family friends, also lawyers, told me this. But you can't imagine it, you can't comprehend it, until you feel it. Law school is so hard it hurts. Your brain actually aches, as do your shoulders, your neck, your eyeballs, and your backside, not to mention your bruised and battered pride. The night before my first day of school, a day that would include Civil Procedure and Torts, I spent eight hours in the library trying to dissect two cases regarding Rule 35[39] sanctions. I would later realize how bat-guano insane it was to begin a civ pro class with Rule 35, but at the time I was young and naïve and thought it was all my fault. I had always done well in school. I had always gotten good grades, and sailed by with little-to-no effort. And not just because I was a theatre major, mind you—I had taken some theory courses. It wasn't all singing and dancing.[40]

But still, *Sibbach*[41] and *Schlagenhauf*[42] vexed me, and continued to vex me into the wee hours of the next two weeks. As is typical for first-year students, I would wake up in a cold sweat, bolt from my bed, and rush to my books, just to look up one footnote. I spent every waking hour at the library, closing it down most nights. I got back my first ever subpar grade, on a writing assignment in Legal Methods, and realized that knocking something out the night before it was due just wasn't going to cut it this time around. The horror of my situation began to dawn on me: I would have to apply myself.

Luckily, I was not alone. In the first few weeks of my journey, I met several fellow travelers. The friends you make in law school are like the

---

37. RICHARD MICHAEL FISCHL & JEREMY PAUL, GETTING TO MAYBE: HOW TO EXCEL ON LAW SCHOOL EXAMS (1999).

38. Like, totally.

39. FED. R. CIV. P. 35.

40. In fact, I got a C+ in Musical Theatre, a feat so seemingly impossible as to engender awe.

41. Sibbach v. Wilson, 312 U.S. 1 (1941).

42. Schlagenhauf v. Holder, 379 U.S. 104 (1964). This case, it should be noted, is so obscure that even Wikipedia barely makes mention of it.

friends you make in a foxhole—the extremity of the situation creates an intimacy unheard of elsewhere. The term "fast friends" was created, I believe, because of the first year of law school. And for me, being so far away from home and the life I'd had before, these men and women became my family. We supported each other in class,[43] we drank with each other after, and in all the moments in between we just made each other laugh like hell.

As stupid as law school could make me feel, it was nice to know it wasn't just me. In my group of friends, one had a graduate degree from the University of Chicago in International Relations, one was a former executive with Valero Corporation, and another had taught high school in the Bronx. But all of our previous experience was of only modest assistance in the face of the new legal language we were being asked to learn and speak. Day would become night, and day again, and still we would be no closer to the answers we were seeking. It would take months to realize that the pursuit of knowledge itself was the answer.

"I'll get you, my pretty, and your little dog, too!"

There is one moment from my first year that I will never forget. In order to understand this moment, however, some background is necessary. We have all had professors, I am sure, who cultivate an air of insanity. Not just wackiness or zaniness or good-natured absent-mindedness, but actual madness, with an added dose of malice. My Civil Procedure professor was such a woman.

Now, it was rumored at the time, and has since been verified by my own empirical data, that this was all an act for the 1Ls. This particular professor, it was said, was an absolute joy, a peach, in her upper level classes. But to us, she was terrifying. She had a formidable legal mind, first of all. She could strand you in a mental forest of logic so dense you'd be eaten by wolves before you ever saw daylight again. Her weapon was not diabolical laughter or flying monkeys or the ability to throw fire; it was a stare from behind glasses that actually reflected the heat from the sun at you. When she had fixed her attention on you to recite a case or answer a question, the air was literally sucked out of the room.

---

43. Mostly this support was in the form of hurried g-chat messages when someone had failed to read the night before.

Naturally, we fixated on what we perceived to be her gentler attributes, in an attempt to make her less frightening. This professor had an affinity for rather feminine outfits, consisting of bright colors, patterns, flowers, and various pairs of tights. She was known to wear her long, blond hair in a giant pink bow. But somehow, this seemingly warm and soft manner of dress made her even more terrifying. She looked so approachable, and then she went for the proverbial jugular. She was a walking, human Venus Flytrap.

The second day of class, we began predictably. As previously mentioned we were dealing with Rule 35, and as she looked at the seating chart for her next victim, the classroom door opened. Class had been going for about five minutes, and we had been told in the first day's lecture that lateness would not be tolerated. Yet in walked a girl from our section. She was wearing a yellow tube top and jeans, and for some reason, her outfit made her lateness even more egregious, as though her bare shoulders were an added insult. As this girl sauntered from the door diagonally to her chair, which was of course in the farthest possible corner from the door, time stood still. The professor fixed her gaze on the yellow tube-topped one with laser precision, stopping mid-sentence to watch as the girl walked right past her without so much as a nod of apology. She watched as the girl sat down. She watched as the girl pulled out her books, her laptop, and her water bottle. She watched as the girl carefully avoided her stare. The rest of us watched the professor watching the girl. It was for situations such as this that the phrase "baited breath" was in invented.

Finally, the professor spoke. "So nice of you to join us," she said, sweet as you please.

No response from the girl, other than a deer-in-the-headlights glance upwards. No one could save her now.

"Why don't you tell us what state remedies Ms. Sibbach could have pursued before availing herself of the federal court's protection," the professor continued, knowing full well that no one in that room, other than herself, was prepared to answer such a question. The girl in the yellow tube top made some noises that may have been words, but not in any language I had ever heard. The professor's impossible questioning continued as the girl sank lower and lower in her chair.

Fear is a questionable pedagogical methodology, but one that seemed to work on us, a room full of overachieving Type-A head cases. The best we could hope for was to keep our heads down, and try to weather the seventy-five minute, twice weekly storm with as little damage as possible. We all believed we were in for the roughest semester of our lives.

Our first inkling that this professor's antics came from her belief that 1Ls should all endure a bit of hazing, and not instead out of an actual desire to destroy what little was left of our collective dignity, came on Halloween. She arrived into class dressed as a witch, complete with tall pointy hat, tattered black robes, spider web tights, and a broom. She gave us chocolate. Dark chocolate.

"I am the Great and Powerful Wizard of Oz!"

But no amount of chocolate can get you through some bad days. There are days in law school where it feels like you will never have the right answer. You will never be smart enough. My mother once told me that there will always be someone smarter, faster, prettier, more popular, or more successful than you—hopefully not all at once. So it is important not to compare yourself to other people, and to strive instead for your own personal best.

Anyone who has ever gone to law school can tell you what a crock that is. First-year classes, for most schools, are graded on a curve. At my school, the curve was particularly steep, set at about a C+ for the first-year curriculum. You are told not to talk to anyone about your grades. You are told that an A paper might still get a B- because of the curve. You are told that competition can ruin friendships and your health. You are told that grades are not necessarily a predictor of your success as a lawyer.

I was told all that, and still I found myself crying in the fetal position on my kitchen floor when I found out I had a C in Property. Property being a five-credit course over one semester, I had basically tanked my GPA, and with it any opportunity I would have to ever get a job, my own home, a family, or retire. I was going to die alone, with my face eaten by my own cats (of which there would of course be dozens), because I had performed below the curve on an exam.

The view from the cold linoleum that day was not pretty. I had gotten all the way to the Emerald City of my educational fantasies, and had been told that I couldn't hack it. My fears of inadequacy, my jealous and competitive nature, my sheer physical exhaustion after the mental marathon of finals, all combined into a toxic plume of sky-writing, and what it wrote was "Surrender, Hala."

I was ready to give up. I wanted to go home, not even completely sure where that was anymore. I'd worked so hard and for so long, and my successes had been a quiet few, while my failures, I felt, were insurmountable. A great and powerful voice boomed loudly in my head, telling me I would never be good enough, that I would never succeed. And I was frightened.

But as I sat up from my dirty kitchen floor, I thought about what I had accomplished in the previous nine months. I had learned to speak this new legal language; I had made space in my brain for an astronomical amount of knowledge. I had been able to use my new knowledge to help people, and to continue my activism in areas close to my heart. And most importantly, my friends and I had proceeded through one of the toughest years of any of our lives with courage and aplomb, with grace, and most of all, with laughter. We had been there to catch one another when we stumbled, and I knew they would be there to catch me now. I had the three things I needed to succeed: smarts, heart, and courage. The booming voice in my head was just my own insecurity, hiding behind a curtain of fear.

EPILOGUE

It is hard to understand without experiencing it how epic the struggles of the 1L year can seem. It may seem foolish, or exaggerated, to those who have not lived through it. But those two short semesters are the beginning of a journey, not from point A to point B, but from who you are to who you wish to become. You may return to your old life, to your old hometown or the people who knew you before, but you won't be the same old person. As for me, my life is now in Technicolor, and there is no going back.

Contested Meanings:
Achievement and Ambition at
an Elite Law School

DEBORAH WAIRE POST

Every year, after one of my students discovers that I attended Harvard Law School, I am asked the inevitable question. What is the difference between Harvard Law School and the law school they are attending, the law school where I teach, Touro College Jacob D. Fuchsberg Law Center? This is a question that is unanswerable, at least in the few moments that would be available in a classroom context. In many ways, more ways than my students would suspect, law school is the same wherever you go. In other ways, elite schools are radically different from the schools in the tiers that lie below. If I am to tell the story of my first year of law school in a way that would allow my students, and other students who might be in a similar position, to make a comparison that has any meaning at all, I would have to place my story in a historical and socio-cultural context, which is what I will attempt to do.

Every story has to begin somewhere and the story of my first year in law school, like *One L*, begins with an explanation. How did I end up at Harvard Law School?[44] When I applied to law schools, my former employer and mentor, Margaret Mead, assured me that I did not have "a snowball's

---

44. Anecdotes about my first year of law school also appear in an essay that I wrote for the Tenth Anniversary of the *Harvard Blackletter Law Journal*. Deborah Waire Post, *Homecoming: The Ritual of Writing History*, 10 HARV. BLACKLETTER L.J. 5 (1993).

chance in hell" of getting into Harvard. But then Dr. Mead also thought she had no right to ask anything of the Museum of Natural History, where she had her office, or of Columbia, where she taught stadium-size anthropology classes as an adjunct faculty member without tenure. The world was changing, and she played a not inconsiderable role in the transformation, but that doesn't mean she always understood the particularities of the change. I don't think I did either.

Harvard University and small towns in upstate New York, where I grew up, exist on different planes of existence. As a friend once said to me "you are where you are from." Even as we are changed or transformed by time and experience, gaining sophistication and knowledge, the world view with which we began life is a vestigial sensibility, leaving its mark on our initial reaction to new or unusual events or circumstances and shaping our expectations. In the absence of some intervention or external influence, admission to Harvard is not within the contemplation of poor or working class students from small towns, even though every year Harvard admits students who come from such places.[45] When I was growing up, I did not have a grand plan for my life and if I had had a plan for my life, it would not have included Harvard Law School.[46]

I was surprised when I got to Harvard and discovered other people there like me—students who probably had not grown up with the expectation that they would attend Harvard Law School. In my Contracts class I was flanked by two people who had a great deal in common with me and with each other, although they were very different in appearance and in the values they embraced. Steven J. Eberhard,[47] a native of Lubbock or some other small city or town in Texas, a graduate of Texas A & M, class

---

45. Elite schools like Harvard have only recently begun to focus on the class divide that is far greater now than it was when I entered the law school. *See* Karen W. Arenson, *Harvard Says Poor Parents Won't Have to Pay*, N.Y. TIMES, Feb. 29, 2004 (describing the elimination at Harvard College of parent contribution for parents earning less than $40,000); Paula Wasley, *Stanford U. Increases Aid to Cover Tuition for Low-Income Students*, CHRON. HIGHER EDUC., Mar. 31, 2006.

46. MARY BATESON, COMPOSING A LIFE 38 (1989) (the child who has dreams, but no or few resources, may not include in his or her dream a "realistic and realistically imagined next step.").

47. Spencer Abraham included a tribute to Steven Eberhard, co-founder of the *Harvard Journal of Law and Public Policy*, on the occasion of the Journal's 30th anniversary. *See* Spencer Abraham, *A Founder's Retrospective: The Journal at 30 Years*, 31 HARV. J.L. & PUB. POL'Y 1 (2008).

president, and proud member of the Corps of Cadets, sat on one side of me. He came to class every day with a Styrofoam coffee cup from the Hark, and I assumed, erroneously it turned out, that he was sipping coffee all through class. Actually he was depositing his "chaw" in that cup. Fern Fisher,[48] who became my best friend, sat on the other side of me. Fern was a former cheerleader from Riverhead High School in Long Island, the daughter of a single mother, and a summa cum laude graduate of Howard University.

It is true that there were many children of privilege at Harvard at the time I was admitted. There were legacy students whose parents attended or taught at Harvard, but there were also a lot of people who came from interesting and unusual backgrounds. Not all of them had been through the pre-school to private or prep school pipeline I learned about only after I graduated from law school and went to work at a firm in Houston, Texas. Why Harvard chooses particular applicants over others is unknowable because of what I call the "human factor." A mathematical formula only goes so far: some combination of grade point average, LSAT score, and a multiplier derived from a ranking of colleges narrows the field and then human beings get involved, subjective judgments are made, and values and ideals come into play. In the late sixties and the seventies, schools addressed past injustices and the structural barriers that kept women and minorities out of law school. We have since moved beyond that singular moment of clarity when there was a collective moral certainty that the almost total exclusion of women and minorities from law schools was wrong and that redress was necessary.[49] There still are today, however, admissions professionals and faculty who are purposeful in their desire to create an interesting and diverse mix of students and an educational environment

---

48. Fern Fisher would later become Deputy Chief Administrative Judge for New York City Courts, charged with state-wide responsibility for access to justice issues.

49. In the iconic anti-affirmative action case, *Regents of the University of California v. Bakke*, 438 U.S. 265, 318 (1978), Justice Powell referred to the "non-objective factors," including race, and the educational benefits of diversity which were articulated in the admissions standards of Harvard College, which he appended to the opinion. *Bakke* ended the era of self-reflection and remediation of past discrimination through an explicit policy of integration that was the hallmark of the civil rights movement and began the era in which "diversity" became the rhetorical and political tool for the creation of a more inclusive student body.

that approximates and furthers the goal of creating a "successful society." A successful society acknowledges and respects a broader definition of merit. If Harvard Law School were as capable of accommodating competing definitions of merit in its hiring criteria for faculty as it has been in its standards for the admission of students, it might legitimately claim that it is, in fact, an example of the successful society described in the theories of some of its own faculty.[50]

For years I have claimed that the Harvard described by Scott Turow in *One L* is not the Harvard I knew as a first-year student. There is probably more than one explanation for this disclaimer, but the one that is most obvious to me is the place from which we each started. Scott came to Harvard from a teaching position at Stanford. What I didn't know when I started law school, but I do appreciate now, is that Stanford and Harvard are two sides of the same coin. Stanford definitely has more athletes, more sunshine and fountains, a mind boggling assortment of mini eco-systems, a lake, golf course, and riding stables. Harvard was in 1975, and pretty much still is today, quite gray and very, very old and venerable looking. What Harvard and Stanford have in common is the function they both serve. These are two of a handful of institutions that train most of those who assume positions of power and influence in politics, popular culture, business, and, not so surprising, legal education. Coming from Stanford, Scott would have known a great deal about Harvard before he got there.

I left a job as an executive secretary to Robert Rahtz, editor-in-chief of the school book division of Macmillan Publishing Company, to come to a place I knew nothing about and where I knew no one. For a year or more I had been sitting outside the office of Mr. Rahtz reading unsolicited manuscripts and typing monthly reports on a Selectric typewriter with the

---

50. The Canadian Institute for Advanced Research has had a Program on Successful Societies funded in part by the Weatherhead Center for International Affairs at Harvard University. One aspect of a successful society discussed by Harvard sociologist Michèle Lamont and referenced in this essay is the extent to which a society is inclusive. In a successful society, members of minority groups are afforded "social recognition and cultural citizenship." Michèle Lamont, *Responses to Racism, Health, and Social Inclusion as a Dimension of Successful Societies, in* SUCCESSFUL SOCIETIES: HOW INSTITUTIONS AND CULTURE AFFECT HEALTH 151 (Peter A. Hall & Michèle Lamont eds., 2009). Successful societies "sustain competing definitions of a worthy life and a worthy person, which empower lower status groups to contest stereotypes and measure their worth independently of dominant social matrices." *Id.*

aid of carbon paper and white-out. For a year or more, a high powered attorney, outside counsel for Macmillan, walked right by me into Mr. Rahtz's office without stopping at my desk or addressing me in any way. When Mr. Rahtz told him I had been accepted at Harvard, that attorney made a point of shaking my hand and congratulating me. It was the first time I experienced the power of an institution to confer prestige and status.

A yellowed newspaper clipping is not as romantic as a madeleine, but then I am not Proust and in any event the written word provides a better measure of reliability where my recollections are concerned. I still have a copy of a *Daily World* news story dated October 22, 1974, which one of the union organizers at the Colliers Encyclopedia research division distributed to Macmillan employees the day the company fired approximately 200 employees. The article refers to the "Columbus Day massacre" at Macmillan.[51] The company fired eager young employees who were trying to persuade white collar workers to join Local 153 of the AFL-CIO Office & Professional Employees International Union. It also fired a lot of women, including some who must have complained to Louis Lefkowitz, the attorney general of New York State at that time. Prior to the firings, which many thought were retaliatory, Lefkowitz filed a sex discrimination complaint against Macmillan with the New York State Human Rights Division. Women employees had also filed a complaint with the EEOC.

The newspaper story of the Macmillan firings shares the page with a story about the trial of the National Guardsmen who fired on the students at Kent State. On the reverse side there are stories about the Watergate trial and resistance to school desegregation in Boston. The events related in each of these stories remind me of the many contests, small and large, that were occurring in 1974 between those who wanted the world to change and those who wanted to preserve the status quo. Law was everywhere part of those contests, and that may well have been the reason why I began to think about the law as an alternative to a career as an editor in a publishing company.

If I had been reading that newspaper more carefully back then, I might have understood that there are limits to the transformative power of

---

51. Janet Shulman, *Looking Back: The 1974 Macmillan Massacre*, PUB. WKLY., Apr. 10, 2008.

the law.[52] I was too busy walking the picket line with women who were fired because they complained when they were paid less, promoted less frequently than their male colleagues, and denied the maternity benefits provided to the wives of the male executives. Mr. Rahtz protected me while I was out on strike and I still had my job two weeks later, but law school certainly seemed like a better plan to me as I sat down to write the essay portion of my application to Harvard Law School.

All of this is preface to the real subject of this essay, my first year of law school. You might think that after all that, law school would be a disappointment. You would be wrong. The first case I read in law school was *Monge v. Beebe Rubber Co.*,[53] a New Hampshire case about the retaliatory discharge of a woman who complained about sexual harassment. Considering where I had been and what I had seen, I can't imagine anything more relevant to my own life than that case. Sure there was some wise guy in that first legal methods class who raised his hand and referred to "the instant case" or "the case at bar" and I had no idea how he knew to do that. If he wanted to make an impression, this he did because after all these years, it is one of my clearest recollections of my first year in law school. Even so, it is not an unpleasant memory. I was startled and amused, perhaps, but not frightened or intimidated. It was obvious to me that this student was either a quick study, picking up on language in the case and repeating it in class, or he was already familiar with the jargon used by lawyers (in cases or briefs, if not in ordinary conversation).

The only real pain I experienced as a first-year law student was vicarious. One of the many professors at Harvard reputed to be the model for Professor Kingsfield in the movie *The Paper Chase* judged the oral arguments that were the culmination of our legal methods or legal process class. It was an interesting case involving the constitutional rights of a class of inmates convicted of rape and sentenced to life imprisonment without the possibility of parole. I defended the sentences on behalf of the State of Kentucky, not an easy task for me. After we finished our arguments and received the comments and critique of our arguments, both teams left the room. It was after the formal critique when I saw this professor pinch the cheek of a woman on the opposing team, the way your great Aunt Agnes

---

52. It took eleven years, from 1974 until 1985, before Macmillan signed a consent decree and paid damages to some of the women against whom it discriminated. *Id.*

53. 316 A.2d 549 (N.H. 1974).

might do while murmuring something like: "Aren't you the sweetest little thing." What the professor said to her, sotto voce, was something along the lines of "if you had written an exam for me the way you wrote that brief, I would have had to fail you." I doubt his overly familiar gesture was meant to soften the blow. He must have realized that it simply compounded the humiliation: she was treated like a child while her intellectual ability was called into question.

Perhaps I was not disappointed with law school because law school was different from my undergraduate experience when I felt, more than might have really been the case, that my small town or rural background created social distance between me and my classmates. Law school also was different from the anthropology department at Columbia where I was enrolled as a graduate student and employed as Dr. Mead's teaching assistant. While I was at Columbia, I had a class with Marvin Harris who criticized Franz Boas and Dr. Mead for being "eclectic" —that is to say, he thought them insufficiently theoretical in their approach to anthropology.[54] It didn't take very long for me to realize that faculty with grand theories need or demand acolytes and that I probably would never be "sufficiently theoretical" in the estimation of Marvin Harris and others like him. In contrast, the first day at Harvard, I knew I had found a place where I fit in, a place where it did not seem to matter if you were eclectic in your approach to legal theory. You might not think so, but this is one of the advantages of a large school with a diverse student body.

At Harvard I became part of a community. My first weekend in Cambridge, the first year black women at Harvard Law School organized a potluck brunch, which we held at my apartment on Pine Street, just past Central Square. There were nine black women, or nine women who chose to identify as black, in the first-year class of 500 law students at Harvard in 1975.[55] If my memory is correct, the day was bright and the sun lit up the

---

54. The more polite version of this criticism became Harris's description of cultural anthropology in the tradition of Boas as "historical particularism," though the term "eclecticism" still appears in his critique. "Eclecticism . . . is often little more than a euphemism for confusion, the muddled acceptance of contradictory theories, the bankruptcy of creative thought, and the cloak of mediocrity." MARVIN HARRIS, THE RISE OF ANTHROPOLOGICAL THEORY: A HISTORY OF THEORIES OF CULTURES 284–85 (1968).

55. Patricia Williams wrote a small piece on the ten black women in her class, the class that graduated in 1975, the year I entered Harvard Law School. Patricia Williams, Notes from a Small World, NEW YORKER, Apr. 29, 1996, at 87–91. In contrast to my class experience,

plants lining the shelves on my front room window. The smell of burnt sugar from the Necco factory on Massachusetts Avenue filled the apartment. I was happy to be in Cambridge as I opened the door and welcomed the women who had climbed three flights of stairs with dishes and platters of food. It was a good day and an auspicious beginning to my law school experience.

Like Scott Turow, I was invited to join a study group, but my study group was composed entirely of African-American students, four men and three women.[56] We had our share of drama around the preparation of outlines, but I never doubted for a moment that the purpose of the group was mutual support and friendship. The debates we had about the meaning of particular doctrines or the theories that were discussed in class were important to our intellectual development, but the friendship we practiced daily sustained us throughout law school and beyond. Since graduation, I have been back to Harvard for only three reunions. One was Celebration Fifty, commemorating the fiftieth anniversary of the admission of women to the law school. The other two were reunions of black alumni. I travel back to Cambridge for these reunions because I know I will have a chance to see the members of my old study group.

I am ashamed to admit that I read *One L* for the first time as I prepared to write this essay. As I said at the beginning of this essay, I had always believed that the experiences Scott had in his section were different from those of students in my section at law school. When I finally read the book, I discovered that both sections had pranksters, although the practical jokes devised in our section were considerably funnier, and that intolerance when it comes to theory is not such a rare commodity among academic overachievers. "Just give me what I need to know" is a demand that I associate with my students, but clearly this is an attitude that spans time and social strata.

Most surprising was the fact that both of our sections rebelled at some point during the school year. The gendered nature of the rebellion in my section is vociferously denied to this day by many of my classmates, espe-

---

Pat writes of her black women classmates that "[w]e didn't spend much time together back then, though each of us, I learned, had imagined that the others were off nurturing tight friendships and circles of support." *Id.* at 88.

56. The members of my study group were Fern Fisher, Kenneth Frazier, Marsha Mosely, Charles Ogletree, Reginald Thomas, and Keith Williamson.

cially the women.[57] My section attacked a novice, a first-year law professor and one of only four women on the faculty. Turow's section picked a fight with one of the more powerful faculty members, a much less likely choice from a structural standpoint. I might be inclined to say that rebellion was habitual for my generation because we were living in the aftermath of the 1960s, except that I have now witnessed the same phenomenon on a recurrent basis. Law students often gang up on the least powerful member of a faculty. It is all about anger and displacement.

I know that *One L* is part of the mythos in the legal profession, the trope of education by ordeal.[58] *One L* is social commentary and psychological thriller, the law school equivalent of *Lord of the Flies*. It is a story of men fighting, not for survival—survival was never an issue at Harvard since most students were assumed to be smart enough to pass the exams—but for dominance. These men cooperated with one another, but I do not believe they really liked each other. The relationships and the cooperation were calculated and instrumental, a means to an end, not an end in themselves. Women in this story are incidental, wives that suffer silently and one woman student with children who is made to look particularly pathetic because she allowed herself to be used and then discarded by a Machiavellian male classmate. The desire for success that spawned the fear and the insecurity of the people described in *One L* might have been there in my section or in my study group, but I don't believe it had the same sort of debilitating and disintegrative effect. More importantly, I do not understand why Scott thought this was Harvard's fault. He blamed Harvard for not saving the students from themselves—from the obsessive compulsive, self-destructive behavior that could only end in anger and disappointment.[59]

Somewhat late in the tale, Scott notes that women and minorities weathered the law school experience far better than the men who were

---

57. *See* Deborah W. Post, *Reflections on Identity, Diversity and Morality*, 6 BERKELEY WOMEN'S L.J. 136 (1991).

58. LOUISE HARMON & DEBORAH POST, CULTIVATING INTELLIGENCE: POWER, LAW AND THE POLITICS OF TEACHING (1996).

59. Pat Williams' version of the competition for grades and status by men is nowhere near as dark as mine. Instead of men at one remove from savagery, she saw men who "looked like an eternally roiling mass of puppies, always chewing on one another's legs." PATRICIA J. WILLIAMS, OPEN HOUSE: OF FAMILY, FRIENDS, FOOD, PIANO LESSONS, AND THE SEARCH FOR A ROOM OF MY OWN 217 (2005).

part of his cohort. I think he conceded that this was more sane and reasonable, but I do not think he really believed it or at least he didn't believe it completely. He couldn't believe it and subscribe to what he called variously the "standard of excellence" or an "achievement ethic" that was the principal justification for the competitive ethos he writes about.[60]

What then must he really have thought about the rest of us, the women and minorities, who did not participate in the rituals of competition? The almost footnote about the progress of blacks in the guise of Chris Edley, now Dean of Berkeley Law School, who made law review, or Susan Estrich, erstwhile talking head and former campaign manager for Michael Dukakis, who was elected president of law review, felt contrived, a politically correct afterthought.[61]

I have often confessed, sometimes apologetically, to my son and to various friends that my sisters and I share one common characteristic. We are all workaholics. What we are not, I suppose, is ambitious. There was a time, when I was in grade school and high school, when I felt compelled to achieve the highest score on every exam, to win every award that was on offer for academic performance, to be number one in every class. During my childhood and adolescence I learned that success has its rewards. I also learned that those rewards need not include either social acceptance or happiness. It was a lesson I took with me to law school.

Michèle Lamont, a sociologist at Harvard, has written extensively on race and especially on the response of racial and ethnic groups to inequality and discrimination. In a chapter from a book she co-edited, she describes interviews with working class blacks and black elites during which the strategies they used to deal with inequality and discrimination were elicited. I was struck by the difference between the response of the working class black man who said his strategy was to show his white co-workers that he could do "anything they do just as well as them"[62] and the remarks of the subjects she labeled "African American elites" who said that they had to be "twice as smart" or "smarter than" their white colleagues.[63]

---

60. *See, e.g.,* Scott Turow, One L 82, 178 (1977).

61. *Id.* at 241.

62. Lamont, *supra* note 50, at 159.

63. *Id.* at 160.

I think it is predictable that those whose success is defined in terms of the "dominant social matrices" would be those least likely to engage in the very strategy that Lamont uses to define a successful society—a strategy that rejects the criteria built into those matrices. It may well be that this research, where there might not have been many opportunities to observe the subjects interacting with others, does not reflect in its entirety what Lamont labels the "cultural repertoire" used by people of color to contest racism.[64] If I were describing the strategy that I have used in my life, I would say I have lived my life in a way that does indeed express a "competing definition of a worthy life" and this strategy is one that was already in place when I entered Harvard Law School.

What Harvard had to offer that I needed was an opportunity to develop this "competing definition of a worthy life." In my first year, I was happy to be back in school, happy to be reading and studying and discussing law. I took from Harvard what I needed to know, relished the parts that had meaning for me, the cases and the materials and the people and the relationships that are still important and relevant to my life. What I wanted back then was a good life, and a good life included a career that would have meaning and make a difference. And that is what I have.

In my twenty-five years of teaching I have met many Harvard graduates. I would put them into two categories. At one extreme are those who are uncertain in their affection for Harvard. They do not understand why they have not risen to the top of their professions. Certainly their admission to Harvard, and the degree they earned, was portentous of a larger role on a bigger stage. Some of them believe that Harvard was the high point in their lives. Their disappointment makes me sad.

At the other extreme there are those who are vociferous in their condemnation of Harvard and skeptical about my politics because I do not understand their passion on this subject. In *One L* they would be the character who ran for class marshal on a platform that he would make sure no one ever gave money to Harvard. The progressive cum radical faculty who are critical of Harvard see it as a site of privilege in a society characterized by extreme and unjustified disparities in wealth. Harvard, as far as they are concerned, perpetuates a sense of entitlement, training each new

---

64. *Id.* at 161.

generation to think and act in a way that preserves and perpetuates social injustice. I do not disagree.

At the same time, I am not convinced that Harvard is entirely to blame. I know that for me much more than for any of them, a Harvard Law degree gave me the power to carve out a space in this world where I could write and teach in my own way. I came to Harvard with a world view that could be expanded, but not destroyed, and a value system that could be challenged, but not erased. Law students for generations have believed that law school changes them, but the changes do not reach to the core of who they are as human beings. So, many, many years after the so-called "Macmillan Massacre," I still recognize injustice when I see it. Only now, I have the opportunity to write and I teach in a way that I hope will change the world.

I ♥ Crits

CAMERON STRACHER

If, as some have claimed, hating law school is a prerequisite for enjoying the practice of law, then those who love their first year best will be the most miserable.

It is September, 1983. I am waiting tables at a local restaurant in Cape Cod, and writing the Great American Novel. The Cape is dull, gray, empty, and cold—nothing at all like the summers I remember. Endless days in front of the typewriter like Jack Nicholson in *The Shining*. Nights crawling bars like Nicholas Cage in *Leaving Las Vegas*. The strip is dark, the lights shut down, and there is no Elisabeth Shue.

There's no one, in fact, except my two roommates: a pre-med student working at the labs and an unemployed prep school teacher. At the restaurant my fellow waiters are a sorry lot: older, divorced women supporting their kids; high school drop-outs with too much time to drink; an older man who has already beaten them to it. My soon-to-be-ex girlfriend has fled to Oslo, Norway, and tells me she can't afford the phone calls. Mail takes weeks, and the distance between the words is endless.

In my back pocket, however, is an acceptance letter from Harvard Law. It's been rubbing a hole there for nearly a year since I deferred my admission to follow this dream. A philosophy major in college, I scorned the idea of law school and applied only at my parents' prompting. Law keeps your options open, they promised, as people with no idea what they are talking about often say. What they really meant was: Get a job. But I was young, naïve, and still believed in romance.

A year of failure, however, can harden anyone's heart. After the cafés and the vodkas, it was time to write, and the writing did not come easy. It turned out that dressing the part was so much easier than living the part. Writing meant having something to write about, and my middle-class angst was not interesting—even to me. The blank pages stared up from my desk, mocking me with their emptiness. Meanwhile, Harvard Square, with its red brick and willowy blondes, beckoned like Oz at the end of a golden road.

So I boxed up my novel and left it on a shelf. I bought a futon, a desk, and a bookcase from Goodwill. Then I rented a van and drove myself and my possessions to Cambridge, to a three story walkup on Hancock Street near Central Square. My apartment was on the top floor, a "railroad flat" with five bedrooms stacked end to end and a small kitchen at the back. There was one closet, and one bathroom which I shared with three women and a good friend from high school. The women, Harvard undergrads, were nimble and quick, and their friends were wannabe poets, musicians, writers, and performance artists. The smell of garlic and curry soon emanated from our kitchen, and patchouli and pot from the bedrooms. One evening two guys showed up with a drum set and a guitar, and a small concert erupted in the living room until the police came to break it up.

At a salon in Inman Square, I pierced my ear and dyed my hair. I bought skinny black jeans, pink shirts, and black boots. I walked around Harvard Yard like a man in a foreign country, each building and every undergraduate a source of wonder. There really was ivy on the walls, climbing beneath the shade of ancient oaks and maples. The dirt pathways and stone walkways were worn thin and smooth, and I couldn't help thinking about the feet that had trod there over the decades. The wealthy, famous, pedigreed, and manicured. Supreme Court Justices and United States presidents. CEOs and billionaire drop-outs. I returned home excited, exhilarated, and burning with nervous energy.

The first day of orientation was held on the law school campus in a modern classroom building next to the imposing library. I sat between a championship squash player from Princeton, and the valedictorian from Southern Illinois University. There was a professional basketball player in my class and a circus acrobat, a Broadway lyricist, and a former U.S. Congressman.

We were assigned to Section Four—the "Hollywood" section, as it was known because of the star power of the faculty who taught us. Professor Alan Dershowitz, our Criminal Law professor, was the author of best-selling books, represented Claus Van Bulow, and appeared regularly on *Nightline*. Charles Fried, a noted conservative, would depart our Contracts class in the Spring semester to become the United States Solicitor General under President Reagan. Arthur Miller, who taught Civil Procedure, had a regular television show and a treatise named after him. But the figure who loomed largest in our lives was our Property professor Duncan Kennedy.

Kennedy was the de facto leader of the "Critical Legal Studies" movement. The Crits were hot, as Karl Marx had once been in an earlier academic era. Kennedy, with his unruly hair and beard, looked a little like Marx. He was taller and thinner, however, and spoke with the drawn-out vowels of a Brahmin accent. When he lectured, he paced the classroom and gesticulated with his long arms and hands, stroking his beard and pushing his hair back from his prominent forehead. He didn't call on students so much as lure them. While the Socratic method was alive and well in the hands of formidable practitioners like Professor Miller, Kennedy was the avant garde of a new breed of cajolers, flatterers, and Svengalis. Students were more than mere foils for his superior intellect. They were joint venturers, kindred travelers, spiritual cousins. Kennedy made us feel as if the law were an inside joke and he was giving us the punch line. In his class, the jester was king.

The Critical Legal Studies Movement had inherited the tradition of Karl Llewellyn and the legal realists.[65] The Crits argued that law was "indeterminate," that it reflected the political choices of lawyers and judges, and yielded to whomever wielded the most power. Rather than a neutral, objective reality, law was not only subjective, but entirely unpredictable and, in a sense, meaningless. The mere attempt to explain it, changed it. Kennedy's famous article, *Distributive and Paternalistic Motives in Contract and Tort Law*,[66] was a classic in the genre. Clocking in at nearly one hundred

---

65. For more on the Critical Legal Studies Movement, see Note, *'Round and 'Round the Bramble Bush: From Legal Realism to Critical Legal Scholarship*, 95 HARV. L. REV. 1669 (1982).

66. *See* Duncan Kennedy, *Distributive and Paternalistic Motives in Contract and Tort Law, with Special Reference to Compulsory Terms and Unequal Bargaining Power*, 41 MD. L. REV. 563 (1982).

pages, but with only thirty-two footnotes, the article argued there was really no difference between courts, legislatures, and administrative agencies, except as was necessary for the "false consciousness of the public," or as demanded by the particular political agenda of a given decision-maker.[67] But even more compelling was Kennedy's "little red book"—*Legal Education and the Reproduction of Hierarchy*.[68] Like Marx's manifesto, it argued for a revolution against a system "that train[s] students to accept and participate in the hierarchical structure of life in the law."[69] To smash the system, Kennedy called for law schools to admit all qualified students by lottery and quotas, abolish distinctions between tenured and untenured faculty, pay all law school employees the same salary, and make janitors trade places with professors for one month each year. These proposals, Kennedy claimed, were "counterhegemonic" and designed to "reduce illegitimate hierarchy and alienation within the [law] school and to reduce or reverse the [law] School's role in promoting illegitimate hierarchy and alienation in the Bar and the country at large."[70]

Heady stuff, and smoothly seductive to a boy who knew just enough philosophy to be dangerous. I joined a left study group, as suggested by Kennedy, where we didn't outline our courses or prepare for midterms but, rather, read the works of Marx, Derrida, Foucault, Gramsci, and Lacan, the Crits' intellectual progenitors. We argued about "deconstructionism" until the early hours, and buzzed about how to transcend hierarchy and patriarchal values. When it was time to interview for summer jobs, I wore jeans and a gold hoop earring, and did not get a callback. My interviewing was pure theater; I had no intention of working for the corporate state. My friends were going to Legal Aid, the poverty law clinic, a fellowship with the ACLU, and I was certain I would follow. Who needed money when your parents were writing the checks?

One night, at a party, I met a redheaded classmate with green eyes and an attitude. Thus followed the first of many tempestuous relationships: slammed doors; three a.m. phone calls; other men. She broke my heart

---

67. *Id.* at 565.

68. A shorter version of the book, which Kennedy self-published in 1983, appears at 32 J. LEGAL EDUC. 591 (1982).

69. *Id.* at 591.

70. *Id.* at 614–15.

in the way that only a romantic can have his heart broken: willingly and repeatedly. Liz wanted to be a federal prosecutor, and didn't understand how indeterminacy would help her. "I can't tell a judge it's all politics," she said. Critical Legal Studies was pointless solipsism, she claimed, interesting only to pointy-headed intellectuals. We argued late into the nights, then agreed to disagree until we didn't agree about anything anymore.

Kennedy had that effect on people. Love him or hate him, it was difficult not to be in a camp. The Crits upended convention, and had left detritus in their wake. Faculty meetings, reportedly, were tense and splintered. Tenure decisions were bloody battles. The first year curricula was torn and battered. But Kennedy, himself, was aloof from the fray.

In those days, students had little interaction with faculty. There was no e-mail, and no one would have thought to visit a professor's office or, worse, call him on the phone. It was not *The Paper Chase,* or even *One L,* but there was still fear and loathing between those who did the teaching and those who received it. Yet Kennedy's egalitarian ramblings made him seem different. In class he eschewed the suit and tie for a threadbare jacket and faded denim work shirt. The bravest among us called him "Duncan," and peppered his name in our conversation. He was less than father figure, and more like a big brother who was home from college with a duffle bag of bootlegged tapes he might consider sharing.

We were surprised when he declined an invitation to visit our study group. Instead, he sent his best wishes, and urged vigor in the struggle. When he saw us on campus, he couldn't remember our names. After class he was anything but warm and fuzzy, and few of us dared approach him at the podium.

I didn't know then that Kennedy's wife—"Mopsy"—was a social columnist for the *Boston Globe,* or that he favored expensive cigars and could be found smoking them with his feet perched on his enormous cherry desk. He had never actually practiced law, and except for a short stint in the CIA(!), never really had a "professional" career except as a law professor. But I don't think knowing any of this would have mattered. CLS appealed to my essential rebelliousness, my conflict between following my heart and selling out. It was a conflict that would plague me for the rest of my life. CLS was perfect for me—the law student who was not interested in the law, *per se,* but was at law school as an antidote to boredom, to have heady conversations and meet girls.

Many years later I realized CLS was simply the philosophical patron saint of frustrated lawyers. Men (and some women) who never wanted to be lawyers in the first place. Academics—the worst kind of lawyers—who fled practice as soon as they could in order to teach. What better theory than the meaninglessness of legal reasoning? If everything was a power grab, then training lawyers to actually practice law was irrelevant. The only thing that mattered was exposing the sham. Once exposed, Kennedy offered utopian proposals that couldn't possibly be enacted. It was enough to prove he was the smartest kid in the class. His reward: a cozy tenured professorship at Harvard Law School.

The hierarchy Kennedy wanted to invert, it turned out, was the one that privileged practicing law over teaching it, that made corporate lawyers rich and professors dress in threadbare jackets. It was an old trick, the same one Lenin had used with Marx's help, and owed more to Nietzsche than Foucault: Today's revolutionary was tomorrow's cigar-smoking, Jaguar-driving, upper-middle class, plasma TV watcher. Kill the king, then bed his wife and take his throne.

CLS appealed to me, and plenty of my classmates, because we didn't want to learn that law was a vocation like plumbing or carpentry. Spending our lives in the service of bankers and real estate magnates who would get richer through our labors was not what we imagined when we constructed the future. Much better to embrace the theories of the cool kids, and to smile with smug self-assurance at the stupidity of the masses.

Kennedy's final exam was the ultimate betrayal. After a year of deconstructing orthodoxies and challenging hegemony, the exam was a classic issue-spotter, where Black Letter Law ruled with an iron fist and a reign of terror. It turned out Kennedy's revolutionary fervor only extended so far. He could have resisted conforming to university norms and created an exam consistent with his anti-hierarchal pedagogy, but I suppose he realized at some level he wasn't quite so powerful as to ignore the market forces that kept him tenured. It was one thing to teach that law was power; another thing to risk his job by subverting the system that kept him well-employed. He let students call him "Duncan," but he wouldn't give up his podium, his seating chart, or his bluebook exam. (I should have known from the first day he paraded around the lecture hall that he was a sucker for hierarchy.) In the end, he didn't really care whether his students were prepared for careers as attorneys; all that mattered was the illusion of preparedness. If nothing else, CLS was brilliant at conveying that illusion. It taught us to "think like lawyers" and talk like lawyers. We just couldn't practice like lawyers.

Once upon a time, law, like life, was full of promise. I was in love with the philosophical debates, and the act of deconstruction itself. The buzz after Kennedy's class and the espresso in the café with Liz. All was new, fresh, and shiny, and CLS was going to change the world.

But the world, it turned out, was filled with document production and interrogatory responses. It was filled with partners who assigned work on Friday nights and called on Sunday mornings to follow up. Colleagues who never left the office and frightened the cleaning staff. Memos that were written and never used. Takeout food that congealed in Styrofoam. Misery. Isolation. Irrelevance. Despair.

CLS never taught us about any of this because it couldn't. It wasn't a theory for lawyers really. It was a theory *about* lawyers. It made some of its practitioners famous and, if not rich, well-off. In a certain crowd, Kennedy was a rock star, and he carried himself like a man who appreciated being the center of attention. (Does any professor not enjoy the egomaniacal thrill of a classroom of acolytes scribbling his every word?) He held sway over Harvard through the 1980s, until a chill wind blew CLS away.

Duncan, you sweet-talked and seduced me, misled and deceived me, led me to water and told me what to think. I miss you every day.

Part IV
Two and Three L

According to a familiar adage, students are scared to death in the first year of law school, worked to death in the second year, and bored to death in the third year. For 1L students, studying law is a fresh and exciting endeavor, but it comes with a large dose of anxiety about exams, grades, and the nagging suspicion that you don't really deserve to be there and that you got accepted to the school only because of some sort of clerical error within the admissions department. Having survived the first year and mastered the basic skills of legal analysis, research, and writing, one might think the 2L year would be a breeze. But second-year law students tend to find themselves with a host of things to do on top of just keeping up with homework and attending classes. Students get involved in a diverse array of extra activities. Some get positions as editors of law journals. Some land spots on the teams that will represent the school in mock trial, moot court, negotiations, client counseling, or other competitions. Some become deeply immersed in the school's legal clinics, getting valuable hands-on experience representing real clients. Others become research assistants for professors. Students also get the chance to venture beyond the law school's walls through a variety of internships, externships, clerkships, observerships, and fellowships. Many students juggle part-time jobs, such as clerking at a law firm, while keeping up with their studies. The 2L year is also when students invest a lot of time and effort in looking for jobs for the upcoming summer and beyond. Between classes, they rush to send out résumés or get to interviews.

By the time they reach their third year of law school, many students start to feel anxious to move on and start the next phase of their lives. Some already have a job lined up, while the employment search continues to weigh heavily in the minds of those who do not. With two years of study and training already under their belts, some get restless and feel like classes have become just more repetitions of an already familiar routine. Some law schools have recently begun to experiment with significant reforms of the third-year curriculum, searching for ways to distinguish it from the first and second years and to give students a culminating experience that better prepares them for the transition to practicing law. A few schools unveiled radical revisions of curriculum, such as having 3L students participate only in experiential learning opportunities, from simulations to live client clinics.

The upsides of the second and third years of law school include a lot of choice in classes. Most schools have few required courses past the first year, and offer a wide array of useful and intriguing upper division classes, ranging from Antitrust and Electronic Discovery, to Negotiation and Trial Advocacy.

One L in a Different Voice:
Becoming a Gay Male Feminist
at Harvard Law School

MARC R. POIRIER

My project here is to reflect on my first year at Harvard Law School, but I will begin with a vignette from my last semester there. In February, 1978, Boston received more than two feet of snow over a couple of days. The city shut down. Governor Dukakis declared a state of emergency. After two days, the Law School reopened despite the emergency order still in effect.[71] Dean Albert Sacks simply would not let Harvard Law School be humbled by mere weather. He personally walked in from Belmont.[72] His refusal to acknowledge the ongoing weather emergency epitomizes the intransigence and arrogance that the Law School administration appeared to me to bring to many common sense problems and demands during my time there.[73]

---

71. Ken Gormley, *Blizzard Break Brings Bellyflops*, HARV. L. REC., Feb. 17, 1978, at 2; J. Ezra Merkin, *Sacks Explains Decision to Hold Class*, HARV. L. REC., Feb. 17, 1978, at 4–5; Editorial, *The Right Decision*, HARV. L. REC., Feb. 17, 1978, at 10.

72. Merkin, *supra* note 71, at 5.

73. One unnamed administrator described the decision as evidencing "the basic analness" of Harvard Law School, and was concerned with how reopening so soon would appear to "the little guy in the Square who obeyed the governor." *Id.* at 5. The Dean explained that he preferred to avoid four days of makeup classes, which would have inconvenienced students more than requiring them to attend classes during the emergency. *Id.* Keep in mind that cars were banned from the streets and there was no local public transportation. The administra-

Considering how much I disliked Harvard Law School, it still surprises me sometimes that I eventually became a law professor. Once graduated, I thought I would never set foot in a law school ever again. My last semester, I was elected for long term office—those guys that are supposed to help the class stay in touch and perhaps help the school raise donations—on the campaign slogan "Not One Penny Ever." A bunch of us ran on that slogan. I came in tied for the last slot. The election did not make any difference. The Law School simply asked other, more willing folks to collect the money.

I was not prepared for Harvard Law School. I had found success and happiness at Yale majoring in literature—not English, not comparative literature, but the theory of texts and stories and the ways that they construct and reproduce understanding and identity and history and civilization. Probably a fancy name for what I studied would be "applied hermeneutics." I wrote my honors thesis on Martin Heidegger's approach to poetry. It had just about nothing to do with what was going on at Harvard Law School.

Harvard was not prepared for the likes of me, either. For one thing, I may have seemed something I was not. I applied from Paris, France. I went to Paris after Yale because I wasn't crazy enough to try to become a professor of literature. At that time, graduate schools were glutted with young men who had been avoiding the Vietnam War. It was clear there would be no meaningful professional openings in the humanities for a generation. I didn't know what else to do and thought I might as well be a confused youth in Paris for a while. Paris had been welcoming confused American youths for quite some time. Part of my particular confusion was that it had become clear that I was homosexual ("gay" was just emerging as an alternative term in this time frame), and I needed to sort that out. Paris had a long history of welcoming confused homosexuals, too. But with a French name and a job at a French oil company, I might have appeared to Har-

---

tion expected students to walk in the snow up to an hour each way to attend class. Merkin, *supra* note 71, at 4. To be sure, the Law School recorded many classes on those two days. *Id.* And the Dean had checked with Governor Dukakis first. *Id.* Still, Harvard Law was the only non-emergency institution in the area open during the emergency. I recall a headline that the Governor was not happy about the reopening, though the only inkling of this in the *Harvard Law Record* is from a talk that Dukakis gave the following year; when asked, he did not recall any negative comments. David Quinto, *Dukakis Reminisces on Governorship: What Went Right, and What Went Wrong*, HARV. L. REC., Dec. 8, 1978, at 6, 7.

vard Law to be another ambitious young European would-be executive, the kind of future leader that Harvard Law likes to imbue with American values and turn loose on the world.

Actually, Harvard Law was not prepared to deal with a fair number of the students in my incoming class in the fall of 1975.[74] The Zeitgeist of the early 1970s led many top law schools to admit more students of color and women, along with some attempts at economic (class) diversity. I suspect the idea was that the racial turmoil of the late 1960s and the emerging claims for social justice articulated by various feminisms would be resolved by training a more diverse class of students as lawyers mostly in the traditional mold. There were role models in the civil rights movement and in the emerging constitutional and statutory litigation around sex/gender. As to role models, however, Harvard Law itself had almost no faculty of color and almost no women faculty throughout my stay, let alone any openly gay professors. There were to be sure several young faculty operating in Critical Legal Studies mode. They were often on our side, critiquing the law and the Law School from within, occasionally effectively. Their critiques did not translate for me into a sense that the law school was responding to student concerns either about local matters or broader social justice. Harvard's faculty did feature some avatars of public service—Archibald Cox, for example, walked the halls wearing the honorable mantle of the Saturday Night Massacre.[75] His genteel approach did not correspond especially well to the righteous anger of these incoming students, nor to their sense that corporate business as usual was not all there might be to the study and practice of the law. We were looking for something a little more dramatic, a little more 1960s, perhaps.

One important conflict between the students on the left and the law school administration occurred my first year. A recruiter from a major law firm allegedly joked, to a black law student, that his firm employed attorneys of color, one of whom had gone on to work for Clorox. The student did not find the anecdote funny. She complained.[76] The Law School did

74. My class was Scott Turow's. I did not know him. We were in different sections.

75. *See* Carroll Kilpatrick, *Nixon Forces Firing of Cox; Richardson, Ruckelshaus Quit*, WASH. POST, Oct. 21, 1973, at A1; Kermit Kubitz, *Profs Condemn Firing of Cox*, HARV. L. REC., Nov. 2, 1973, at 1, 3.

76. *See* Susan Gillette, *Large Midwestern Firm Challenged by HLS Student*, HARV. L. REC., Feb. 27, 1976, at 1, 6, 15, 16.

not see the need to sanction the firm for this stray remark. Various student groups got involved, but could not persuade the administration to apply its antidiscrimination policy.[77] By spring the controversy over the failure to respond became part of a much broader attempt to push reforms about placement and other aspects of the institution.[78] In April 1976, a number of student groups insisted on speaking directly to the Board of Visitors, in what was styled a mass protest.[79] It was quite a heated discussion. The Board responded the following fall with recommendations for reform, which the administration appeared effectively to ignore.[80] A number of the reform proposals were, eventually, adopted in some form. But by then I had moved on, recalling Harvard Law as a place of conflict and institutional recalcitrance.[81]

---

77. *See* Susan Gillette, *Law Group Head Demands Action on Discrimination*, Harv. L. Rec., Apr. 16, 1976, at 1, 8; Roger Evans, *Coalition Plans to Pack Committee's Meeting*, Harv. L. Rec., Apr. 23, 1976, at 1, 8, 16.

78. *See* Evans, *supra* note 77; Bruce Howard, *Groups Present Reforms to Placement Committee*, Harv. L. Rec., Mar. 26, 1976, at 1, 4 (reporting that the Black American Law Student Association, the National Lawyers Guild, and the Women's Law Association presented to the administration a proposal, endorsed by a number of other student groups, for reforms relating to placement).

79. *See* Paul Coady, *Board of Overseers Hears Student Groups Sear HLS*, 10 Harv. L. Rec., May 7, 1976, at 1, 8, 16 (describing special meeting between Board of Visitors and many angry student groups); Evans, *supra* note 77, at 16 (describing the students' plan to pack the Board of Visitors meeting and speak "under protest"). The following year, a similar conversation occurred in a much more "placid" atmosphere. Bill Rose, *Visiting Committee Presides; Placid Atmosphere Prevails*, Harv. L. Rec., Apr. 29, 1977, at 1, 2, 9, 16. By two years later we were back to the "annual open meeting with students." J. Ezra Merkin, *Visiting Committee Comes Back to School*, Harv. L. Rec., Mar. 17, 1978, at 1.

80. Charles Jordan, *Overseers Recommend Reforms*, Harv. L. Rec., Oct. 22, 1976, at 2, 6, 16; Editorial, *Pick Up the Gauntlet*, Harv. L. Rec., Oct. 22, 1976, at 10 (chastising the Law School administration for unresponsiveness to the Overseers' report).

81. A few months later an outside investigation exonerated the law firm, finding either that the offending statement had not been made or that it was innocent. David Remes, *Bowman Disappointed: Study by Gorman Neglects Evidence*, Harv. L. Rec., Oct. 8, 1976, at 1, 3, 15 [hereinafter Remes, *Bowman Disappointed*]; David Remes, *Chicago Firm Exonerated of Discrimination Claim*, Harv. L. Rec., Oct. 1, 1976, at 1, 5, 12, 16 (concluding that the offending statement either was not made or was made innocently and the student overreacted). The Law School Placement Committee did not adopt this conclusion, however, concluding in its own report to the Dean that it could not resolve the dispute either way. Remes, *Bowman Disappointed*, *supra*, at 16.

Jointly organized demonstrations occurred every year I was at Harvard Law about something or other. My third year, one big issue was that Chief Justice Warren Burger had been invited to preside over the annual upper level moot court competition. Students on the left observed (this was in the fall of 1977) that the Burger Court was rolling back what we considered the advances of the Warren Court in a number of areas. Several student groups worked together to write a pamphlet critiquing the Burger Court's retrenchment; we also organized a teach-in and a demonstration, though one intended not to disrupt, only to make dissent visible.[82] I participated through the Harvard Law chapter of the National Lawyers Guild. The outcome of all this? At the last minute Chief Justice Burger had back trouble, and Justice Thurgood Marshall came to Cambridge to preside instead.[83] So the protest was blunted.[84] The teach-in was a success.[85] The teach-in and demonstration were the first times ever, so far as I can tell, that gay activists spoke at Harvard Law School.[86]

In addition to the unpleasant discovery that this was not graduate school in the humanities, there were in fact pervasive problems with the educational method: large classes taught ineffectively, a fostering of counterproductive competitiveness (there really were cases ripped out of the reporters), a disconnect between what happened in class and what was expected on exams, systematic failure to address skills development, the

---

82. Barbara Kritchevsky, *Teach-In Speakers Blast Burger Court Stands on Blacks, Women, Gays, Poor*, HARV. L. REC., Nov. 23, 1977, at 3, 7, 16; Bill Ross, *Protest of Court Decisions to Mark Burger Ames Visit*, HARV. L. REC., Nov. 4, 1977, at 1, 3, 7; Larry Zelenak, *Law Guild Leads Protests Against Burger Decisions*, HARV. L. REC., Nov. 23, 1977, at 1, 9.

83. Zelenak, *supra* note 82, at 1.

84. Less than 100 people showed up. *Id.* at 9. The following year, the scenario repeated itself. This time Chief Justice Burger actually came; there was a protest (with some 200 people), a jointly-produced pamphlet, and a demonstration; and Chief Justice Burger met with some of the students. Pat Hanifin, *Burger Meets Court Critics Before Ames*, HARV. L. REC., Nov. 21, 1978, at 8, 12, 13.

85. *See* Kritchevsky, *supra* note 82, at 3.

86. *See id.* (Marge Ragona, Pastor of the Metropolitan Community Church of Providence, Rhode Island, spoke at the teach-in); Zelenak, *supra* note 82, at 9 (Joe Martin, a Massachusetts lobbyist for gay rights, spoke at the protest, and there were many signs for gay rights in the crowd). To be sure, the upper level moot court competition problem for 1976 had involved a lesbian teacher who had been fired. Terry Keeney, *School Board Lawyers Win Ames Competition*, HARV. L. REC., Dec. 3, 1976, at 1, 6, 14. That provided some sort of visibility for LGBT issues the year before.

occasional professor as bully. Everyone knew it, the question was what you did about it.

For the most part the only way to learn writing skills was from other students, via participation in a journal or one of the student volunteer groups focused on litigation.[87] The best educational experience of my first year was a Federal Litigation seminar, under the supervision of David Shapiro. A limited group of students worked a hypothetical mass tort invasion of privacy lawsuit through a set of in-class exercises, with seven required writing projects and one or two oral exercises for every student. But only a few students could get into this seminar; it was hugely oversubscribed. I also benefitted from participation on the *Harvard International Law Journal*, eventually as an articles editor. Those skills live on in my academic work.

Self-help was essential. I sought sanity in martial arts courses,[88] piano playing, Harvard Square's restaurants, and many, many foreign films. With friends, I developed reading groups. Most important for me, under the aegis of the National Lawyers Guild, a number of lesbian and gay students from Boston area law schools began an anti-sexism reading group. That is where I acquired my grounding in feminist theory, one still useful to me in my academic work. The Lawyers Guild, especially that student reading group, was also the only place where I encountered fellow LGBT folk[89] in a reflective political context.

The whole matter of feminism, theoretical or applied, seemed a gaping void at the Law School. Not only was feminist social critique missing from the curriculum, *women faculty* were missing. Harvard Law had never had more than one or two tenured women faculty,[90] and although it was looking for candidates it considered qualified, there weren't very many of them,

---

87. While I was at Harvard Law, though not in my first year, Gary Bellow and Jeanne Kettleson undertook a systematic restructuring of the clinical program. This led eventually to the Jamaica Plain center. In my third year I did a clinical placement directly at Greater Boston Legal Services, supervised by then-LL.M. student Walter Heiser. It was an extraordinarily useful experience, one of my best memories of law school.

88. My instructor was Bill Paul, an LL.M. student at the School of Education. The next time I saw Bill was at the 1979 National Gay and Lesbian March on Washington. At the 1987 March, I saw only his AIDS Quilt panel. Bill had died of AIDS.

89. If I may be allowed an anachronism, for "LGBT" is a product of the 1990s and the 2000s, not the 1970s.

90. *See generally* Mary Elizabeth Basile, *False Starts: Harvard Law School's Efforts Towards Integrating Women into the Faculty, 1928–1981*, 28 HARV. J. GENDER & L. 143 (2005)

apparently, and the ones who were hired seldom stayed.[91] My Contracts professor lasted two years. She was treated with extraordinary incivility by some of my fellow students.[92] I can't speak to how she was treated by the law school faculty. For whatever reason, she returned to private practice. The other female professor was Elizabeth Owens, an international tax scholar.[93] She also taught a public lands course, which helped steer me into my environmental/energy practice in Washington, D.C. I did not know Owens was a tenured professor until I researched her this past summer. She had another title, director, I think. When I was on the job market years ago, a typical question would be who my favorite law professor was. After mentioning two visitors (who didn't count, apparently) I would be asked for my favorite *Harvard* law professor. I would name Professor Owens. No one ever recognized her name.

The National Lawyers Guild became an important anchor throughout my time at Harvard Law.[94] There was a Harvard Law Guild chapter, distinct from the Boston chapter. It (the Law chapter) had been founded just the year before I arrived. The Law School recognized us as a student group, but gave us a particularly unusable office space, under the eaves of an old house, crowded and hard to heat or cool. The Boston chapter of the Guild, on the other hand, provided support for us and other local student chapters, in the form of external events, advice, and speakers, as well as some helpful training. In my third year I did a day of field work for the Mashpee Indian case[95] jury selection process, traveling to leafy suburbs to

---

(analyzing the history of women professors at Harvard Law School from 1928 through 1981).

91. *See id.* at 158–89 (describing how Harvard hired but failed to retain women professors in the 1970s); *see also id.* at 193–94 (assessing Harvard's shortcomings in the 1970s as the source of its current relative dearth of women law professors).

92. *See* Deborah Waire Post, *Reflections on Identity, Diversity and Morality*, 6 BERKELEY WOMEN'S L.J. 136, 141–42 (1990-91) (describing one of the incidents).

93. For a sketch of Professor Owens' life and her career at Harvard Law, see Basile, *supra* note 90, at 165–67.

94. Apparently I was at one point the Guild's "putative president," though I don't recall anything like a definitive organizational structure. Randy Phillips, *Harvard Law Guild Gears Up*, HARV. L. REC., Oct. 29, 1976, at 2. I suspect I'm just the guy who happened to be willing to speak to the reporter.

95. Mashpee Tribe v. Town of Mashpee, 447 F. Supp. 940 (D. Mass. 1978), *aff'd*, 592 F.2d 575 (1st Cir. 1979). The tribe sought to recover land allegedly alienated in violation of the federal Nonintercourse Act. The case was dismissed based on special findings by a jury

observe the neighborhoods of prospective jurors, in terms of flags, religious statuary, and bumper stickers. Also in my third year, the Law School Guild sponsored an alternative first year moot court problem, designed to produce actually useful research for lawyers in the Boston Chapter. I supervised this project.

The Lawyers Guild was less helpful with respect to feminism and homosexuality. The larger organization was itself struggling with those issues. Marx had not discussed women or sex, although Engels produced a relevant text.[96] Many Lawyers Guild folk viewed feminist critiques, as well as the emergence of homosexuality as a political and personal issue, with suspicion. They were considered bourgeois deviations from the class- and race-focused crusades of the Lawyers Guild. Nevertheless, typically, an "anti-sexism" committee would be established, as it was in Boston. This group served as a consciousness-raising focal point for interested Guild members. The anti-sexism group could then communicate feminist concerns to larger Guild organs, with varying degrees of receptivity and success.

The Harvard Law Guild served another function. Among dissatisfied student groups at Harvard, the Guild was one that welcomed white men. The Women's Law Association—so effective throughout my time at Harvard,[97] under the leadership of Sheila Kuehl[98] and others —was so far as I

---

indicating that the tribe had ceased to be a tribe at times relevant to the lawsuit's cause of action.

96. FRIEDRICH ENGELS, THE ORIGIN OF THE FAMILY, PRIVATE PROPERTY, AND THE STATE (1884).

97. The Women's Law Association raised and by slow degrees prevailed on many issues: altering the student health services to address needs of women such as reproductive issues and breast cancer; revamping the gym to accommodate women; increasing the enrollment of women; and ever so slowly hiring and retaining women whom Harvard would consider to be qualified. To be sure, in 1972 the Women's Law Association had also filed a sex discrimination complaint against the Law School with the Department of Health, Education and Welfare. *See* David L. Cocke, *Sacks Terms WLA Charge of Male Bias "Groundless,"* HARV. L. REC., Jan. 26, 1973, at 1–2, 4; Editorial, *Women and HLS*, HARV. L. REC., Apr. 13, 1973, at 10 (mentioning the sex discrimination complaint). In my third year the Women's Law Association sponsored an immensely successful celebration of twenty-five years of women at Harvard Law, and the Harvard Women's Law Journal was initiated. *See* J.P. Macon, *Alumni Group Funds First Women's Law Journal*, HARV. L. REC., Sept. 30, 1977, at 5; J. Ezra Merkin, *Ginsburg, Grasso, Bellamy to Celebrate HLS Women*, HARV. L. REC., Mar. 10, 1978, at 1, 8;.

98. Sheila was famous before she arrived at Harvard Law School because she had played Zelda in *The Many Loves of Dobie Gillis*, a 1960s television show. *See, e.g.*, Gary D. Halley, *Ex-*

knew open just to women. That seemed appropriate. The Black Law Students Association and the Chicano Law Students Association were open only to members of those races, so far as I knew. That seemed appropriate. Several groups welcomed progressive students interested in channeling their energy through litigation or law reform work—Legal Aid, the Committee for Military Justice, Students for Public Interest Law, and others. The Law School Council was viewed as somewhat centrist, though its leaders did address institutional change, espousing a restricted giving policy for alumni as a way of coercing the administration into dialogue. But in terms of confronting the administration, the Guild was a haven for left-leaning students, especially for white men.

I have left for last issues of homosexuality and visibility. On a personal level, my year in Paris had turned out entirely celibate. Alas. I arrived in Cambridge bound and determined not to repeat that experience. Alas also, but for other reasons.

Frankly, Harvard Law wasn't dealing very well with sex, let alone homosexuality.[99] Neither was a topic taught in courses.[100] There were no openly gay or lesbian faculty. Or staff. Or students, so far as I could tell. In my third year I did learn that there was a crowd of gay men who partied to-

---

Star of "Dobie Gillis" Leaves Television, UCLA Administrative Post, Comes to HLS, HARV. L. REC., Feb. 6, 1979, at 5, 12. She would go on to become a power player in California politics and would eventually publicly come out as lesbian. But not in law school.

99. The most extensive discussion of illicit sex I ever encountered was furtive folk knowledge, in the form of advice handed around to go look at the twelfth volume of the second series of the Southern case reporter. When you pulled out the volume it would fall open to a case containing a particularly graphic description of oral sodomy. Back at the Langdell Library in 2009, I stopped by the old set of the regional reporters in hard copy. Twelve Southern Second is all grimy from handling. It still falls open to *Lason v. State*, 12 So. 2d 305 (Fla. 1943) (construing "the abominable and detestable crime against nature").

100. Bill Rubenstein, writing about his experience at Harvard Law several years after mine, describes just two Law School courses and an undergraduate seminar that touched on homosexuality. William B. Rubenstein, *My Harvard Law School*, 39 HARV. C.R.–C.L. REV. 317, 319 (2004). The Law School courses were taught by Martha Minow and Kathleen Sullivan, neither of whom had yet been hired when I was there. Rubenstein also describes spending an evening as a first year student in the mid-1980s looking for references to homosexuality using standard law research apparatus. He found absolutely nothing. *Id.* at 318. He wrote, "In the vast majestic expanse of Harvard Law School's library . . . the absence of legal materials about my life was deafening." *Id.*

gether, though not at the law school, and without any apparent thought that homosexuality might have anything political about it.[101]

It certainly would have helped to have had role models from *somewhere* on how to integrate the personal and political aspects of homosexuality. They were almost nowhere to be found in the media. Harvey Milk emerged from obscurity and was elected to public office in 1977. Locally, openly lesbian politician Elaine Noble worked for a state antidiscrimination law, an effort that was not successful during my time at Harvard. Barney Frank was a year ahead of me at Harvard Law. He was already a star, in the state legislature and at school.[102] But he didn't come out until 1987. By 1977, gay politics were in the news thanks to Anita Bryant's "Save the Children" Campaign in Dade County, Florida. But she was the *anti-gay* role model. For me, there was basically no one there, no one to model myself on, professionally or personally—except for those other, equally bewildered, gay and lesbian law students in the Lawyers Guild reading group.

In terms of my personal life, this was an era when gay men met other gay men in bars, baths, and through personal advertisements. I turned to all three.[103] Nothing ever resulted in a relationship. Though truly, how could it have? I had no car. After my first year, I shared an apartment with friends to whom I was not out. There is much to be said for a room of one's own.[104] Looking back, law school did not foster a particularly healthy set of habits. My behavior certainly was in the spirit of the times, though. Open homosexuality in the 1970s often meant, for men at least, plain old sex.[105]

The squeamish should skip the next three paragraphs. They are about sexually transmitted diseases. STDs were a significant aspect of my law school experience. I missed a lot of school because of them. I mention

---

101. Compare Brad Sears's description of closeted, wealthy, apolitical gay men at Harvard Law School circa 1992. Brad Sears, *Queer L*, 1 Nat'l J. Sex. Orientation L. 234, 238–39 (1995).

102. Frank was the subject of a personal interest feature in the *Harvard Law Record* his first year. Robert E. Mack, *State Legislator Barney Frank Enjoying One L Status*, Harv. L. Rec., Oct. 4, 1974, at 14–15.

103 . Bill Rubenstein says something similar. "Most of my learning at Harvard . . . took place in bars around the city." Rubenstein, *supra* note 100, at 320.

104. *See* Virginia Woolf, A Room of One's Own (Harcourt Brace Jovanovich 1989) (arguing that women's independence is intimately linked to economic status).

105. *See, e.g.*, Frances Fitzgerald, Cities on a Hill: A Journey Through Contemporary American Cultures 63–65 (1986) (describing intense sexual activity among gay men in the Castro district of San Francisco in the late 1970s).

them here not only in the interest of a fully honest description, but because generally speaking coerced invisibility and shame about sex and sexuality led, and continue to lead, to foolish behavior, to poor information, to incompetent medical diagnoses and treatment, and to unnecessary suffering and death. Coerced invisibility and stigmatization of homosexuality result in systematic injury through unacknowledged risk and untreated disease. This is, in a small way, genocidal. Nowadays this is about HIV and hepatitis C. Back then it was mostly about smaller stuff.[106]

While in law school I contracted (in chronological order) crabs, gonorrhea, hepatitis A, and mononucleosis. The first and second were easily cured. I believe the third, hepatitis A, may actually have come from polluted shellfish encountered during a summer clerkship in Richmond, Virginia, though I will never know. I certainly managed to communicate my hepatitis to a friend without ever having exchanged bodily fluids. By the time I got mono in the fall of 1977, I was used to being sick at law school.

The hepatitis was the worst; I missed six weeks of law school while recovering from it. That was my best semester for grades, ironically. The case of crabs was also instructive. The doctor at the Law School health service extension office shrieked, as she reached for her gloves, how disgusting it was to see this parasite in America. After that, I always went down to the main health service in Harvard Square. The doctor at the law school apparently wasn't ready for sex.

In a read-through of old issues of the *Harvard Law Record* this past summer, I found an editorial that criticized the developing identity politics of the decade, the very politics I needed and could not find.[107] It was published in the fall of 1978, perhaps not coincidentally the semester that Harvard Law acquired its gay and lesbian student group.[108] The author

---

106. *See id.* at 66 (discussing the prevalence of sexually transmitted diseases among gay men in San Francisco in the late 1970s).

107. Editorial, *Splintering the Movement*, HARV. L. REC., Nov. 16, 1978, at 10.

108. Harvard Law's gay and lesbian student group was formed in the fall of 1978. J. Ezra Merkin, *HLS Recognition Sought by Gay Rights Group*, HARV. L. REC., Oct. 20, 1978, at 1, 7. The administration encouraged the students to join some other existing group instead, but they declined. *Id.* at 7. The following spring the administration announced it was adding homosexuality to the list of protected categories for admissions and placement, a move requested by the new student group. *Harvard Announces Ban on 'Gay' Discrimination*, HARV. L. REC., Apr. 27, 1979, at 15. Despite some early influence, however, the Committee on Gay

argues that at the beginning of the decade the civil rights community had been united in its concern to combat injustice through law.[109] Then the women, the Jews, and the gays had gone and formed special interest groups at the Law School.[110] These groups were, selfishly, looking out for themselves rather than seeking to contribute to a collective interest in achieving social justice.[111] This editorial utterly failed to recognize the importance to subordinated groups of being able to be amongst their own, to articulate their own experience, in both positive and negative dimensions, and to formulate their own agendas both for personal fulfillment and political change.[112] As members of dominant groups so often do, the author assumed that the world was transparent to him/her, and that whatever s/he didn't see didn't exist or wasn't important to anyone. Putting specific faces of diversity on injustice was unacceptable, threatening. Despite good intentions, the editorial articulates an attitude hostile to group visibility that, from the student side, contributed much to the alienation that I felt at the Law School.[113]

Change on issues of homosexuality at Harvard Law did indeed come, but it has come very slowly. In researching this essay I discovered three other autobiographical essays from gay men who were Harvard Law students and now are law professors (or were—one died).[114] Spaced at intervals of about five years each from my own experience, these essays do not show things getting very much better. None of the three authors was happy there, and visibility continued to be an issue. Brad Sears for example

---

Legal Issues may not have amounted to much for quite a while. Brad Sears reports that in 1992-1993 it only met twice, with an average attendance of five. Sears, *supra* note 101, at 237.

109. *Splintering the Movement, supra* note 107.

110. The Women's Law Association, the Jewish Law Students' Association, and the Committee on Gay Legal Issues are the three groups specifically mentioned in the editorial. *Id.*

111. *Id.*

112. The author wrote, "Groups don't have civil rights—people do. Classifying people into groups for the purpose of determining their civil rights is itself a violation of the fundamental civil right not to be pigeon-holed or stereotyped, but to be treated as a unique individual." *Id.*

113. Even in 1992, Brad Sears wrote, many students just didn't get it—incomprehension or hostility to visibly gay students continued. Sears, *supra* note 101, at 236.

114. Peter M. Cicchino, *An Activist at Harvard Law School*, 50 Am. U. L. Rev. 551 (2001); Rubenstein, *supra* note 100; Sears, *supra* note 101.

reports that even in 1992, "There were only a handful of students in the entire school who were out."[115]

In 1993, my fifteenth reunion year, I decided to attend a reunion at Harvard Law as a way of catching up with two former law partners. In a large lecture to a truly august assembly, an eminent professor used a hypothetical homosexual rape (in a locker room! of two football players! and under the influence of drugs! and with witnesses!) to pose the question whether a coerced contract could be enforced. I raised my hand to comment and wound up in the front of the room, explaining to three hundred people what my problem was. It became clear that this kind of slander was not likely to stop until there were tenured LGBT faculty. So I modified my "Not One Penny Ever" pledge, to "Not One Penny Until There Are Tenured LGBT Faculty."[116] Harvard Law finally hired Janet Halley away from Stanford in 2000.[117]

Things are considerably better at Harvard Law now, not just on the issue of LGBT visibility, but on other fronts that made me feel so out of place and unwelcome—feminism, gay studies, and queer studies in the curriculum, the role of women at all levels of the institution, the presence of clinics, a more respectful and humane attitude towards students from the administration. One cannot expect a hugely wealthy and powerful institution to be where I would be politically. Because of its size and reputation, however, I somehow expected Harvard Law to be prepared to support students like myself, to be truly diverse, and to be cutting edge intellectually and educationally. Back then, it was not particularly good at those things.

POSTSCRIPT

I landed well. I wound up at a small Washington, D.C., boutique firm, Spiegel & McDiarmid, doing something arguably public interest-like while making a decent living. Quite by accident, the firm was incredibly gay friendly; one of its founding partners, George Spiegel, had two gay sons.

---

115. Sears, *supra* note 101, at 237.

116. I had already relented to the extent of giving Harvard Law money earmarked for summer public interest fellowships for students doing LGBT-related projects.

117. On the importance of Professor Halley's presence and visibility at the Law School, see Rubenstein, *supra* note 100, at 331–32.

The partners were happy to allow me as a junior associate to work on the logistics of the 1979 National Gay and Lesbian March on Washington. I ended up a Security Marshal on the day of the March, carrying a walkie-talkie and wearing a special sash, charged with keeping peace. It was by this chance that I happened to encounter again my friend and martial arts teacher from Harvard, Bill Paul, and law school classmate and Harvard Law student leader Sheila Kuehl. This time, though, it was on the occasion of an event where we could all be openly and politically gay.

One L and Beyond

GERRY SPENCE

I am a country boy. Was then and still am. I didn't know where Harvard or Yale were located—in what city or state I mean. I heard of Yale but I don't know how I came to hear of it. We didn't have television. I didn't read much. Probably some professor mentioned those places in passing.

During the Wyoming summers when I was a boy, I'd sleep in a tent behind the house while my parents rented my room to passing tourists. The doors of the hours were never locked, and the tourists always paid. It was a different time.[118]

> We had a sense that *we* were in control of our lives. We didn't need a lawyer to sue a corporation for false advertising. We made our own or did without. We didn't need a lawyer to sue for the botulin in the corn that had been canned in some distant factory. My mother canned it herself. We didn't need to sue Delta Airlines for the loss of our luggage or our lives. We never flew in an airplane. There was no need to sue Ford for a car manufactured with defective brakes. We putted along in our Model A at thirty miles an hour on empty country roads. There was no call to sue for the rights of women. Few were thinking of wom-

---

118. Gerry Spence, With Justice for None: Destroying an American Myth 37 (1989).

en's rights—least of all, women themselves. Martin Luther King, Jr., had yet to march to Selma. Civil-rights suits were unheard of.[119]

While most members of the bar understood their duty to represent the poor, the scorned, and the forgotten, the "gentlemen of the profession" represented banks, utilities, railroads, and insurance companies:

> I thought it strange people didn't realize that whenever the bank gave the nod, the *gentlemen* of the bar would foreclose on the people's homes and farms, and whenever the people were hurt or their loved ones killed, the *gentlemen* of the bar, for their standard hourly fee, would defeat their just claims, while the *rabble* of the profession still fought for the little guy.[120]

Before I left high school, I had decided I wanted to be a lawyer, and rejected other paths, such as preacher or schoolteacher. I didn't want to be trampled over by a bunch of adolescent kids, like the one I used to be. "Preachers and teachers were mostly wimps anyway . . . I wanted to be somebody with power."[121]

After a stint in the Merchant Marines, I was twenty-one when I entered law school in 1949. The school sported two classrooms above the library at the University of Wyoming and a few small cubbyholes for four professors and the dean. It had a large room for the main library—not much larger, however, than my present living room, which isn't an auditorium. Some stacks existed behind in intimidating rows. Bad lighting back there too. I tried to stay out of there as much as possible.

We had about twenty students who graduated from our class. Maybe thirty began the trip. All white. Most were returning veterans from World War II. Couple of women. I was scared, twenty-one years old and married with a couple of kids. We didn't languish around in the world in those days. We got after it and got it done. I was the youngest in our class and I had no staggering prelaw history as a student or scholar. I still had pimples.

---

119. *Id.*

120. *Id.* at 32.

121. GERRY SPENCE & ANTHONY POLK, GERRY SPENCE: GUNNING FOR JUSTICE 37 (1982).

The ubiquitous fear was flunking out. It was like a battleground. We soldiers with less than passing grades were picked off with little mercy. George flunked out. So did Sam. Bye. My God, the next one is me. And the second year and third, as well, they kept flunking us out. Out. Out. I graduated as the valedictorian only because I couldn't get over my fear of flunking out, even to the last.

I would take copious notes, go home, and redo the notes by hand into a bound notebook we were required to keep. We typed our briefs on small tissue sheets that we glued into the notebook. I read these for my exams like a dying priest over the gospel. I'd been an English major because I liked writing, and our tests were all essays, so I excelled. Then I became the first honor graduate from the University of Wyoming to flunk the bar. Big Mamma up in the Sky was having her usual fun.

Our bar exam was totally essay as well. The chair of the Bar Selection Committee barely knew how to read although he had read enough to pass the bar. Never attended law school. He ended up representing the Union Pacific Railroad. The year I graduated he flunked that year's top student (me) and bottom student. The bottom student became a judge. I know I couldn't pass one of those word puzzles that today these intellectual athletes who never tried a case and never looked an accused in the eye call a bar exam. But I have been able to write a brief or two and make a passable final argument, and I can tell a story, if not here, well, elsewhere. But I didn't learn any of that in law school. So it goes.

When the graduation ceremonies were held, I was so poor I couldn't rent a cap and gown for the graduation. I stayed home. Doubt that I missed much. Anyway, I'm told they throw those caps out into the air at the end of the ceremony. Besides, it was then that the work began—the fight for justice.

Justice. What could possibly be more American? But, what has happened to justice in America? There stands the courthouse, solid, stately. Inside, we still find great judges, men and women dedicated to the law, presiding over our cases. In the courtrooms, we hear our hometown lawyers pleading to a jury of our neighbors. But there will be no justice, for a new king dominates justice in America, a sovereign whose soul is pledged to business and whose heart is geared to profit. The new king, an amorphous agglomeration of corporations, of banks and insurance companies, and mammoth multinational financial institutions, maintains a prurient passion for money and demands a justice of its own, one that is stable and predictable, one that fits into columns and accounts and mortality tables, one that is interpretable in dollars, so that a little justice is a few dollars and a lot of justice many. The new king cannot deal with the soul, the fire, and the unpredictability of human justice. Profit is the lifeblood of business, and if there is no profit in justice, people are not likely to receive it.[122]

And this is why I have always represented the people, why I fight for the little guy. I still believe in that revered duty, which was taken for granted all those years ago. Because, "[w]hen we zealously defend the lowest, the forgotten, and the damned, we preserve the system that protects us all."[123]

In short, my tenure in law school was not among my most favored memories. If I had to do it all over again I might have taken another avenue—maybe painting or writing. Maybe bank robbing. If I come back I want to come back as a bank robber. In my own way I have robbed a few and find it very satisfying.

One thing I know, though. Fear, the abject terror I experienced in law school, has never left me. It has stayed with me as a friend. I have been equally afraid of losing a case for a client. Fear energizes me to prepare, to work hard, to care, both for my client and myself. I would have rather gone to school and learned to pick daisies and chew Juicy Fruit gum. I think they offer courses something like that today, but I'm not sure. But I do know that, in some ways, what I learned in law school was equally valuable.

---

122. SPENCE, *supra* note 1, at 3–4.
123. *Id.* at 31.

Tales from the Back Bench

ROBERT R.M. VERCHICK

Just beyond the Harvard Law School's campus near the university's music building stands a handsome tree, perhaps elm or maple (I don't inventory such things), its exposed roots elaborately knotted into the lumpy ground. At the base of the trunk is a hollow, so dark that even in full sun you can't see inside. Nailed to the trunk above the hollow, is a hand-painted sign that reads: "Pooh."

That was the scene when I attended Harvard as a 1L. Pooh still lives there. In fact, the bear's now got a small yellow door hinged to the trunk. I suppose that law students passing by wonder, as I did then, who keeps the place up. Undergraduates, most likely. *Maybe* a bored bassoon player avoiding her dissertation. But not law students. They would *never* stoop to such whimsy.

My move to Harvard Law was an exciting, but sometimes frustrating transition. The law school community was large and anonymous, the famous Bauhaus dormitories (designed by Walter Gropius) part Habitrail and part shoebox factory, the eyes of campus administrators a baleful gray. I had come with a bachelor's degree in English (English!) from a west coast university that called itself "the Farm," a campus known for fragrant eucalyptus and a pride of lion-colored hills. Harvard Law was certainly no "Farm," and to my eye it was no "Hundred Acre Wood" either.

Whimsy? Forget it.

At the law school we were all scared. Herded into cavernous classrooms with impressive molding and portraits of dour judges, we sat in swiveling seats each marked with an assigned number. The professors would enter from doors behind the lectern (you wouldn't want them sashaying past students from the rear) and pull out an enormous cardboard seating chart from a special bracket on the wall. "Ms. Johnson . . ." you'd hear one of them say. Thank God, you'd say to yourself. It could have been me.

This went on for weeks, months, with little end in sight. Meeting people was hard, I found, because it was nearly impossible to dig beneath the surface. Students seemed always to be sizing up other students—the schools you'd gone to, your former jobs, the countries you'd visited, your comments in class. Or not. We each had campus mailboxes in the student center into which organizations and departments would stuff urgent flyers about all the stuff you should be doing—hearing a Nobel Laureate, becoming a Big Sister, fighting world hunger, or joining the CIA. All of this would immediately go in the wastebasket as fast as I could shovel it. But on a day in late October I found something else, a single colored sheet formatted like a newspaper. It said:

THE BACK BENCH REPORTER
A publication by, for, and about Section 1
October 24, 1986 – Vol.1, No. 1

It was a newsletter, printed in the unmistakable style of a Macintosh computer with a dot-matrix printer. Like the tracts of Thomas Paine and Alexander Hamilton, authorship was concealed. The title was taken from the practice at the time of allowing unprepared students to sit near the rear of the classroom—on "the back bench," where they could silently listen and perhaps finish a crossword. But, importantly, there was, really, no news. Instead a quiz! ("How many Section members rowed in the 1986 Head of the Charles?" "Ms. Johnson was the first person called on in Prof. Miller's class. Who was the first in Prof. Sargentich's class?") And a ranked list of funny quotations from professors and students overheard and scribbled down in our classes. Who could forget when J.T. said, "You look out the window and you see the Taj Mahal and you say—'Mother of God!'" (What was that all about?) Or Prof. Arthur Miller's creepy smile when he assured, "Yes, Virginia, we do wash your brains here." (A number one ranking!)[124]

As leaves fell off the damp trees and dissolved into mush, the *Back Bench Reporter*, or "*BBR*," as students called it, hit its stride, and became a necessary diversion to my law student life. Every week the *BBR* would publish rankings of quotations, light-hearted profiles of students you wish you had met, occasional advice columns and fictional movie reviews, like this one based on *Regina v. Dudley & Stephens*,[125] you know, the case where three sailors in a lifeboat eat the cabin boy:

JUMPIN' JACK FLESH [British Title: "Four Men in a Tub"] (PG-13) Adventure on the high seas as "somebody's got to be lunch." Starring Dudley, Stephens, and Will Parker. "I'm sick; feast upon me!" —J.T.

I loved the 1L profiles. For the most part, they seemed genuine, not showy or posed. They always featured the student's "facebook" photo, taken in the days of dime store photo booths and inevitably a little goofy looking. You could find out who obsessed over Korean food, who giggled too much in college, who liked Jimmy Stewart movies. Once in a while you found a real hero, like K.L., a doctor who described once "meeting Jimmy Carter while on a trek in Nepal at 14,000 ft. and treating Rosalyn [Carter], who was sick."

The 1L profiles always featured students' "ambitions," some real, some tongue-in-cheek.

C.S.: "To find happiness even if it means being a lawyer"

J.R.: "To practice law on an Indian reservation/To be a village magistrate coordinator in Alaska"

---

124. Quotations from the *Backbench Reporter* are taken from the publication's first year in print, available in THE BACK BENCH REPORTER: A PUBLICATION BY, FOR, AND ABOUT SECTION 1, VOLUMES ONE THROUGH THREE: THE WHITE ALBUM 1986-1989 (on file with the author). Many thanks to Doug Ulene, Harvard Law School Class of 1989, for making this work available to me. For the reader's convenience, I will not cite individually to each publication's issue. Also, I have taken the occasional liberty of changing punctuation or reformatting text, in the interest of clarity. Finally, I have replaced the names of students with their initials for reasons of privacy; the professors, on the other hand, are on their own.

125. [1884] 14 Q.B.D. 273 (D.C.).

R.H.: "To be a lawyer and a wife and a mother (stable family life is as important as career)"

C.S.: "To be a fat judge"

J.T.: "To emerge from here psychically unscathed"

D.U.: "(Public) Corporate grind; (Private) Author, househusband, entrepreneur, rabbi"

M.M.: "(Pleading in the alternative) (1) To end oppression; (2) To chuck all this for a commune in Vermont . . ."

So sweeping was the *BBR*'s knowledge, so intimate its detail, that people began to suspect there must be spies everywhere. I imagined them as nervous birds scurrying about the wood in search of silver buttons and tangled string. Almost whimsical, I know, but you get the idea.

The quotations poll often captured a moment in class of laughter or at least a smirk. And I came to realize that class really wasn't all that serious if you remembered the funny bits. Gradually students were crawling out of their shells, and professors seemed to enjoy that.

It happened in Criminal Law:

PROF. DANIEL MELTZER:	Give me the difference! Why is this case not like *Katz*? One word—Mr. Albert?
M.A.:	Hoffa!
PROF. MELTZER:	No, "consent." "Hoffa" is not bad, though.

And Property:

PROF. LANCE LIEBMAN:	You've chased a fox? Did you catch it?
D.B.:	Yes.
PROFESSOR LIEBMAN:	What was it worth?
D.B.:	Not nearly as much as the energy you spend chasing it.

And Criminal Law again:

D.G.:	It seems to me you can look at sex in one of two ways . . .
PROF. KATHLEEN SULLIVAN:	I think there are more.

Sometimes a student would say something he might never live down:

> R.N.: I don't know what Camplin was so upset about, just because the guy bugged him.
>
> PROFESSOR CHARLES OGLETREE: If I told you that *bugger* meant "sodomize," would that change your mind?

But then, again, so would professors:

> PROF. MELTZER: "You walk through Harvard Square and people ask you if you want to buy drugs . . . . Does that happen to anyone besides me?"

How I yearned, back then, to see one of my witty phrases published on that page. I know others did too. Sometimes both students and professors *tried purposely* to get on that page by planning some line and then just letting it fall out. You could tell when people did that.

When it came to skillful sound bites, Professor Miller, our Civil Procedure instructor, was surely in a class of his own. Dressed always in a three-piece suit, a ridiculous watch fob dangling from his vest pocket, he managed to elicit both laughter and horror. There were more rumors about him than anyone else. It was whispered that Miller served as model to Scott Turow's fictional Professor Perini, that Miller once taught *Erie Railroad Co. v. Tompkins*[126] dressed as a train conductor and once in drag (*Erie* marked a 180-degree reversal—get it?), that he once stormed out of the classroom when a student was unprepared. I have no idea if such claims were true, but they circulated constantly. And say what you want, the guy knew how to make the abstract concrete, like the rules concerning the waiving of objections and the joining of motions:

---

126. 304 U.S. 64 (1938).

Rule 12(h) is the stiletto—it's the knife coming in; Rule 12(g) is the twist.

Or this explanation of the Full Faith and Credit Clause:

I've got that judgment for $83 billion, and I can wander around the country with it, can't I? Like Diogenes with a lamp . . . trying to ferret you out. My judgment is a *vacuum cleaner*, and it's in your pockets no matter where your pants are . . . .

It's true that class with Miller could get a little rough. At times it seemed as if he had graduated from the Don Rickles School of Education and Pedagogy.

I don't know; the answer isn't on *my face*. It's in the tan pamphlet [containing the Federal Rules of Civil Procedure]. Or haven't you taken the cellophane off yet?

But for the most part, he toyed with the good students, like this graduate from Harvard College.

I mourn the fact that you are the product of an inferior primary, secondary, and undergraduate education. I realize that your world vision is where the best nachos are in San Diego.

And he *did* urge you not to take it personally, as he did once on the return from the hospital:

I hate doctors. I hate needles. I hate clinics. I hate this university. I haven't had any coffee, to which I am addicted. . . . So the only possibility is taking it out on you.

A few students, instant heroes, got sassy right back.

PROF. MILLER: "Why isn't it a *res judicata*/claim preclusion case?
K.S.:   Because it's in the Issue Preclusion section [of the book].
PROF. MILLER: "Everyone's a sit-down comedian today."

In winter I liked to walk across the Anderson Memorial Bridge from Cambridge to Allston across the Charles River. The structure's brick and stone evoked a colonial history I was not used to on the west coast. Admirers of *The Sound and the Fury* know that Quentin Compson, William Faulkner's most famous misplaced Southerner, had once been similarly drawn to this bridge—before he threw himself over it. It wouldn't have worked the day I was there, of course, since the water's surface was completely frozen. I stared at the sheet of white ice anchored between the river's shores. Faintly, but unmistakably, I made out a message scratched into the top frosty layer of ice, communicated in simple block-letters about five-feet tall. "Harvard Sucks," it said. Poor Quentin, I thought. But of course, he had nothing to do with it. Yalies? Resentful town kids? Who could know? But again, surely not law students.

I no longer shared that frigid sentiment, but that is not to say I did not have issues. My girlfriend of several years had broken up with me. (In fact, she announced this decision just a few days before my first law school exams.) She was working in New York City at the time, and I was amused and strangely touched that she had asked one of her roommates to call me regularly to make sure I was "O.K."

I guess I was doing all right. The intellectual atmosphere of the classroom was no longer frightening, but instead spiked with creativity, insight, and devilish wit. And I was told by no less than writers for the *BBR* that romance, like many contracts disputes, understandably boiled downed to "impossibility and frustration."

Reflecting an almost Jurassic sensibility, the *BBR* early on sponsored a student survey seeking the names of men and women with whom members of the opposite sex would like to be stranded on a South Pacific Island. My favorite published responses (both from women) were "Dudley & Stephens" and "This is insulting—I hope [student] money isn't being spent on this trash." But the *BBR* offered more intelligent insights on law school romance too, noting, for instance, that the heterosexual male student body was *not* so easily divided between men who had "no clue" about women and men who had girlfriends. (There were not many married folk in those days.) It turned out there was a significant number of men who could claim allegiance to *both* camps, a status dubbed "Advertent No Clue," or "Unreasonably Having of Girlfriend." Who knew my life was so easily explained?

In February, the *BBR* published valentines too:

Dear C.,
    I'm looking for a short, beer-drinking guy with curly hair who's man enough to fall asleep in class; I'm looking for you big guy.
                              The Woman of Your Dreams

And,

To whoever voted for me in the South Sea Island Poll: Get LOST.

Most classmates I knew came to Harvard Law School with an impression of the institution borrowed from popular culture. For some, it was *One L*, for me it was the film *The Paper Chase*, which I must have seen twenty or thirty times. My favorite scene, believe it or not, was the one where James Hart slips away one night with a classmate and sneaks into the library's sprawling stacks. Like the Phantom spelunking Parisian sewers, Hart and friend float through dimly lit corridors, waxing spiritual and casting long shadows. I'm slightly embarrassed to say I did the same thing, or something like it. This was the '80s, of course, so investigating the notes of a conventional scholar like Mr. Kingsfield was not my style. No, I was ensorcelled by the Crits, and the feminists, and the emerging prose poetry that would become Critical Race Theory. I recall combing the music library's jazz collection in search of Billie Holiday's "Body and Soul," because Mari Matsuda had cited it in a draft article.[127] In the basement of Langdell Library, I would run my fingers down the spines of the *Stanford Law Review* until I came to the absolute fattest one of all—volume 36, the fabled "Crit Symposium" issue, wherein lay the *Finnegan's Wake* of legal scholarship, the Alpha and Omega, Peter Gabel and Duncan Kennedy's shocking and unreadable *Roll Over Beethoven*.[128] And like a kid reading Kerouac for the first time, I would marvel at the nerve of a top-tier law review that would accept as a scholarly coinage the term *intersubjective zap*.

---

127. Mari J. Matsuda, *Looking to the Bottom: Critical Legal Studies and Reparations*, 22 Harv. C.R.–C.L. L. Rev. 323, 337 n.62 (1987).

128. Peter Gabel & Duncan Kennedy, *Roll Over Beethoven*, 36 Stan. L. Rev. 1 (1984).

Heady days, to be sure. But reality killed the buzz. Soon Harvard's faculty was engulfed by a tenure dispute involving a feminist scholar, beloved by some and spurned by others. The affair got ugly fast. Tenure was denied and a wedge was driven through the faculty. Some professors refused to talk to one another after that. Many students also began choosing sides. We 1Ls were somewhat immune, since most of us had little time for ideological battles. But the record, as captured in the *BBR*, will reflect that philosophy and social science did infiltrate our classrooms.

> PROF. LIEBMAN: You think moral relativism is scary?
>
> J.T.: If you're just gonna go with the climate of the times, if you're just gonna throw up your hands and say, "Whatever," yeah, I think that's pretty scary.
>
> PROF. LIEBMAN: You've got a problem in the 20th century.

At one point in Contracts, Prof. David Charney suggested a student had "been reading too much Posner." It used to be, he mused, "that in the first year of law school the one thing you were sure to have learned was how to read a case. Now the one thing you are sure to have learned is how to generate cheapest-cost-avoider arguments."

In Torts, our beloved Professor Lewis Sargentich opined on the history of a manufacturer's liability in tort, with a riff that to this day I cannot hope to comprehend. "We have undergone a sea-change," he explained, "a plate-tectonic development: tort was being subducted under contract, but now there is an equal clash of continents."

After the snow melted (in April) and the robins returned, it appeared that we, like that boy in the Hundred Acre Wood had finally outgrown the fantasy. We were focused on jobs now. As even Miller had taught us, "When you get out there, you're not paid to think. You're paid to win." As exams approached, more and more students piled onto the backbench, and Prof. Charney announced that "[n]ext class will be taught from the back of the room so you can all hear me better."

Nonetheless, the *BBR* did continue, published anonymously for three years, although in the end most of us had discovered the small band of classmates behind it. While students *and* professors sometimes questioned its standards, it must be said that this newsletter is cited not once, but twice, in the annals of the *Harvard Law Review*.[129]

Some of the great personalities I came to associate with Harvard Law School are no longer there. Professors Liebman, Miller, and Sullivan eventually moved to other schools. Professor David Charney, at age forty-four, died unexpectedly from a brief illness in 2000, his life cut way too short.

The students? A runner-up on the infamous South Pacific list went on to become a central player in a wildly successful internet retailer. (I won't mention the name, but it rhymes with "spamazon.") The skinny kid who hadn't opened his "tan pamphlet" is now the Elizabeth K. Dollard Professor of Law at Yale and among the most-cited legal scholars in any field. The young woman who once hoped to end oppression and join a Vermont commune built a career representing municipalities in complex litigation and helping tribes and local governments develop their economies. She is also a Buddhist monk. There are so many people in my first section who have been blessed by rich family lives, satisfying careers, rewarding volunteer work, and adventure of all kinds.

As it turns out, the break-up with my girlfriend didn't last. The next year, we got married and remain so. And on January 16, 1987, a modest plea for help issued by me in Contracts was ranked *first* among the editors' list of favorite quotations for that week's issue.

"I'm not sure exactly where I'm lost . . . but I am."
—R.V.

Back then perhaps. But not anymore.

---

129. *See* Note, *Intergovernmental Tax Immunity*, 102 Harv. L. Rev. 222, 229 n.49 (1988) (quoting Laurence Tribe: "irony—in and of itself—is not unconstitutional"); Note, *Over-Protective Jurisdiction? A State Sovereignty Theory of Federal Questions*, 102 Harv. L. Rev. 1948, 1957 n.79 (1988) (quoting Daniel Meltzer: "*Pullman* is not so much a case as it is a doctrine. The *Pullman* case is, obviously, a prime example of the *Pullman* doctrine.").

Part V
Taking the Bar

After finally making it through all the work and worries of law school, those who want to become lawyers face another daunting hurdle: the bar examination. In 1763, Delaware administered the first American bar exam, and the practice soon spread to the other colonies. Today, most states offer the bar exam twice a year, once in late February and again in late July.

Taking the bar exam is a notoriously grueling affair. The exam usually takes place over two days, but some states have mercilessly added a third day of testing. The format varies from state to state, but the exams typically include several hundred multiple-choice questions on core legal subjects like Property, Torts, and Criminal Law. The questions can be very difficult, even for someone who knows the law quite well. Rather than simply offering one unequivocally correct answer choice for each question, the test writers often force students to make tough decisions about which one of several plausible answer choices is "the most right" or "the least wrong." In addition to the maze of tricky multiple-choice questions, the bar exams typically contain a series of essay questions that can delve into a wide array of specialized topics like family law, conflicts of law, negotiable instruments, and secured transactions. In recent years, some states have added new components to their exams that are designed to test practical skills such as drafting a legal document or preparing a summary of advice for a client.

While taking the bar exam is not fun, preparing for the test is the real ordeal. Most people begin studying for the bar exam just a few days after graduating from law school. They pay to attend daily bar review classes that will cover all the key material that might be on the test. For weeks on end, they write outlines and make flash cards. They memorize definitions, elements, rules, and exceptions. They work their way through thick books of practice questions. While people entering other professions, such as medicine or accounting, also face tough exams, none of them can match the daunting reputation of bar exams.

The weeks after the test can be even more stressful than those that preceded it, as the nervous would-be lawyers await the results and most convince themselves that they have failed. Overall, about 60 percent of them breathe a huge sigh of relief when they receive the good news that they passed. The pass rates vary widely, however, with the odds of success barely reaching 40 percent in some jurisdictions such as California, but with some lenient states routinely passing more than 70 percent of their applicants. A majority of the states have now adopted the Uniform Bar Exam (UBE), a standardized test that allows portability of the results to other jurisdictions accepting the UBE.

The stories in this section include one by Wanda Temm, based on her years of experience helping students prepare for and pass the bar exam. She describes the stress that students endure and the unexpected twists they often face just before or even during the exam.

Given the amount of work and pressure involved, failing the bar exam may feel like the end of the world. But some people have shown remarkable persistence, taking the bar exam dozens of times before finally passing. And some people who had trouble with the bar exam have gone on to great success in law, politics, or other endeavors. John F. Kennedy Jr. needed three tries to pass the New York bar exam. Hillary Clinton did fine on the Arkansas bar exam but failed the D.C. test. Pete Wilson and Jerry Brown failed the California bar exam, but each went on to become that state's governor. Richard M. Daley passed the Illinois bar exam on his third attempt, and later became the mayor of Chicago. Antonio Villaraigosa gave up after failing the California bar exam four times, but he went on to be the mayor of Los Angeles. Kathleen Sullivan failed California's exam for lawyers already admitted to practice law in other states, a remarkable result given that she had 20 years of experience as a law professor at Harvard and as dean of the law school at Stanford.

Most states require those taking the bar exam to be law school gradu-ates. But in a handful of states such as California, Vermont, and Virginia, the tradition of "reading the law" persists. This method enables a person to take the bar exam after several years of studying law under the supervision of a judge or practicing attorney. Marilyn Skoglund's story describes how she took this route, passed the bar exam, and went on to become a member of the Vermont Supreme Court without ever attending law school.

A Coney Island for the Mind

THE HONORABLE MARILYN SKOGLUND

My favorite astrologer, Rob Brezsny, offered this to Aquarians last week:

"You really need to tell your stories. It's not just a good idea; it's down-right urgent. There's a backlog of unexpressed narratives clogging up your depths. It's like you have become too big of a secret to the world. The unvented pressure is building up, threatening to implode. So please find a graceful way to share the narratives that are smoldering inside you—with the emphasis on the word 'graceful.'"[130]

Actually, I'm not an Aquarian, but, hey, it was all the encouragement I needed to accept the invitation to provide my narrative to this venture. Granted, I know next to nothing about law school, but, as a comparison study to the erudite essays elsewhere in this volume, my story may amuse. I am an aficionado of learning. It is an addiction. My legal learning experience was not typical, but any student of any discipline can relate to the thrill when comprehension dawns and nascent skills become recognizable. What a rush.[131]

---

130. *Free Will Astrology*, THE STRANGER (July 19, 2011), http://www.thestranger.com/seattle/free-will-astrology/Content?oid=9123815.

131. My "first year" was a Coney Island for the mind. It was sparkly, scary and exciting. I riff on the book of poetry by Lawrence Ferlinghetti who took the title from Henry Miller's *Into the Night Life*, self-published in 1947. *See* LAWRENCE FERLINGHETTI, A CONEY ISLAND OF THE MIND (1958).

First, life tricked me. I thought I'd grow up to be my mother. My father said, "if a woman has to work outside the home, it should be in one of the helping professions—a teacher or a nurse." Poor dad. I went to college, got married, had a child, then I grew up.

My husband, with his MFA, was a serious artist. If any of you have lived with a "serious artist" you may already have shuddered. And, to be fair, when we married, I was a serious artist wannabe. But if I analyze the marriage contract from a legal perspective, there was no meeting of the minds. Or, perhaps after eleven years of marriage, what broke the contract was impossibility of performance, because there came a time that one of us had to give up dreams of the MOMA and think seriously about working for a living, earning money for food, that kind of thing. We had a child. Low paying, odd, part-time jobs that left us free to "make art" were not cutting it. My BA in sculpture turned out to qualify me in the Vermont job market to carve grave stones.[132] I will not trouble you, dear reader, with that debacle.

I did have some skills. I could write. And, good writing is critical to good legal argument. My education into the written word was unconventional as well. I was in advanced English courses throughout high school. I could dissect *Beowulf* with alacrity but had no clue what to do with a comma. In a required English course in college, a teacher who saw talent but no skills took pity on me and tutored me in writing. After college, I got a job as an editor/writer at a local college. (Do I need to continue pointing out that my jobs were all part-time?) My depressed boss taught me that passive voice was the devil, that too much pluperfect had been found to be just annoying, and that commas are our friends.

I wish I could identify some laudable, altruistic goal that led me to the law, but I cannot. In evaluating my options, I gave great importance to professions that came with a license that would allow me to work for myself. While selling real estate and styling hair may have been fun, I had no interest in either. However, the law sounded like a good fit, a profession that would allow me to play with words and wits. Of course I wanted to go to law school—formal education was the model I knew—but that idea never got off the ground and was kicked under the sofa to live out its days with the dust bunnies. I took the LSAT; did well. However, back then, in

---

132. The next town over is a huge granite producing area.

1977, the folks at the Law School Data Assembly Service had a practice of not counting credit hours or grade points from courses in the fine arts, and my BA was in fine arts. According to the LSDAS, I had only accumulated 80 semester hours, when, in fact, having attended university for seven years taking any course that interested me, I graduated with around 215 credit hours.[133] As a result I looked like a dullard who did well on tests. There was also the question of money. We had none.

But, I'm from Vermont, where you can still "read for the law." For four years you apprentice yourself to an attorney and if you pass the multistate and the Vermont essay part of the bar exam, you are a bona fide, genuine lawyer, minus the diploma for your wall. So, I began. First, I enrolled in a six month course in how to be a paralegal. I learned how to find the law library and how to use it. I read about civil procedure and attended a few criminal arraignments. That was about it. Then, I saw an ad for a law clerk at the Office of the Attorney General, applied, and borrowed a dress for the interview.[134] Meanwhile, my husband watched as I prepared to enter the conventional work force and decided I was "selling out" by "working for the man." This was not a happy time.[135]

At my interview, the Attorney General was not fooled by my disguise as a conventional twenty-seven year old, and he said, "You realize that we prosecute people who smoke marijuana," and asked how I would feel about being seen as not wearing a white hat. Well aware of his pending lawsuit to stop an atrocious tire-burn at a dump across the lake in New York State, the fumes of which were trespassing into Vermont's relatively clean air, I was ready for him. I spoke about that lawsuit and assured him that many in his office wore white hats and that I'd be proud to join the posse. He smiled. Actually, he told me later that what got me the job was the fact that I had worked part-time as a graphic designer for R. Buckminister Fuller

---

133. In 1971 I was married and pregnant with my first child. I thought it might be a good idea to go ahead and get the BA because, and I honestly remember thinking this, it might be a while before I could go back to school. This is your first clue as to how my mind worked back then. Sometimes it went off the tracks, sometimes it didn't even notice that there were tracks.

134. It was a hideous brown and orange wrap-around polyester shirtdress.

135. Besides, The Band broke up that year.

during my years as an undergraduate.[136] He was suitably impressed. And so, in 1978, I became a "Special Assistant Attorney General." And so, my husband left and moved to Illinois.

I paid the twenty-five dollar fee and registered to "read for the bar." In those days, that was all it took. Today, people reading for the bar are required to submit reports every six months detailing their course of study.[137] I had no lesson plans. Really, I had no plan, period. As a four-year clerk, I needed a lawyer to be my sponsoring attorney. My luck held and the late Louis Peck took me on. Louis went on to be a Justice of the Vermont Supreme Court, but in 1978 he was the Chief Assistant Attorney General, overseeing the civil and administrative law divisions. He was also a card carrying equity actor. Years before, one of his roles was in an off-Broadway production of *Dracula*. He and I were usually the first in the office each morning. While he made the coffee, he would start in his very best Bela Lugosi voice, "Listen to them. Children of the night [referring to the wolves howling in the dark Transylvanian Alps]. What strange music they make." I would then slip into my side-kick character of Renfrew, Count Dracula's assistant who had a taste for flies, and respond, "Flies, Master, flies!" We'd alter roles as the mood struck. After hours, I'd help him run lines when he had a community theater production coming up. That only got awkward when he was playing the psychiatrist in Equus. Clearly, not your typical 1L experience.

Reality reared its ugly head on about day four of the job. I was assigned to work with an attorney in the civil law division defending a new complaint filed against the state in federal court. The attorney was going over the claims for the Deputy Attorney General. I stood to the side, just listening, trying to follow along, when she announced that the case was "a 1983 case." Now, it was 1978 when I woke up that morning. I was pretty sure about that. Pondering this ripple in my reality, nothing else said in that meeting registered. After the meeting was over and I was alone with the attorney, I casually asked, "What makes this a 1983 case?" She pointed

---

136. Bucky hired me because he learned I was the only girl in high school to take a drafting course. This was my first lesson in the benefits of serendipitous educational decision making. I took the drafting class because it interested me. This attitude and love of learning is why I spent seven years as an undergrad.

137. Rules of Admission to the Bar of the Vermont Supreme Court 10 (Sept. 2017), https://www.vermontjudiciary.org/attorneys/admission-vermont-bar.

me to 42 U.S.C. § 1983 and I read cases until I understood the federal civil rights action. I also understood that I was woefully unprepared for the job.

This was my method: get an assignment—go to Black's, key word digests, case reporters, treatises, whatever, and read and compare cases until the principles made sense and I could understand how they applied to a set of facts. Consider this my version of the Socratic Method without the public humiliation and snickering of fellow students. As I understand it, the Socratic Method of continued questioning based on initial responses is designed to teach students to rummage through the layers of an issue like excavating a garbage receptacle for bottles to redeem. I am not sure about the use of humiliation as a teaching tool, and what snickering peers add to the process escapes me. And, I do not know that thinking like a lawyer is that much different than thinking like any problem-solving professional. (Granted, plumbers do not routinely deal with life-altering problems involving emotional pipes with attitudes.) In figure drawing I was taught that one should understand the skeletal and musculature systems of the body before one tries to abstract the human figure. It follows then that, in law, one must examine the guts, glue, language, and armature that goes into a legal principle before one can appreciate and apply it. The challenge of figuring out how and why the law worked became my favorite part of the job.

My job was that of a clerk, no one was paying me to be a student. But, also, no client was being billed for my hours of research and writing, so whenever possible I went beyond what was necessary for my assignments to study the law's evolution and learn why the law was as it was, another symptom of my addiction.[138] I would study for hours, sorting through the law like a woman separating strands of silk from a worm's cocoon using

---

138. Just this year I learned that, in the Qur'an, when a man wishes to divorce his wife, he must abstain from her for four months. Divorced women shall "wait concerning themselves for three monthly periods. Nor is it lawful for them to hide what God has created in their wombs." QUR'AN 2:228 (Abdullah Yusuf Ali trans., Tahrike Tarsile Qur'an 25th ed. 2009). This is the best explanation I've heard for the nisi period in divorce law. *See, e.g.,* 15 VT. STAT. ANN. § 554(a) (2010) ("A decree of divorce from the bonds of matrimony in the first instance, shall be a decree nisi and shall become absolute at the expiration of three months from the entry thereof"). When I sat as a judge in the family court, I was told the decree nisi period was to allow for people to change their minds about divorcing. I thought that a bit paternalistic on the part of the state. Now I believe the three month wait was originally designed to establish paternity and protect a progenitor's line. Fascinating.

fingernails that have each been filed into several little points to act as a carding tool. To pull apart the issues from a wad of legal argument so that each thread can be clearly seen was so satisfying. In my study of the law, the pure logic, historical shadows and basic societal need for and human reliance on the rule of law began to tingle like ginger ale poured directly over my brain. I fell in love with the law.

It was a solitary, self-motivated education, but I am disciplined. Soon I was being assigned to all parts of the office to do research, draft complaints, write memoranda, and absorb the collective knowledge of the attorneys in the civil, criminal, administrative, environmental, consumer protection, and civil rights divisions. In the central office of the Attorney General in 1978, I was the only student with about fifty "teachers." Each attorney had his or her own focus and style of instruction. I knew I'd earned an "A" when the attorney submitted my draft memorandum to the court without major changes. Here's a concept that is apparently alien for a 1L—there was no competition. And, being the only sponge walking the halls, I became a project for the office. Nor was my ego on the line. The attorneys were on the high wire, I was learning to walk. And, as Karl Wallenda, the head of the Flying Wallendas, once said, "Life is on the wire, the rest is waiting."[139] I wanted to be on the wire real bad.

If all this sounds just lovely, there was a separate reality that should be acknowledged. While I was putting in an eight hour day at my job, my eight-year-old daughter was getting off the school bus and walking a half mile to a small shepherd's cottage that we called home. The cottage was located on a five-hundred-acre dairy farm owned by an amazing old farmer, Walter Smith. Many people helped me grow into a lawyer—Bucky Fuller who ingrained in me concepts of intuitive engineering and anticipatory design which I used as a litigator to build my case and plan for the opponent's tactics; my depressed boss who taught me to write; all the attorneys at the A.G.'s office who took time to explain and critique; and my mentor, Louis Peck, who showed me what dignity and character looked like. But, I could not have survived without Walter. He taught me it was okay to ask for help sometimes, and he gave me courage.

---

139. Karl was killed in March of 1978 walking a high wire in San Juan, Puerto Rico. I watched it on TV. I cried.

The only source of heat in the un-insulated cottage was a wood burning furnace in the cellar, so when my child got home from school in the winter, she had to go into the cellar and shove some wood into its maw. Walter gave me free firewood—an early version of fuel assistance. I would not ask for food stamps (those were for really poor people, and I refused that label), but Walter let me dip raw milk out of the bulk tank and he gave me eggs when the hens were laying and tomatoes to can (I'd do the work and split the results with him) and when he killed a cow or pig or chicken, he always gave me some meat.

If I avoided the stress, the competition, the overwhelming intensity of *One L*, it was because I loved my work and, when I left work, I was privileged to go home, sit on the floor playing with Legos or coloring with my daughter, read her a book, and put her to bed. She anchored me and put everything in perspective. My stress came from being hired to work a full time job for $7,000 a year.[140] There was not a lot of time for worrying. And, besides, when we needed to, we could walk to Walter's house up the road and eat Campbell's chicken noodle soup and mayonnaise sandwiches, which was pretty much his daily dinner. I had Walter.[141]

In May of 1981, the office gave me a two month leave of absence so I could focus on taking the bar in August. While my four years at the Attorney General's Office exposed me to constitutional, contract, civil and criminal law, and the rules of evidence, civil and criminal procedure, etc., etc., etc., the work of the Office provided no experience in, for example, bulk sales and secured transactions. By August, it looked like a crayon box threw up in the cottage. Color coded three by five filing cards were everywhere: by the sink, the toilet, the bed. They detailed everything from priority of creditors to grounds for divorce. They were kind of pretty. I took the bar and passed.[142]

---

140. In 1978 gas sold for sixty-nine cents a gallon.

141. Walter died in 1995. He lived long enough to see me sworn in as a District Court Judge. He was very proud.

142. After four years as a "special" Assistant Attorney General, I continued at the office for thirteen more years as a real one. During those years, I was made Chief of the Civil Division, then Chief of the Public Protection Division (Environmental, Consumer Protection and Civil Rights). In 1994, the Governor appointed me to the trial bench. Then, in 1997, the Governor appointed me to the Supreme Court.

After thirty years in the fields of law, *ancora imparo*.[143] In 2017, I again stood for retention,[144] and I can continue as a Justice of the Vermont Supreme Court for another six years. Under Vermont law I do not have to retire until I am ninety years old. (Not a good visual for me.) This much I know: learning is as critical to my well-being as wine and chocolate. And, I believe, if I continue to study everything that interests me and makes me wonder, my mind will not go soft. But, if I am wrong and I appear to have spent too much time on the Tilt-A-Whirl, then, it will be time to make my dogs' dreams come true and give them my heels as chew toys and do something I've always dreamed of doing: cutting pie and pouring coffee in a nice, friendly diner.

---

143. This Latin phrase is generally translated to mean: "Still I am learning." It is often attributed to Michelangelo.

144. I come from a state where judges are appointed after going through a Judicial Nominating Board process that sends names of "qualified" persons to the governor who interviews those that interest him and appoints a nominee who then goes next door to the Senate Judiciary committee for confirmation. Then, every six years, a retention committee reports to the joint House and Senate their recommendation as to whether the judge should be retained for another six years. In a joint session, the legislators vote by secret ballot.

Conquering the Elephant

WANDA M. TEMM

I sit in the stands every spring and watch the horde of smiling faces. The graduates cross the stage, shake the dean's hand, shake the chancellor's hand, and shake the hands of university dignitaries that they never knew existed and who attend perhaps just to enlarge the sense of pageantry. Graduates wear the gowns and hoods that most will never wear again. They grab their diplomas and frequently raise their arms in celebration to the shouts of family and friends. And there are the family and friends congregated *en masse* with equally smiling faces who attend to cheer; to photograph; to embed this moment, this achievement, in the history of their lives.

But the graduates know they are not done. You can see it in their eyes and wary smiles when you greet them afterwards. Often, it is evident in the forced cheeriness when they nervously laugh and say "oh yes, need to take that one more exam." For they know the time has come. The elephant that has been present in the room since the first day of law school is now visibly blocking their path. They must conquer this beast to reach their end goal—the reason they went through the last three years of angst—to practice law, whether to assist the underdog or to take over Wall Street. If they cannot conquer the elephant, they cannot reach their goal. It is that clear-cut. The stakes are that high. And they know it.

I'm watching, too. I watch as each one crosses the stage. As one heads toward the dignitary line-up, I inwardly smile knowing that this particular student is well-equipped to tackle the beast, but tends to get in a tizzy when the stress piles on. I will need to keep reminding her that she is not striving for an "A." The next student has done decently in law school and with the right amount of encouragement and hard work will be just fine. Next is the student that I have been concerned about for some time. Perhaps I had him as a first-year student and he just could not seem to handle analysis or his grammar was woefully deficient. Perhaps I chaired the committee that oversaw and decided the readmission after academic dismissal, knowing the student was still at risk for not passing. My anxiety comes and goes as each student crosses the stage. Then, the students want me to meet their families and I assure each one that they will vanquish this beast with hard work and motivation, I know they will do it, and they will be fine. Their family glows with pride.

The elephant is the bar exam. A two- or three-day exam that purports to test many of the skills necessary to practice law. Much discussion about the validity and reliability of the bar exam has ensued for several decades without any major reform in the exam itself.[145] Movement towards a national bar exam has progressed steadily with the advent of the Uniform Bar Examination (UBE). Students who take the UBE can potentially transfer their score to numerous states while only taking one bar exam.[146] Possible reform is another story for another day. The reality for today's law student is that they must pass the exam as it exists in order to practice law in their chosen jurisdiction.

Every law professor plays a role in preparing students for the bar exam. Analytical skills are the foundation for all lawyering tasks. Analytical skill development begins at orientation and is part of every law school course, trial advocacy team, appellate advocacy team, law journal, in-house clinic,

---

145. The National Conference of Bar Examiners did introduce the Multistate Performance Test (MPT) to replace some of the essays in the late 1990s. The MPT is a ninety-minute question that combines legal analysis with drafting a particular document a law firm partner has requested. This task requires the student to focus on the audience and purpose of the document in addition to synthesizing the law and applying the facts to predict an outcome or advocate for a client. The goal is to have a more realistic assessment of writing skills other than by essay. Two MPT questions are included in the Uniform Bar Examination.

146. Each jurisdiction decides for itself what minimum score it will accept. Each jurisdiction will also do its own character and fitness determination and may set other requirements for licensure such as mandatory Continuing Legal Education courses or another assessment of the particular state's law. As of 2018, thirty jurisdictions have adopted the Uniform Bar Exam.

externship, and simulation exercise. Writing projects push students to articulate analysis, communicating it clearly and concisely. Attorneys use their analytical skills from the first initial client interview through the completion of the transaction or the end of the litigation. At every step along the way, analytical skills are needed to decide the best course of action to reach the client's goals and then to competently take that action.

But analytical skills are not enough to pass the bar exam. Bar exam preparation is an endurance course requiring intense motivation and hard work to stay on track. An inordinate amount of time is required to prepare. Commercial providers keep a running list of uncompleted tasks for students that is often bewildering and petrifies students so much that they cannot discern, much less finish, the key tasks that must be done.

In the early 2000s, my law school experienced a dip in bar passage rates. A blue-ribbon faculty task force was created to study the issues. Their conclusion: multiple factors impact bar passage—low law school G.P.A., working during the bar preparation period, failure to finish course requirements on time, lack of motivation, lack of finances, anxiety. There is not one major reason why a graduate fails the exam and; thus, there is not one magic cure-all to boost a law school's bar passage rate.

As the faculty was trying to reach a consensus on what to do, a certain curmudgeon on the faculty decided that he knew what to do about it and was just going to do it. He decided to have refresher lectures on topics. But he also recognized that skill development—taking essay and multiple choice-style questions—was critical. He stopped by my office and asked me "to grade a few essays." That started me on my path towards identifying my passion—teaching, coaching, counseling, and helping students prepare for and pass their chosen bar examination. To date, I have taught more than fifteen hundred students how to prepare for the bar examination, I have graded their essays and MPTs, I have worked on strategies and tactics to attack questions in each specific topic, I have created mind-maps[147] to assist in issue identification and memorization of rules, and I have tried to keep their anxiety at a healthy level.

Each student has her own story. Certain similarities emerge, but many have unique experiences. I choose some of these stories to share here and

---

147. Wanda Temm, Clearing the Last Hurdle: Mapping Success on the Bar Exam (2d ed. 2018).

to convey to each bar prep class to reinforce the lessons I want them to learn:

* preparing step-by-step to see how these early steps are then used at crunch time;
* practicing essay skills to learn how to structure an analysis and to go step-by-step through an analysis, ensuring sufficient detail in their rule statements and in their application of the rules;
* avoiding procrastination;
* dealing with anxiety, which is often crippling;
* taking the necessary breaks to maintain emotional health and to deal with stress;
* taking care of physical needs to be in the best shape possible on test days; and
* dealing with personal crises that arise.

DEALING WITH "NORMAL" STRESS

In my over fifteen years of teaching bar prep, I have seen all kinds of crises. First, everyone experiences some form of stress. When it reaches a peak—that feeling you have incurred massive debt for a legal education to reach your goal of becoming a licensed attorney that is all for naught due to the bar exam—predictable reactions occur. These "normal" reactions include anxiety, sleepless nights, panic, crying, sobbing, etc. At the beginning of each bar prep season, I forewarn my students that it will come and it's perfectly normal. It's not a question of whether they will experience heightened anxiety, but a question of when. Continuing to study in a state of heightened anxiety is virtually worthless. My tried-and-true remedy? Take a break from studying. Take regular breaks, including a day off every few weeks. Bar preparation is a marathon, but long-distance runners have scheduled breaks in their training and bar students should, too. That break must be a true break—no thinking that they should be studying. Instead, spend time with family and friends, enjoy the latest movie, or play that round of golf. Then, when they hit the books again, the nerves will be calmer.

Other students have crippling anxiety. While I have a counseling degree and training, I know enough to know when I am in over my head. I refer students for professional help. I tend to focus on traditional anxiety treatment, such as counseling. But I have had two students who sought a rather non-traditional method—hypnosis. Both students had failed the exam at least once. Both felt their anxiety was a major factor in their performance. Traditional counseling had not worked for them. Each student's counselor recommended hypnosis. Now, I am a true skeptic of hypnosis. But each student experienced immense relief. Part of their experience was how to deal with stress while they were studying and the other part of their experience was on dealing with the stress during the exam itself. Both passed the exam with a sizeable margin. I am still a skeptic; but hey, it worked for them!

One year, long after the results were posted, I asked my students to share with me how they got through their stress. I was inundated with responses. Here are just a couple.

* I told myself that I wasn't alone in how I was feeling. That probably 75 percent of people were feeling exactly the way I was feeling. That the feelings of being overwhelmed, stressed, and defeated were not unique to me. Then, I thought of all those people in years past [who] must have felt this way as well, but stuck with it and passed the bar exam. I also thought that if I didn't pass the bar exam and that was the biggest problem I had in my life, that I was one lucky individual who will just have to figure out another plan of attack.

* I can vividly recall feeling like there was no way that I was going to pass. I even remember the subject I was studying (Property). My wife suggested that I take a break, but the thought of taking a break and losing out on valuable study time made me more stressed. So, I spent several hours frozen by stress, where I wasn't studying but wasn't relaxing either. Then I remembered you said that it was okay to take a break. I took the rest of the day off and just relaxed.

My words of wisdom are: It's okay to take a break. If you're feeling stressed and overwhelmed, you won't be able to study effectively. Don't try to tough it out—that will probably only make things worse. Instead, take the rest of the day or evening off. Relax. And come back the next day fresh.

DEALING WITH PERSONAL CRISES UNRELATED
TO PREPARING FOR THE EXAM

These personal crises run the gamut from relationship issues, babies, illness of themselves or others close to them, to the death of a loved one. One student simply could not handle the death of his dog. At first, I could not understand why this was having such an impact. I realized then that this student really had no other support system. He had been a loner in school and did not have family nearby or that were particularly understanding of the intense study necessary for bar preparation and its resultant stress. I could empathize then. I suggested delaying the exam and he decided to take it and failed. He passed the second time.

Relationship issues may even venture into sabotage. A student's spouse threatened to leave her every semester or so throughout law school, not coincidentally around finals. He bumped up his manipulation during bar prep. He had access to her phone and kept checking her texts. He questioned everywhere she went and who she was meeting. Apparently, he thought she was being unfaithful. He locked her out of the house and took the children to his parents without telling her where they were. He filed for divorce days before the bar exam. During this entire time, she tried to focus on the tasks she needed to accomplish each day. While not all tasks were completed, she focused on the most important ones and had a good support system with friends. She passed and kicked him out of the house!

A married couple had worked at the same large law firm before going to law school. They decided that she would go to law school first while he supported her. Then, he would go to law school, while she supported him. She did a federal judicial clerkship for two years and then was an associate at that same large law firm. He was a summer associate for that firm and then was to be an associate after the bar exam. They would be working in the same section of the firm, but for different partners.

The wife was a high-strung individual throughout law school. A perfectionist, she always had high anxiety and frequently sought assurance. During bar prep, she was a regular visitor to my office. His personality was not exactly the opposite, but he differed in significant ways. More laid-back and extroverted, he made many friends and was a leader in everything he did. While she did well in school and was in the top ten, he was number one in the class every semester with seemingly much less effort and definitely with much less anxiety.

About ten days before the exam, she suggested that he take a break and they go to a restaurant. She then dropped the bomb. She was filing for divorce. He was to move out of their townhome immediately. He must find another job and not come to the firm where she was practicing. Oh, and she was keeping the dog. He was stunned. He did not see it coming, although he later admitted things had been rocky. All of her demands meant changes not only to his vision of his life with her, but to his career. He immediately sought advice. My advice was to tell her that he would address all of these issues after the bar exam. He was not moving out. She could, if she wanted. He was going to the same firm. He was going to keep the dog. They'd discuss the townhome later.

He was on the roller-coaster of emotions that many individuals experience while divorcing or during the breaking-up of a long-term relationship. He swung back and forth from concentrated studying to sobbing. The blessing—he had a wonderful support system. Not only a group of friends that rallied around him, but family with whom he could talk about everything. He was a daily visitor to my office. He pondered whether to postpone taking the exam. I encouraged him not to. While I don't like to think about relationships as a win-lose proposition, I did tell him that not taking the bar exam at all meant she succeeded in sabotaging his career. I reminded him that even though he was number one in the class, he had still done every single task I had asked of him and the only thing he needed to do was to memorize as much law as he could and try to do that in one-hour increments. Try to focus for one hour and then take a break to deal with emotions.

Later, he told me that studying for the bar in those last ten days is what kept him going. While he had the potential to ace the exam and be the top scorer in every category, he did not score extremely high, but he did pass the exam with a significant margin despite everything that had happened. He did move out of the townhome as they agreed to sell it and split the equity. He did start at the firm and he did keep the dog. He learned very quickly that she was being unfaithful with a partner in the firm. Unfortunately, the partner was in the office next door to the student's—no doubt the reason his wife dropped the bomb when she did. He stayed with the firm about nine months before he left for a position in another city. We keep in touch and he's doing great with a job he loves and a family he adores.

Illnesses and death affect individuals so differently. For one, the death of a grandparent is devastating emotionally and for others it seems a brief interlude of grief with that grief not impeding their study. Illnesses vary as well, from a cancer diagnosis to sudden surgery for appendicitis. Whether those students take the exam depends on their individual needs and goals, whether a delay would completely forestall those goals, and the timing of the illness/death. A surgery in the first couple of weeks is quite different from surgery the week before the exam. The key to passage for these students is whether they have been preparing step-by-step before the event happens. If they have, they are usually fine. If not, then I may recommend delaying. They don't necessarily take me up on it, but I don't hesitate to give that advice if it is warranted.

DEALING WITH EXAM DAY CRISES

These are my game day instructions:

Be prepared. Have everything together and ready to pick up and go that morning— photo identification; any bar paperwork required to get in the room; laptop; power cord; pens, pencils, and ear plugs (unless prohibited or the board of bar examiners provide for you); a sweater or light jacket in case the room is cold (if allowed); and anything else you might need that is allowed. Leave your cell phone in your hotel room or car. You don't want to have to run back to your room or car to get something. Your heart rate will sky-rocket and you won't be as calm when the exam starts.

A colleague had a potential disaster occur. He was waiting in line to be let into the room. Everyone was tense, naturally. That tension swelled when an applicant collapsed and seemed to be having a seizure. Some applicants just stepped over him. Others motioned for the bar staff to assist. He could feel his own heart rate increase. As my colleague got to the front of the line, he was not allowed into the room and was told to step aside and wait. He waited until everyone else was in the room and then they started the exam! He wasn't in the room! What was happening? He nearly fainted. The proctor told him his law school failed to submit some paperwork and he would not be allowed to take the exam. The examiners had sent him a letter at his parents' address and his parents had been out-of-town. He asked to speak to a supervisor and then had to track her down in another part of the hotel. She let him take the exam in a separate room and she gave him the full time to take the exam. He was given a warning that the paperwork must be received within a few days. He then had to calm his heart rate before he could start. This is less likely to occur with online registration and submission of paperwork, but the lesson is clear. Don't give up. Try to be calm and wait for a final word from someone with the authority to give it.

Another colleague experienced a calamity that would have sunk most people. His car broke down and he was staying with friends. The friends would not be there to take him anywhere on the days of the exam. Public transportation was available, so no problem. He waited and waited at the bus stop. No bus. He started running towards the conference center, even though it would take him about three hours to run the entire way. But he saw a bus on the horizon. He ran faster, but just missed it. He watched it and tried to catch up, but again failed. He finally caught a different bus that would drop him off at a stop a few blocks away from the conference center, but he still took it. He arrived at the registration line literally nine minutes before the exam began. Soaked, out of breath, unkempt, and needing a shower, he must have been a sight. He received quite a lecture, but was allowed to take the exam.

He sat across from a woman who was panting and sweating more than he did. She was nine months pregnant and her water had just broken. She ultimately left with EMTs after about two hours. With all that had happened, he kept on going and found a peace within himself for the rest of the exam. He decided that he had the power to choose how to react and respond to this situation. He decided to keep pedalin' because what was the worst thing that could happen? Many things in life are much worse than failing the bar exam.

HAVING A MANTRA HELPS

I tell my bar prep students that having a mantra can help deal with stress because it keeps you grounded and not worried about failure. Here are a few that have worked for others:

* I kept reminding myself that the exam was only testing to ensure I have basic competency. I only need to be proficient. If I put in the time and learned the foundational basics, I would be able to make it through.

* When I felt like I wouldn't pass the bar, the one thing I would repeatedly tell myself was "I can do this. I put in the hours. I studied. I can do this."

* Just keep on going. If you don't quit, you'll win!

* I kept telling myself that I worked hard and did everything I was supposed to do. Thousands of people passed the bar before me and thousands will pass in the future; I will pass, too.

* When I was feeling like a failure, I would stop studying and put in a motivational movie. My favorite choice was one of the Rocky movies. In *Rocky Balboa*, Rocky says to his son "It ain't about how hard you hit, it's about how hard you can get hit and keep moving forward . . . that's how winning is done."

* "Trust the process." By trusting the process of studying, no task was too big. By narrowing my focus on the next task or study tool in the process, success was inevitable.

* If you take the bar exam seriously, you will pass.

* I had to stop and remind myself that I did not HAVE to take the bar, I GOT to take the bar. There are many people, even class-mates, who were not going to get that opportunity. I used it as a tool to keep myself motivated and appreciate that the hard work was also a privilege.

* I really am not going to die if I fail. Failure was always a motivat-ing factor, but never a paralyzing influence because I had my friends around going through it with me.

* Failing isn't the end of the world, my wife will still love and support me, my family will still love and support me. I will be able to take it again.

* When I was really feeling sorry for myself (thank you Property questions) I just thought of all of the worse things that people go through. The hardships that other people overcome, like cancer or divorce or a disability. And it really just helped to keep things in perspective. In the grand scheme of life this is 2 days and if other people can battle through MUCH worse things, then I have NO reason whatsoever to get down on myself, complain, or think negatively.

* One day on a break from Property questions that I had just bombed, I watched this really uplifting video about a developmentally disabled boy and his dog named Haatchi. I actually cried and afterward was mad at myself for getting down on myself about a test. Any time I had any doubt after that I just thought about that video and realized I could do this and just kept moving forward.

* From a repeat taker, "Am I a victim, or am I a survivor?"

Teaching bar prep students has been immensely rewarding. The teaching dynamic is drastically altered as the teacher is not the ultimate evaluator. The teacher is now a coach. A coach teaches skills, motivates players, builds a sense of team, encourages her team when they are down on themselves, and kicks butt when appropriate. And that is what teaching bar prep is all about. It is a team effort—us versus them. I tell every single class that my goal is for each of them to achieve their goal. Their goal is to practice law and that requires passing the bar exam. I strive for each of them to do just that.

Part VI
Job Search

One of the biggest worries of any student contemplating entering professional school, whether law, medicine, business, or dentistry, is graduating with enormous debt and slim job prospects.

These worries have been fueled, in large part, by articles splashed across the pages of popular media, stories of law grads moving back in with parents or waiting tables just to make ends meet while they search for legal jobs. Yet the grim stories and dire predictions of a jobs crisis do not match actual employment data. While employment statistics across the country went down in the years after the financial crisis of 2008, even in the worst years, 85 to 90 percent of law school graduates reported that they were employed nine months after graduation and about two-thirds of the total number of grads were employed in jobs that required a J.D. Rural areas already suffer from a scarcity of lawyers, and given anticipated retirements over the next decade (amounting to as much as a quarter of active attorneys), forecasts indicate likely shortages of experienced lawyers. And although many proclaim that "there are too many lawyers," truth be told, there are never enough good ones.

Law students and lawyers have a wide range of experiences in the job search process. Some people (particularly top students, those at elite schools, rainmakers at firms, etc.) get wined and dined by potential employers. Instead of actively searching for a job, this group of law students and lawyers has employers that come looking for them. For others, the job search is quite different—it's a long process, and one that requires lots of ingenuity and a great deal of resiliency.

While all law schools have career services offices, which sponsor on-campus interviews (usually with larger firms), résumé reviews, job fairs, and strategic planning sessions, among other services, savvy students utilize the career development office as just the first step.

Although successful legal job seekers today may begin with the career development office, most are doing innovative things to credential themselves in ways that set them apart from the crowd: a student with a tech background and a *summa cum barely* J.D. makes a pitch to larger firms about his computer expertise and anticipates the firm's needs for an electronic discovery coordinator; another takes the equivalent of a Master's in Business through Coursera's free online classes while in law school; a third attends any community or law programs she can find on bioethics and starts a Health Law Society at her school; other students satisfy their school's research and writing requirement by drafting an article in the area of law in which they want to practice. Even during law school, students are strategizing to make themselves uniquely valuable in a particular niche.

In some of the newspaper stories about law job prospects that have been so negative and received so much publicity, the reporters interview law school grads who can't find jobs and who will say something along the lines of "I send out 20 résumés every week" or "I've sent my résumé to 200 law firms and never received any responses." Perhaps they're not following a good strategy, if they do the same thing over and over and it doesn't work. Most career professionals will suggest not to paper the town with résumés or to cold-call prospective employers—apart from the judicial law clerk application process. And this process is exactly what Josh Blackman describes. He engaged in one of the most work-intensive methods imaginable of searching for a federal judicial clerkship.

When students enter law school, studies indicate that more than half express an interest in public service work. Upon exiting, however, only a fraction of those students actually enter the public interest area. Although loan repayment assistance programs are on the rise, it can be particularly difficult to find jobs in the public interest sector. Even for top students from big-name schools, who could easily get jobs at big firms, it can be tough to find a job in some areas of public interest work simply because there are fewer openings and more people seeking those jobs. The result is somewhat ironic—that sometimes a low-paying job is harder to find than a high-paying one.

There is a lot of serendipity in searching for jobs. People can do extensive job searching but then get a job in an odd or unexpected way. Students who take the initiative and ask for informational interviews just to learn about certain areas of practice—like the entertainment or bankruptcy practice in a city—do tend to find serendipity working for them. The ones who seem to have jobs fall into their laps are the ones who network and attend bar events, lectures, wine-tastings, ball games, and young lawyers meetings. Although the people they meet may not have jobs for them, the person they met at the bar association luncheon may be the one who introduces them to the golfing buddy, who happens to know the lawyer who is working as a talent agent and who needs someone to review contracts. It is a cascade that looks like a proximate cause problem in Torts. Prospective employers are much more likely to consider hiring someone who comes recommended.

Once lawyers are in practice, the dimensions and routes of job searching change. Because more than four out of five lawyers change jobs during their career, most periodically contemplate alternative arrangements or possibly better deals. Some people go through life always seeking greener pastures elsewhere. But it is hard to be happy when you have one foot out the door. Moreover, most attorneys must continue to seek new clients to ensure that their practices remain lucrative.

While many practicing lawyers who are currently employed may not be looking for another job, in the literal sense of finding a new employer, many lawyers are always searching for the next job in terms of marketing to find new clients or new work. Indeed, the marketing outreach for rainmaking purposes is continual: writing bar articles, advertising, writing a blog, utilizing social media such as Facebook and Twitter, attending reunions, working on bar committees, networking through community volunteer work, doing speaking engagements, and becoming an authority in a specialized area. With more than two-thirds of lawyers practicing in solo or small firms, the process of bringing in new business is almost neverending. This is the story of stamina and innovative hustle as told by small firm lawyer, and former Olympic Trials marathon runner, Jon Little.

From Being One L to
Teaching One L

JOSH BLACKMAN

When I applied to law school, I knew next-to-nothing about law school. I really walked into it blind—I would say legally blond, but I am brunette. I had no friends or family members who were attorneys. The only political science class I had ever taken was in high school—and I distinctly remember mistakenly writing on an exam that Thomas Jefferson, and not James Madison, wrote the Constitution. I didn't know what a tort was. I had no idea what the Socratic Method was. I didn't know what Law Review was. I didn't know what "clerking" was. At orientation there were thirteen tables, to represent each Circuit Court of Appeals. I didn't know what a "Circuit" was.

I had never read or heard of Scott Turow's classic, *One L*. For that matter, I didn't even know what the term 1L meant. During orientation, someone asked if I was a 1L. I gazed back, and inquired what that was? But just a few years after I stepped into my first law school class as a bewildered evening student, I had clerked for two federal judges (after sending out 1,600 applications), published a bunch of law review articles (the first of which was dedicated to James Madison), and become an avowed Supreme Court nerd.

In hindsight, I know that the uncertainty, chaos, and confusion that is being a 1L is hardly limited to the first year of law school. 2L, 3L, and beyond present greater challenges and tests, that are much tougher than Contracts and Torts. Indeed, 1L is not only preparation for, but truly a metaphor for everything that attorneys have gone through, and everything we will go through. Such poignancy is what makes Turow's writing, and our own memories, so everlasting. With these experiences, in the fall of 2012, I began teaching a whole new wave of 1Ls as a law professor at South Texas College of Law. Having gone from clueless to obsessed, it is perhaps fitting, or maybe ironic, that I was invited to contribute to this worthy collection to talk about my experiences, from being a 1L to teaching 1Ls.

"I THINK I'LL GO TO LAW SCHOOL."

I woke up one morning and said, "I think I'll go to law school." It wasn't a well-thought-out decision. At the time, I was working for the Department of Defense in Arlington, Virginia, as a computer scientist focusing on network security. I had some vague notion of what intellectual property law was—enough to know that it involved computers and the law. Plus, I heard that people with law degrees were guaranteed six-figure salaries! Oh, to be so naïve. Since I was already living and working in Virginia, I limited my choice of law schools to one—the George Mason University School of Law evening program. In addition to qualifying for in-state tuition—a huge reduction at the time—my office was about three miles from the law school. I figured I could make it from work to classes at 6:00 p.m. fairly easily (sadly, in northern Virginia, three miles often takes an hour to traverse). Plus I read on GMU's web site that they had a good intellectual property program! Tuition, commute, and website material were the factors that motivated my law school career.

I took the LSAT after studying from some book for maybe a month. I severely underprepared. My score on the LSAT was a few points lower than my scores on the two or three practice tests I bothered to take. I had no plans on taking it again though, because I wasn't entirely sure that I even wanted to go to law school. I applied to the GMU evening program, early decision, and nowhere else. Mason or bust. A few months later, much to my surprise, I was accepted!

Winter turned to spring, and spring turned to summer. The extent of my preparation for law school during this time consisted of watching Law & Order marathons on TNT. I soon received my schedule of classes, syllabi were posted online, and I ventured to purchase my books. So I was on my way to law school. Now what? I had no clue.

UNPREPARED FOR THE FIRST
NIGHT OF CLASS

My first class of law school, Contracts, met at 6:00 p.m. on August 21, 2006, in room 225. I'll always remember every detail of it. The syllabus for Contracts indicated that "all page numbers refer to the casebook." For the first day of class, we were to read pages 1-34 and 237-252 from the casebook. Of all my pedagogic inadequacies, perhaps my most pressing deficiency was that I didn't even know what a "casebook" was—the sine qua non of Langdell's Socratic case method! Two "required texts" were listed on the syllabus: a book titled *Contract Law and Theory* and another book titled *Restatement 2nd and US UCC Article 2* (whatever that was). For some reason, I decided that the *Restatement* was the casebook. Why, I could not tell you. If only Jack McCoy used a casebook on "Law & Order," then I would've known. I read pages 1–34 and 237–252 in the *Restatement (Second) of Contracts*. These fifty-odd pages of rather dense material broke down to sections 1–19 of the *Restatement*, covering the basics of promises and formation, and sections 216–227, covering conditions in contracts.

When I arrived in class, I noticed that all of my peers had not even opened up the *Restatement* book, but had highlighted and underlined the other book. I soon realized, dumbfounded, that the other book was the "casebook." "Way to go," I told myself. "You read the wrong thing the first day of law school." At 5:48 p.m.—12 minutes before class—I frantically emailed the Professor with a message titled "Contracts Textbook Issue." I pathetically typed, "I apologize for having to send this e-mail on the first day of class, but I have outlined the wrong book for today's class." I was so embarrassed. Rather than outline from the casebook, "I outlined 50 pages directly from the *2nd Restatement of Torts*." Yes, in my panicked haste, I accidentally wrote Torts instead of Contracts. I didn't even know what class I was in. What a horrible first impression. I concluded, "I will not be prepared for class today as I had hoped." Petrified, I implored the professor for empathy, and pre-emptively said, "[t]hank you for your understanding." Yeah, right.

Right before class began—not knowing whether the professor had seen my email—I approached him to tell him about my mix-up. Focused on starting class, he said, "it's alright," and shooed me away. Imagining a Socratic slaughter, I felt a bull's eye painted on my forehead. I had foolishly told the Professor I was unprepared; "easy picking," I thought. After going over the standard administrative matters—office hours, how to contact the professor, the grading policy, etc.—the lesson started.

The Professor asked about *Bailey v. West*,[148] a case I had never read. After a student trotted with a limp through the facts of this case—which apparently involved the sale of a lame horse—the Professor began to ask a series of Socratic questions. Finally, he asked "What are the elements needed for the formation of a contract?" The answer to that question—at least to a neophyte 1L—was not totally obvious from the nebulous-common-law opinion (in hindsight that is why the case was assigned). The professor was met with a combination of stumbling answers and blank stares, as he Socratically waited for the right answer before moving on. Awkward, uncomfortable, silence. He wasn't going to move on until he got the answer he was looking for.

Looking around, almost incredulous, I realized I had the answer ready. Such a black-letter answer is not readily apparent in the casebook. But it can be found in the *Restatement*. In fact, fortuitously, it was found in one of the very sections I had accidentally outlined. I meekly raised my hand, cited section 17, and recited, "the formation of a contract requires a bargain in which there is a manifestation of mutual assent to the exchange and a consideration." The Professor, who was expecting some obscure abstraction from the opinion calmly turned to his *Restatement*, opened up to section 17, and smirked. He asked me some follow-up questions, which I was fortunately able to answer because I had outlined the commentary of the *Restatement* (I quickly learned the place where professors got a lot of their questions). The professor smiled and said, "That is correct, Mr. Blackman." At that point, I smiled too. I was ebullient.

I had no idea what I was doing. I had done none of the correct readings. I didn't even know what a casebook was! Yet I was still able to figure out a law school question, and answer a question that stumped my classmates. At that moment, I realized, "*I got this.*" That moment—in addition to a nerdy revelation when I expressed disappointment at the Supreme Court's abandonment of federal common law in *Erie*—were turning points in my legal education. I found that I loved law school. From that point forward, I never looked back. And I also took care to read syllabi very carefully.

---

148. 249 A.2d 414 (R.I. 1969).

1L: THE MARATHON SPRINT

The life of an evening 1L is like purgatory. During my first year of law school, I worked forty hours a week at my job at the Department of Defense. I would get to work early, most days by 8 a.m., so I could leave before 5:00 p.m. After a full day of work, I would drive the three miles to class as fast as I could—not very fast on most days with inside-the-Beltway traffic—so I would have some chance of getting to class on time. (Professors who mark evening students as absent if they are even slightly late lack empathy).

Getting to class was only the beginning of the tumult. At George Mason University, evening students took four classes, only one less than full-time students (alas I missed Property during 1L year). Preparing for Contracts, Torts, Legal Writing, and Law & Economics (it's a George Mason thing) was brutal. We were in class five nights a week, usually from 6:00 p.m. till 9:00 p.m., some nights until 10:00 p.m. I would usually have no time during the day to complete any assignments. (Professors who change assignments or post new readings the day of class lack empathy.) So, all of my work had to be done in the evenings after I got home from class (usually after 10:00 p.m.) or on weekends, a misnomer if there ever was one for an evening law student. The week never really ended.

I often compared the 1L year to a marathon run at a sprint pace. Every day I was shuffling, from one station to the next. The routine was the same. Wake up. Go to work. Work all day. Go to class. Go home. Study till I fall asleep. Repeat five days a week. Weekends were just a blitz to read ahead for the week (or catch up as needed), work on legal writing projects, and—this usually came last—relax to keep my sanity. I like to think the frenetic pace of 1L as an evening student developed my focused work ethic, but at the time, it was hell on Lexis.

2L: MY FIRST YEAR OF LAW SCHOOL

In many respects my 2L year was my first year in law school. I realized that I wanted to do all the things that a law student does, and so, the summer after 1L year, I decided that I wanted to make law school my full-time vocation. I filed a petition to transfer to the day program for my 2L year. That request was granted. But, I still needed to eat and pay rent, so I continued to work at the DoD, now as a law clerk. Don't tell the ABA, but during my 2L year, I worked about 30 hours a week, and during my 3L year I worked about 25 hours a week. (Regulations limiting the number of hours that students can work, and earn a salary—in light of skyrocketing tuition and ballooning debt—are unduly paternalistic and make little sense.) With this modified schedule, I was able to take classes during the day and at night.

I was elected to the Law Review's Editorial Board, and served as an Articles Editor, which was one of the most trying yet rewarding experiences of my law school career. After the end of the spring semester, I began my first real job as a lawyer-to-be—a summer associate position at a firm in Washington during the BigLaw heyday that was the summer of 2008. I was treated way too nicely. There were daily lunches at gourmet restaurants, numerous happy hours, and perks undeserving of a 24-year-old with two years of law school under his belt. I ate so much steak my first week on the job I gained five pounds. Staring incredulously at the scale, I promptly gave up red meat for the remainder of the summer.

In addition, the firm generously flew all summer associates nationwide to a weekend retreat at the swanky Wynn Resort in Las Vegas. This trip included fully-stocked cabanas by the exclusive pool, dinner in a private room at a Wolfgang Puck restaurant, and clubbing at the posh nightclub Tryst. After this jaunt, we were flown to the firm's Los Angeles office for a weeklong training course on transactional law. We stayed at a chic hotel, described by the *L.A. Times* as a "hotel Austin Powers would love." After a not-so-long day of work, we were treated to tickets to a Dodgers game, a few rows behind home plate. I felt absolutely humbled by all the gifts being showered upon us, and frankly unworthy. I thought to myself, this cannot possibly be economically sustainable. Alas, I was right.

Shortly after we returned to the East Coast, the BigLaw bubble began to burst. A prominent New York firm fired a significant number of associates. Everyone took notice, and collectively began to freak out. *AboveTheLaw.com* became our snarky-yet-prophetic bible, as we read it daily for insights and revelations about our legal-world-to-come. Soon partners started mumbling, and rumors began to fly that associates would not receive offers—a heresy at that point. At the beginning of the summer, we were all assured that if we did our work, we would get offers. Those last few weeks in the office became quite tense. Fortunately, I received an offer, though not everyone in that class was asked to return to the firm.

Perhaps even more heretical, though, I did not accept the offer (nor did I reject it). Returning to the firm was not first and foremost on my mind.

MY ARTICLE III ADVENTURES

At the beginning of my 3L year, I was standing at somewhat of a legal crossroads. Only two years earlier, I had no idea what a federal clerkship was. Yet, for some reason, my mind was set on obtaining one! My odds were slim. Mason sends very few students to federal district courts, and even fewer (maybe one or two a year) to the courts of appeals. My grades were good, but probably not good enough. Fueled in part by my burgeoning Article III obsession and my desire to gain personal and first-hand insights into how judges decide cases, I decided to take a guerilla approach to applying to federal clerkships—apply to them all. All 1,198 active and senior Article III judges—from Acker to Zouhary. Insane! Nuts! Waste of time and money! These were only some of the comments I heard at the time. They were right, but I was not deterred (I seldom am).

Fortunately, 422 of those judges accepted electronic applications through the Online System for Clerkship Application and Review, affectionately known as OSCAR among clerkship aficionados. This made applying to a judge as simple as the click of a button. Unfortunately, 776 other judges only accepted paper applications through the mail. Let's just say I became an outstanding customer at FedEx-Kinkos and the local Arlington post office. I spent more time than I would ever care to count printing, stuffing, and stamping envelopes. Prior to Labor Day, 2008, I mailed out over 776 packages, each including a customized cover letter, resume, transcript, sealed letters of recommendation, and writing samples. A career advisor at GMU later told me that I set the record for clerkship applications—a record I relish with nerdy pride.

I was determined. I was also fortunate. I received one interview with a court of appeals judge, six district court judges, and two non-Article III judges. I did receive this odd quiz from Judge Danny Boggs in Louisville, which asked questions like "What is a Plutoid?" and "Within a factor of 3, how many motor vehicles (4 or more wheels) have been manufactured in history?" I promptly filled it out, but I did not hear back from him. Nine interviews from 1,198 applications was roughly a 1 percent success rate. Not too bad, I thought.

Traveling to those interviews, however, was nuts. Most federal judges adhere to what is known as the hiring plan. Judges who adhere to this plan will not interview any candidates prior to the Thursday in the third week in September. Most judges interview on that Thursday and Friday, and if the vacancies aren't filled, interviews are conducted the following Monday, Tuesday, and if necessary on Wednesday. In other words, all interviews are over the course of five business days. Many judges make what is called an exploding offer—an offer is made on the spot, and an applicant has to accept or reject immediately. Other judges may give some time—not much, maybe 24-hours at the most—for an offeree to make a decision. Accepting any offer made is the equivalent of a legal-categorical imperative—you just have to accept it. It is frankly an Article III race to the bottom.

My schedule for nine interviews in seven cities in five days was insane. Wednesday night I took off from Reagan National Airport to a city in the Midwest, where I was to meet with a circuit judge first thing in the morning on Thursday. That interview went really well. It was one of the most probing, congenial, and revealing discussions I had ever had. The judge had a really good knack for getting to know me well in a short period of time. I left that interview with a very good feeling. The judge told me I would know by Monday, at the latest, whether I had the job.

Immediately following that interview, I was ready to run to the airport to fly to the south for an early-evening interview with a district court judge. Except for the fact that the judge had left me a voicemail at 9:00 that morning informing me that he had already filled the position, and my interview was cancelled. He hired someone for a vacancy an hour after the hiring season began, and a few hours before my interview was scheduled. I never made it there. Fortunately for me, his message came a few hours before that city issued an evacuation order for an impending hurricane. Had I traveled to that city the night before—as I might have if my schedule was slightly different—I would have been stuck for quite some time, and likely missed the remainder of the clerkship season. In this case, a judge cancelling an interview a mere hour after the start of clerkship season began was a blessing.

No rest for the weary. After the cancellation, with the help of my mother/travel agent, I rerouted my flight, and traveled to the east coast for an interview with a district court judge on Friday afternoon. That interview did not go particularly well. After all of that traveling, the judge chatted with me for only ten uninterested minutes, and remanded me to a colloquy with the clerks for the duration of my time there. I later found out that the judge had already filled the position the previous day, and was interviewing me for no discernible purpose. I guess this is a common occurrence.

That evening, I continued my patronage at FedEx-Kinkos and conducted a videoconference interview with a district judge out west. The interview went well enough, and the judge was quite nice, but I felt I just wasn't able to find any chemistry or bond over the videoconference. Exhausted, I returned home for the weekend, collapsed, and tried to catch up on the class work that I had missed from my Article III gallivanting across our republic.

On Monday—after attending class and a law review board meeting—I took the Metrorail to DC, where I interviewed with two non-Article III judges. While interviewing with the first judge, I felt my phone vibrating and peeked into my suit breast pocket—it was the circuit judge calling! Against all orthodoxies, I asked if I could use the bathroom. The judge suggested I use the bathroom in his chambers. I went in quickly, and somehow caught the call before it went to voicemail. I didn't get the job, but the judge praised me, and told me the competition was rather stiff and I just missed it. I composed myself, and continued the interview. Both interviews in D.C. went well, and I enjoyed chatting with both judges.

Later on Monday evening I set off for a place I had never heard of— Johnstown, Pennsylvania. I had scheduled an interview first-thing Tuesday morning with the Honorable Kim R. Gibson. On my way to Johnstown, I noticed some signs on the highway about a Johnstown Flood memorial. "Huh," I figured, "there must've been some flood here or something." "That must be a bad biblical omen!" I arrived late Monday night and checked into a hotel.

The interview with Judge Gibson was extremely enjoyable—I found him to be a warm, amiable, and thoughtful person. All of the questions he asked me were aimed at letting me show my strengths, and illustrating who I am. In addition to asking me about *Erie* and *Daubert*, he asked me where I was from, what my parents did, and what I wanted to do with my life. He mentioned something about the Johnstown Flood. I feigned knowledge, and said I wanted to visit the memorial!

Towards the end of the interview, Judge looked somewhat excited. He turned to his secretary, and said something to the effect of, "You know, I have never in all of my years hiring law clerks made an offer to someone on the spot. I always wait to interview everyone before making an offer." He turned to me, and said, "but you are an exception." Right there he offered me the job on the spot. Success! I was exhilarated! Now, did I do what every law-clerk applicant is told to do, and accept the offer immediately? Against all orthodoxies, doing my best to suppress my unbridled enthusiasm, I told the judge that I had two more interviews in the next twenty-four hours—one in Pennsylvania a few hours away, and one in Atlanta the next morning. I told Judge Gibson I would be able to give him an answer in twenty-four hours. Boy, was that a gamble? Half-expecting him to say no—and I was mentally prepared to accept the offer if that was the answer—he told me, "Yes." I was thrilled and relieved at once. Giving me time spoke volumes about Judge Gibson's character.

After chatting with the clerks, I hit the road for a lengthy drive across the Commonwealth to another district court. That interview was rather anticlimactic. The judge was nice enough, but all I could do was think about the offer in Johnstown, and consider whether this position was a better fit. After a few minutes of the interview, I realized it was not. Tuesday evening I drove home to Arlington, exhausted, thinking it was going to be Johnstown or Atlanta.

Wednesday morning, I boarded an early flight to Atlanta. I had never been to the city, but this was no time for sightseeing. I was scheduled to be there for about four hours, just enough time to interview and go home. After traversing the avian-labyrinth that is ATL airport, I taxied to the federal courthouse downtown, and took the elevator to the chambers of Chief Judge Jack Camp. The interview went amazingly. The judge was a smart, intelligent, and warm person. Towards the end, he told me that of all the people he interviewed, I was his top pick, and that he would likely call me in a day or so to make the offer.

I left that interview uncertain of what I would do. I knew I had to call Judge Gibson very soon to make up my mind. Maybe I should ask for more time, and wait to see if Judge Camp made me an offer? I was truly conflicted. In the taxi on the way to the airport, I called my dad. I remember the conversation quite clearly. I told him that I wasn't sure what to do, and I needed to think about it. He asked me, quite simply, "Did you have the same good feeling about Judge Camp as you did about Judge Gibson?" I thought about it for a bit. I said, "No." The fact that Judge Gibson was willing to give me twenty-four hours to think about it told me that he was someone who would be an advocate for me, and was genuinely concerned about my well-being and best interests.

My dad then asked, "Do you need more time to think about it?" I said, "No." I thought about it for a second, and said, "I'm going to accept the offer from Judge Gibson." After I hung up with my dad, I called Judge Gibson's chambers, and accepted. I was thrilled and ecstatic. Next, I called Judge Camp, and told him personally that I withdrew my application (mind you I had left his chambers maybe 25 minutes earlier, with a tentative offer in hand). He told me that I would have received an offer, but he understood. I then withdrew the remainder of my applications. I landed back in D.C. Rather than going home to collapse, I went to the only place one should go on September 17, particularly after such a legally-draining week—Constitution Day at the Cato Institute. I arrived just in time to catch the tail end of Randy Barnett's B. Kenneth Simon lecture. I told everyone the great news, and we celebrated!

After my acceptance, Judge Gibson wrote me a warm hand-written letter, which is framed and sits on my desk. He closed, "I hope and trust that your clerkship will be all that you expect it to be." It was that, and more.

In hindsight, it was probably a good thing I declined Judge Camp's offer. Judge Camp was arrested on October 1, 2010, on charges that he bought cocaine and other drugs while involved in a sexual relationship with an exotic dancer.[149] The underlying conduct that led to that indictment would have occurred during the spring of my year clerking. He resigned from the bench in disgrace, and was ultimately sentenced to thirty days in federal prison.[150] What a tragic end to a distinguished judicial career. For sure, that would not have been a good way to start my legal career.

Though that was the conclusion of my first clerkship foray, it was not my last.

TO THIRD YEAR, AND BEYOND

On my return to class after I secured the clerkship with Judge Gibson, I felt vindicated. All of my blood, sweat, and stamps had paid off. And just like that, my mind started to wander to what I would do next. During my 3L year, I started to think seriously about going into academia. I loved

---

149. Steve Visser & Bill Torpy, *Stripper Sold Judge Drugs, FBI Says*, ATLANTA J.–CONST., Oct. 5, 2010, at 1A.

150. Bill Rankin, *Ex-Judge Gets Prison Time*, ATLANTA J.–CONST., Mar. 12, 2011, at 1A.

writing, I loved teaching, and I loved law school. What better place for me to work, I thought? Pursuing that profession, though, would be an uphill battle (to put it mildly). George Mason does not have a history of placing academics. The few Mason alumni that have gone on to teach graduated at the very top of their class, and landed prestigious appellate clerkships. So, to give myself any shot at a teaching job, I knew I would need to try again, and secure an appellate clerkship.

I applied again for clerkships during the summer of 2009. With a modified-shotgun approach, this time I applied to every judge on every federal court of appeals in the nation. From Agee to Wollman, a total of 251 applications—114 of which only accepted paper applications. I may have single-handedly kept the U.S. Postal Service out of bankruptcy during those two years. This time around, I received interviews with three judges.

The first interview was in late July of 2010. The interview was mediocre. The judge seemed quite confident that he knew what he was looking for in a clerk, and I realized pretty quickly that I wasn't it. I mentioned that I wanted to be a law professor, at which point he went on a jeremiad about the failures of legal education. I was pretty sure that was not the right spot for me, and I'm sure the judge concurred. During the interview the judge mentioned that he had recently conducted an interview in Washington, D.C., yet I had traveled for a full day, at great personal expense, to get there. To make the situation even worse, the interview was right before the bar exam. Terrible timing! On to the next one.

I scheduled a second interview with a judge to be held on the morning of Thursday, September 16, 2009—Constitution Day! First I met with the clerks. The conversation was okay, but was somewhat awkward. I got the sense that the clerks weren't connecting with me. Next I met with the judge. That conversation went amazingly. She was dynamic, engaging, and very sharp. She took a keen interest in my scholarship, and spent a few minutes questioning and probing me about my most recent article. I could tell we really had a connection. Towards the end of the interview she told me that "She was virtually certain she would make me an offer," and that she couldn't make it now because she promised her clerks that she would interview their friends first." I sensed at the moment that I would be on the winning-end of the deal where judges interview applicants they have no intentions of hiring. The judge told me that she would call me, personally, before 4:00 p.m. that day to let me know one way or the other.

Based on the way she said it, I was virtually certain the job was mine. I thought I had it.

Right after the interview, I got in the car, and drove straight to Washington, D.C. It was Constitution Day after all, and I had to continue my custom of attending Cato's celebration after an Article III interview. As is tradition. This Constitution Day, though, was a bit more stressful, as I was waiting for a call from the Judge. The clock kept ticking. 3:00. 3:30. 3:45. My friends around me could see the dejected look on my face. 3:50. I went outside, hoping that the reception on Massachusetts Avenue would be better than inside. 3:52. 3:55. Nothing. At 4:01, I called. The secretary answered, and perfunctorily told me that the positions were already filled. I was crushed. I later found out that one of the other clerks disliked me and spiked my candidacy.

There was no time to despair. I still had one more interview. For the second time, I received a quiz from the Honorable Danny J. Boggs. Judge Boggs, who at the time was the Chief Judge of the Sixth Circuit, sits in Louisville, Kentucky. His clerkship application process is well-known in legal nerd circles.[151] To screen applicants, he emails a select few a general-knowledge quiz—don't dare call it "trivia," as the information is hardly trivial! He makes the quiz up every year by himself. There are questions about history, science, pop culture, politics, the classics (Judge Boggs is a huge classics buff), logic, miscellaneous calculations (e.g., What is the volume of the moon?), and other topics. And no, you are not allowed to Google the answers. I had received the quiz when I was a 3L, but did not score an interview. The second time around, I was luckier. I was to meet with Judge Boggs on Friday, September, 18, 2009, the day after Constitution Day in Washington, D.C. Judge Boggs graciously conducts interviews in Washington, D.C., in addition to Louisville, to allow people to more easily travel to see him.

By chance, while I was sitting in the F.A. Hayek Auditorium at the Cato Institute, frantically checking my phone waiting for the call from the judge I had interviewed with that morning, Judge Boggs was sitting in the row in front of me. I was pretty sure it was him, and when I caught a glance of his nametag, my suspicions were confirmed. I pecked away an email on

---

151. Jonathan Kay, *The Honorable Answer Man*, NEW YORKER (May 14, 2001), http://www.newyorker.com/archive/2001/05/14/010514ta_TALK_DEPT_OF_TRIVIA.

my Blackberry to a career counselor at GMU. She said try not to be too "stalkerish." Good advice. I introduced myself, and said that I was looking forward to interviewing with him tomorrow. Judge Boggs greeted me, said something to the effect of "see you tomorrow," and focused his attention on Judge Michael McConnell, who was delivering the B. Kenneth Simon lecture.

The next morning I met with Judge Boggs. The twenty-five-minute interview was enjoyable and insightful. First, he started off by politely offering a glass of water. Such a nice gesture, and appreciated when one is quite nervous. Next, he went over the quiz, focusing on wrong answers, and asking how I had arrived at answers (if you cheated on the quiz, you're done here). After that, we had a lengthy conversation about what I've done and what I wanted to do. Then, just as quickly as it begun, it was over. He told me that he would make his decisions by the following Tuesday, at the latest.

I went back to Johnstown feeling nervous and anxious. Monday came, and no call from Judge Boggs. Tuesday came, still no call. I called Judge Boggs's chambers on Wednesday morning at 9:00 a.m. Surprised, the judge got on the phone. He told me, in no uncertain terms, that he had three clerkship spots open (he had previously had four, but recently concluded his term as Chief Judge). He had filled the first two spots, but the third was open. The person to whom he made the offer had not yet accepted. Judge Boggs had given the candidate until 5:00 p.m. that day to accept it. Judge told me that if that person did not accept the position by 5:00, the clerkship would be mine.

The next eight hours were among the most stressful of my life. My hands were shaking and my stomach was in knots. I tried to do some work, but I could not. I just waited by the phone. Finally, it was 5:00. I called chambers. Judge Boggs told me that the person accepted the position. Judge Boggs strongly encouraged me to apply again next year (that would be my third time applying to him). I told him I would. I was devastated, but not lost.

Fortunately, my faith and good feeling about Judge Gibson proved true. On my second week on the job, before I had gone on the interviews—and before Judge Gibson had interviewed anyone for his chambers—with some trepidation, I asked "If I do not secure a circuit court clerkship, can I return to your chambers for a second year?" Originally when Judge Gibson made me the offer, he gave me the option of one year or two. I initially told him one year, so he was planning on hiring my replacement. Judge Gibson agreed, and said as long as I could tell him by Wednesday, September 23, 2009—the effective final day of the clerkship-hiring season, and generally when he made his offers—the option for the second year was open for me. After that fateful call with Judge Boggs—which I took in Judge Gibson's office—I agreed to a second year. Mind you, at this point I had only been working in Johnstown for about three weeks. Had I not made that move, who knows where I would have wound up after I finished my clerking?

Though, in a way I am quite grateful that Judge Boggs did not hire me then. After the rejection, I knew I would have to do something else to distinguish myself on the path to academia, so I started a blog, JoshBlackman.com. The blog became quite popular very quickly. Next, on a lark, I created a Supreme Court Fantasy League, FantasySCOTUS.net, that went viral and burst onto the scene. Soon, I started to develop a following, and a reputation that would serve me very well in my future exploits. From those projects, numerous opportunities blossomed.

Alas, I was still not done with my goal of obtaining a federal circuit clerkship. During the summer of 2010, I applied to a more select group of circuit court judges—a total of about 100 judges, 20 of which only accepted paper applications. My lack of postage-purchases may explain the Post Office's shortfall during this year. This time around, I received two interviews.

At the end of August of 2010, I received an interview with a circuit judge. It went amazingly. I got there at 3:00, and was scheduled to meet with the judge for about thirty minutes, but the conversation was so engaging that I was there for almost two hours. The judge only ended it because he had to leave for the day. We talked about Supreme Court cases, my scholarship, books we had both read, and people we both knew. It was really an excellent interview. At the end, the Judge told me (and I've heard this before) that he was not going to make any offers until he interviewed everyone—he wouldn't be done until after Labor Day—but that I was in a very good spot. I was thrilled.

Shortly thereafter, I received the now-familiar email and quiz from the chambers of Judge Danny J. Boggs. That year Judge Boggs was hiring early due to foreign travels during the clerkship season, and would be interviewing and making offers in early September. For the third time, I submitted answers to the Boggs quiz (this is another Article III record of futility I hold). And, like last year I received an interview to meet with Judge Boggs in Washington, D.C., on Tuesday, September 7, 2010. The interview was almost identical to the one the year before. He offered me a glass of water, went over my quiz answers, and talked about my interests and expectations. The conversation was thoughtful and revealing. I hoped I had not only grown a year older, but a year wiser. At the end of the interview, he told me he would make his decision by that Friday, September 10, 2011. Then, the waiting started.

Anxiously, I watched as the clock ticked away. On the day the decision was supposed to be made, I waited. Waited. Waited. Then, at around 5:30 p.m., my cell phone rang. I had stored his phone number in my address book, so I knew exactly who it was. I answered it, and then ran into Judge Gibson's office while answering the call. It was Judge Boggs. I got the job—on the condition that I not blog while clerking. Ha! I somewhat expected this request, and agreed to his terms. After three tries, the job was mine. The third time was the charm, I suppose. I was exhilarated.

After a long process that stretched three years, 910 mail applications, 639 online applications, 12 cities, roughly 5,500 miles covered, north of $5,000 in postage, printing, and travel expenses, plus countless heartbreaks and disappointments, I had secured the job I wanted.

I withdrew my candidacy from the judge I interviewed with in August. He was disappointed, but relieved I was going to Judge Boggs. He wrote me, "On a personal note, I am disappointed that we won't have a chance to work together next year, but you will be in good hands with Judge Boggs." And, as was tradition, on Constitution Day I attended the celebration at the Cato Institute. But this time, I was not anxiously waiting for a call, or dreading what would happen. My position was secure. I definitely had a special appreciation for Article III that day.

GETTING HOOKED AT THE MEAT MARKET

After three consecutive summers of onerous applications for clerkships, you'd think I would take a break? Not quite. I suppose I am a glutton for punishment. In the summer of 2011, during the waning months of my district clerkship in Johnstown, and before I began clerking with Judge Boggs in Louisville, I applied to the AALS Faculty Recruitment Conference (FRC). The FRC is essentially the law professor hiring market—affectionately known as the "meat market," though some professors would prefer it to be known as the "meet market." After an equally-arduous process (the subject of another writing, for sure), I fortunately got hooked at the meat market by the South Texas College of Law in Houston. In August of 2012, I began teaching Property in front of a class full of 1Ls.

In less than six years, I went from being a 1L with no clue to teaching 1Ls who have no clue. The blind leading the blind, I suppose. And now I can impart on a new generation of 1Ls what I learned, and hopefully make their journey a bit easier. I can start my first class each year by saying, "Welcome 1Ls. That means First Year Law Students. Now, let me explain what a casebook is."

Some Advice

MIKE LAUSSADE

If there is one thing you learn in law school that will continue to serve you well as a practicing lawyer, it is this: Never turn down free food.

(If there are two things you learn in law school that will continue to serve you well as a practicing lawyer, they are probably "Never turn down free food" and "Seriously, do not sleep with that person." But the editors have given us word limits, so we'll stick with food.)

It's common knowledge in law school that if you need people to show up to your informational meeting for the Journal of Law & Roller Coasters or to come and vote on the official theme for the Student Bar Association's Charity Puppy Auction, all you have to do is offer lunch. Nothing fancy. Just pizza or sandwiches. Maybe an upscale trail mix. Law students have no time, but even less money, so they'll sit through twenty minutes of just about anything if it means calories they don't have to pay for. During my third year, I'd routinely count as lunch a red SOLO cup full of Goldfish crackers, because, other than binder clips and printer toner, Goldfish and red SOLO cups were the only things we kept a constant supply of in the law review office. So, if the Federalist Society's Intellectual Property Law Committee was sponsoring a lunch-time seminar on media law, you can bet I'd be there, in the front row, ready to ask insightful questions about the framers' feelings on YouTube between bites of a turkey sub.

When I finally started work at a big firm, I thought this would change. It did not. Even setting aside recruiting season—essentially a single ten-week-long dinner interrupted only occasionally by research memos—free food is still the primary currency of law firm event attendance. This probably isn't surprising, since, if they're like me and "lived like a lawyer during law school," which really means "drank like a lawyer during law school," most associates start work deep enough in the Student Loan Pit of Despair that even though they're making six figures, snagging a free breakfast taco seems like a major fiscal triumph.[152] And it isn't limited to associates. I have seen the seniorest of partners, people who can legitimately bill near or at a thousand dollars an hour for their time, go to extraordinary lengths not to miss out on free food in the office. Every firm has these people. They will stop working, hold client calls, and travel several floors by stair or elevator just because they've been told that there *might* be food. (Welcome Coffee for the New Real Estate Paralegal? Sure! GoogleMaps Training Brunch? Why not?) The habits are built up in school and never go away, even if it would be more economically efficient for certain partners to have lunch catered by helicopter from the Four Seasons rather than waste even one-tenth of a billable hour seeking it out themselves.

I pass no judgment here. As recently as just now I was working on this piece at the end of a long office day and, feeling lightheaded, thought I'd sneak a peak in the breakroom fridge to see if anything useful had been left behind from a lunch meeting. Two pieces of pizza ended up in my body before I had time to think "I wonder if someone was saving those" or "Didn't the Papa John's on Elm close three weeks ago?" I may bleed out internally before finishing this.

---

152. I would like to briefly put the food aside and discuss a grievous wrong that gets little attention: Law Firm Coffee. Drip coffee is being displaced in more and more law firms by something called a Flavia machine. If you've not met Flavia (from the Latin "Flavia" meaning "not coffee") just ask your least favorite aunt—I guarantee that she loves it. She'll tell you how quick and easy it is to pick out a packet labeled something fanciful like "French Vanilla" or "Hazelnut Cream," slip it into the wondrous machine, and walk away with a steaming cup of productivity. But whatever Flavia is, it is not coffee. I don't say this from a place of snobbery: gas station coffee, McDonald's coffee, airplane coffee—they are all coffee, because they deliver enough caffeine to keep me awake during a two-hour conference call. Flavia, preferring foam over function, provides no discernible caffeine rush, instead offering the option to add a "Creamy Topping," which everybody wants. It makes no sense from a managerial perspective, because if there's one thing that you want your billable hour machines to have, it is easy access to stimulants. For a while I thought this problem impugned my choice to go to a "regional" firm, and that the international firms all enjoyed the real stuff. But apparently, Flavia is just as big in New York and California as it in my corner of the world. Crappy coffee cares not about prestige or size. It must be stopped.

None of this is to say that the survival of these foraging instincts is indicative of something bad about the life of a law firm associate. On the contrary, if on a given day you're forced to make a lunch out of two ketchup packets and a pack of saltines that were left in your drawer from last Thursday's desk meal, it's because you're so busy that you've actually achieved some sort of rhythm. You forget to eat because you're so absorbed by the work that you can't even spare the time to take the elevator downstairs for a pre-made sandwich. Believe it or not, that counts as a good day.

A bad day is when you deliberately take the time to walk outside for a leisurely lunch because you're hoping that you'll get hit by a bus so that you don't have to finish document review.

*　　*　　*

I don't mean to be depressing, but the practice of law has been a disappointment.

I came in with reasonable expectations: I'd try cases, win over juries, thrill clients. I'd work in an office full of eccentric but brilliant people, whom I'd run into in the library and the unisex bathroom. Every partner's office would have a wet bar. Every paralegal would look like a Victoria's Secret model. And every secretary would have either a dark past, a secret fortune, or a weird leather fetish. I'd close billion-dollar mergers by quickly drawing up the papers between commercials. And I'd close out every day sipping Scotch, either at the karaoke joint downstairs—where everyone at the firm hangs out every night because we have no spouses, children, or pets—or on an impossibly wind-free balcony with a partner who sees a little bit of me in him. Basic stuff.

But, at least in terms of meeting my TV-based expectations, being a lawyer has fallen short.

And it's really jarring, because as far from the Hollywood fantasy as corporate law practice is, law *school* delivers *exactly* what the books and movies and TV shows promise us. If anything, the pictures we get of law school from *The Paper Chase*, *Legally Blonde*, and *One L* actually fall short of showing just how intense the experience really is. It doesn't matter if you're actually at Harvard, or if you're at a big state school or a small private law school that nobody's ever heard of. Odds are, wherever you're sitting when you learn about hairy hands and Wellington's First Rule of

Occlusion, you're experiencing *more* stress, and observing *more* weird behavior, than in any of the fictional representations of law school.

By the way: Did you know that *The Paper Chase* was actually made into a television series that ran for a season or two in the late 70s on CBS and starred John Houseman in a reprisal of his role as Professor Kingsfield? Did you also know that the show was picked up by Showtime for another three or four seasons and ran from 1983 to 1986? Did you even know that Showtime existed in 1983? Anyway, if you read through the episode recaps available on the web, your first thought is "Wait—'Hart is seduced by a 1L who's simply after his Contracts outline?' That's ridiculous!" But your second thought is "Wait—that totally happened in my class, only it was Property and the girl was a foreign LLM student!" The same goes for every episode down the line. "Students believe their Criminal Law professor to be senile, attempt to get him removed." "1Ls collude to cheat on a notoriously difficult exam." "The law school is paid a visit by the Russian gymnastics team." See what I mean? Tame compared to the actual law school experience. But six years in at a big firm, and the only thing I've checked off of my *Boston Legal* Bucket List is "Have Awkward Conversation with Partner at Urinal."

I probably shouldn't complain. It is likely that at firms much larger than mine or much smaller than mine, life is a lot more like TV, and probably in bad ways. Months-long diligence projects, late Friday afternoon surprise assignments, these things happen to all of us. But while I've never made a jury applaud or break into song, I've also never had a partner threaten me with bodily harm, or even really yell at me. I count myself lucky.

Because, yes, it is rough being the depository for our clients' stress and secrets and mistakes. And, yes, the constant pressure to do as perfect of a job as possible on documents that hardly anyone will ever read and nobody will ever care about unless you screw them up . . . it takes its toll. But if you really evaluate the misery of law firm associates, I'm not sure that the law is the real culprit. I think the billable hour gets a bad rap. It's not the 1950 or the 2400 or whatever your yearly billable target is that kills you. It's the 70-hour week that comes while you have family in town or the 14-hour day while your wife is sick. Or having to stay at the office until 6:45 when your daughter has her only line in the preschool play at 6:43.

But that's not the law's fault. It's just that growing up sucks.

* * *

I blogged my entire law school experience, from just after the LSAT until just after the bar exam. Because most law school classrooms have WiFi, and just about anything seems entertaining compared to CivPro or Partnership Tax, I had a small but respectable number of readers. Once in a while, one of these kind and well-meaning people will ask why I don't write anymore. There are a lot of reasons.

The first is obviously time. Once you can convert an hour of your life into $400 for your employer, and hopefully some reasonable portion of that for yourself, it gets harder to justify spending time on law-related *Office Space* parodies or fake interviews between you and the ghost of John M. Harlan the Elder. But this isn't impossible. I find time for something like five hours of *Bravo* reality shows each week, so if I wanted to write, I could.

The second reason is mental health. For me, writing about law school was an exercise in aggression and catharsis, which was okay for law school because it's only three years long. But to take aim at the practice of law like that, to portray as fundamentally ridiculous something that you might have to do for forty years, that's just not survivable. Enduring life as a working, married adult requires a certain kind of practiced denial that is not compatible with the production of quality satire.

Mainly, though, I don't write about the practice of law because once you get out of law school, there is literally less to joke about. Let me explain. You start law school. You go to Contracts. You learn about promissory estoppel. You immediately head back home or to a friend's house or to a bar and begin inflicting this concept on civilians, working it into conversations about household chores or sexual favors or whatever. And you think these jokes are hilarious. Because, in that time and in that place, they are. You start with estoppel jokes, move on after a few weeks to sovereign immunity and *res ipsa loquitur*, and the next thing you know you've just stayed up until 4 A.M. arranging an *a capella* parody of Deep Blue Something's "Breakfast at Tiffany's" that explains the Rule Against Perpetuities.

That shared discovery of law school, that huge store of common experience—you never get that again. You start practicing, everyone is in different jurisdictions, different markets, different specialties, and while you can all commiserate over hours and compensation, it's really hard to talk about what it is that you're working all those hours on and being paid all of that compensation for. Sometimes you can't even have a conversation with the attorney in the next office, let alone someone in a different practice group, about what you're working on because they wouldn't understand half of what you were saying. If you're a securities lawyer, you can't just strike up a conversation with a litigator about qualified interests under section 3(c)(5)(C) of the Investment Company Act. In fact, even if you're at a conference that's actually titled *Qualified Interests Under Section 3(c)(5)(C) of the Investment Company Act*, you'll probably want to think twice before using it as a conversation starter.

And that's fine. We spend all day serving our clients . . . Practicing Law. The fact that we're, to a large extent, unable to talk shop when the meter stops running forces us to talk about other things, like sports, and houses, and kids. Things that matter. I think the trade-off is worthwhile. If I'm really desperate for a friendly, non-billable conversation about the finer points of securities law, there's always a CLE available to register for. And they usually provide lunch.

Hustle

JONATHAN LITTLE

When you practice solo or in a very small firm, you are always thinking about and searching for your next job. But that is a big part of the fun of it—as long as you enjoy rainmaking.

The hustle for me began long before I passed the bar and started practicing law. It began even before law school. I ran cross-country and track and field first at Rutgers then at Indiana University. I was an Academic All-American at Rutgers and a two time New York City Metropolitan Champion in the steeplechase. I transferred to IU, which has been historically one of the best distance running programs in America, because I wanted to be an Olympian. My teammates at IU were NCAA champions and Olympic medalists. I witnessed firsthand the dedication it took to be the best in one's profession. It took me three years in Bloomington as well as my entire three years of law school to fully apply these lessons to my athletic endeavors.

My 1L year of law school was something of a blur, since my time was spent running one hundred miles each week in anticipation of my first marathon in January of 2005. Each morning I would meet another local runner at 6 a.m., in a parking garage and get in a workout before class. During the school day, I would go to the library between classes and after class I would go a local high school where I coached track and get in my second workout of the day with the team there. Weekends in law school were spent traveling around the Great Plains with other local Kansas City runners, looking for races and track meets where we could win prize money, to pay my living expenses. I did some reading for class in the car and in the hotel rooms at races, but during the week I was able to get most of the reading done on breaks between classes. I also worked two nights a week at a local running store, selling shoes and on slow nights squeezing in some reading for class. One of my friends from law school said that after first semester he never saw me at law school social events; that would be a pretty accurate accounting of my law school social interaction. My running friends and I would do our workouts in the summer after the sun went down around 10 p.m. When we finished we would run down to the Country Club Plaza in Kansas City, dressed just in running shorts (and adding a shirt to get service), and inhale beers and food.

When I was in law school, the big firms in Kansas City and St. Louis would host parties in the student lounge at school. On more than one occasion I went to the law firm parties in my warm up clothes after a run. Although I had zero interest in working for a big firm—and probably less of a chance of being hired by one—the food was free. My classmates, on the other hand, were all dressed in their best corporate attire mixing with the lawyers from the firms. More often than not, I sat at a table with mounds of free food in front of me, totally content to eat and go home and go to sleep.

Running is a sport that rewards fair play. There is no amount of political connections that can win a race; economic wealth may actually inhibit performance—the top runners tend be from poverty stricken East Africa. To me, running was the complete opposite of the law, where money and connections can overcome many an obstacle. The first class that really piqued my interest in law school was Criminal Procedure. I was appalled at the tactics law enforcement used to get what they sought from people who were often poor, uneducated, and lacking the capacity to defend themselves. Particularly alarming was the number of innocent men who had spent decades in prison as a result of the state bending the rules. One story stands out in my mind: my professor took me out to eat lunch one day with a guy who was in his early thirties and had spent a decade or more in jail for rape. DNA evidence subsequently exonerated him.

In the summers of law school I took a class or two to make up for the classes I missed during the academic year when I spent the afternoons coaching. I never had any law related jobs in law school, and I cannot honestly say I wanted one either. Immediately after law school I moved to Flagstaff, Arizona, to train for the upcoming U.S. Olympic Marathon Trials in November 2007. I got a part time job at the Coconino County Attorney's office. I had passed the bars in Arizona and Indiana, but after getting laid off from the County Attorney's office in March of 2008, I had no job prospects of any sort. My parents had moved to Indianapolis when I was in college so I figured I would go back there and take advantage of the free rent and start my own law practice in a relatively big city.

I had no idea how one would actually start a law practice, or any sort of business for that matter, but I figured I needed an office. This would prove to be my first major mistake. I rented an office in suburban Indianapolis (my second mistake). I added $800 per month of overhead to my business before I had my first client. I should have gotten a P.O. box and met my clients at Starbucks to keep the overhead low. Furthermore, I should have located my office downtown near the courthouse and jail. When you represent people, you have to be available all the time. As a criminal defense attorney, my "people" are at the jail. The second thing I did was print business cards (my first good move). My first case was a family law matter for a guy who worked at an office down the hall. I had no idea what I was doing.

Early on I realized that handing out business cards was the best form of advertising I could do. Lawyers like me represent real people. Procter & Gamble is never going to hire my firm. I give my cards to everyone. I have had great success giving my cards to waiters, bartenders, and restaurant staff. Think of the number of people with whom a waiter interacts, the number of conversations he overhears. He will remember that some lawyer gave him a 25 percent tip and he still has the card in his pocket. I cannot count the number of referrals from waiters I have received. (I have also been hired by many a waiter). I always hang my cards on community billboards too. One time I hung my card up in a Quizno's and got three criminal clients out of it.

In August 2008 I caught the biggest break of my career. The first time I went to visit my new client at the county jail I was fortunate enough to run into one of the most respected criminal defense lawyers in Indiana. He and I talked, and I offered to help for free on any jury trials he had coming up and he took me out to breakfast. Years earlier he had left the local prosecutor's office and had gone out on his own. I did three jury trials with him for free. In the first one, I only cross examined one witness. Most of my work was doing things like finding a projector screen and running the power point presentation during trial. In the last trial we did together I gave the opening statement and cross examined half of the witnesses. I also received the big benefit of being associated with him. Criminal defendants saw me as his sidekick and it gave me credibility and judges associating us together gave me further credibility.

My new mentor asked me how much money I wanted to make. I told him I had no idea. He asked, "What do they pay at the Public Defender's office?" I said, "Maybe $50,000." He said, "Well, you have to make more than that, or you should go over there and start working for them." He said, "How many dollars an hour is $50,000 a year." I did not know. "$25 an hour," he said. He had me explain what my fixed overhead was at the time: $800 a month for rent, a little less than $100 a month for insurance, and $400 or so for student loans. All totaled, it added up to less than $1500. He said, "You need to approach your practice like this: you want $25 an hour for 40 hours a week, 50 weeks a year. Add your overhead to the $25 an hour and keep track of everything you do on each type of case so you know how much money you are making working on each case."

I started tracking each case I worked on. I learned that a Marion County OWI (operating a vehicle while under the influence) takes me two hours to depose each police officer, at least four trips to court (one hour each trip, including the commute), and two hours or so to write a motion to exclude a bad test, for a total of ten hours. If the case is in Hamilton County, I need to add ten more hours for the extra driving. Back when I was starting out, anything that did not net $25 an hour was a waste of time. For example, anything involving the Bureau of Motor Vehicles. I could do traffic tickets all day, but since the BMV in Indiana is rife with mistakes and ineptitude, once the case was resolved in court, the risk of the BMV making a mistake applying the court order to my client's driver's license made the risk of the case becoming a ten hour mess too great. Now, with increased overhead, I must bring in $125 an hour to cover the cost of our firm, so a $1,500 OWI in Marion County is worth my time, but the same case in Hamilton County, to be done well, is not.

The other key piece of advice from my mentor was to make sure that everyone in my community knew I was a lawyer. This was going to be critical since I did not live in Indianapolis before moving there in 2008. If your community is a church, buy an advertisement in the church bulletin.

Coach a little league team. Whatever your community may be, just make sure the other members of it know that you are a lawyer.

Another good move I made early on was to make friends with a young associate at a large law firm in Indianapolis. My friend sent me just about everything that came in the door that he did not do. I took everything he sent. I pride myself on my communication with my clients and I do not nickel and dime them on their bills. Word got back to the large law firm that I was taking care of their referrals and to this day, that firm is my biggest source of new clients.

I have also done a lot of real time marketing. Last year when the Indiana legislature was passing a bill to outlaw collective bargaining, organized labor held many rallies in front of the capital to voice their opposition. I bought coffee and gave it away to the union workers; the coffee cups had my business cards taped on them. I also offered to represent anyone that was arrested for protesting, free of charge.

At another rally for Occupy Wall Street, I spent $50 on Little Caesar's pizzas for the protestors. Again I offered to represent anyone who was arrested out of those protest activities for free (this time several group members were arrested). But I also got several unrelated criminal matters and a personal injury case from Occupy Wall Street referrals.

My partner speaks Urdu and Hindi, so he has an instant community. The only publications we advertise in are the local Hindi and Muslim phone books. Further we are currently producing a commercial that will air at the local Bollywood theater. One of my criminal clients is a freelance photographer. After looking at some of his work, I told him I would do his OWI for free if he would help us make a couple of commercials. My partner and I decided that the best use of his services would be to produce a 30 second spot in Hindi for the local Bollywood theater. For starters, no other attorneys are advertising there. Also, everyone goes to the movies and "everyone" has criminal, bankruptcy, or family law problems, and we are one of the few firms in Indiana that can address those problems in their native language.

Our firm has several websites, covering specific topics from athlete abuse to consumer protection work. We have experimented with purchasing Google key words (good idea) and Facebook advertising (not such a good idea). We have had websites aimed at picking up college kids who get tickets for possessing pot or drinking underage (broke even). The internet is in my opinion the best place to focus your marketing. We are not listed in the phone book and do not plan to ever be. It costs too much and when I get a phone book at home I throw it away, which is what most of the people I know do with them.

Your best advertising is really you. This is why getting out, to bars, restaurants, meetings, political gatherings, and whatever else interests you, is going to bring you the most business. Your community needs to know you are a lawyer and your community needs to be as big as you can make it.

You have to have the right attitude to be a solo or small firm practitioner. You must practice in high demand areas, criminal, family, and bankruptcy. Remember you are running a business and that business is you. You need to handle uncertainty well. You need to be ready to immediately respond when people need you, because you are selling availability. And you have to like to hustle.

Part VII
Game Changers

Eighty-five percent of all lawyers change jobs at least once in their careers, and the average is three times. Most lawyers, in other words, will make a change at some point in the game. But in that respect, law is actually much more stable as a career choice than most other occupations. In the twenty-first century, a college-educated American can expect 11 job changes over a 40-year work life.

Some lawyers may be tremendously change-averse. Perhaps they are people who have gravitated toward law in the first place because they like the certainty of rules. And changing direction isn't easy, especially once someone has developed some expertise and a client base. It is even hard to move within a firm from one section to another, unless you have a lot of business. And even then there are all sorts of strings holding you where you are. Maybe it takes a distinct opportunity to change the course of a life in a big way.

There is a lot of randomness in life. For many lawyers, an initial job may be the result of a fortuitous meeting, a summer clerkship, or a networking event. In addition, some law graduates must take the first job they can get because they have student loans and need the income. It takes time and strategizing to land where you want to be. Even later, your biggest client might go broke or your firm might collapse or merge—like some yuppie version of the Joad family, packing briefcases and moving on down the road to a new firm. A Friday afternoon assignment to research a bankruptcy problem could make you the bankruptcy expert at a small firm. There may be a life event or a single case or question that changes the course of your career. Or maybe you help somebody in a particular situation and then start caring about other people in that situation.

Often people take a new job for a few discrete reasons—a different type of work or more satisfying work (public interest work comes to mind), relationships with colleagues, a better lifestyle, or more pay. Some women (and men) change course once they have children. Prior to having children, many of them planned to do it all—continue working full time and being a mom or dad. But when the child comes, they seem to have a change of heart. In many cases, it isn't that the firms are too demanding. Rather, it's that they simply come to value their families more than their careers, and their priorities change, even when they didn't think they would.

People do change over time. A book, a passion, a change in geography, an idea can alter the direction you might take. It is hard to predict the sweeping social and technological changes that will come over a career. (Even though fledgling computerized legal research was available to people who began practicing law in the 1980s, electronic discovery was not on the horizon.) Maybe for some people, there is one distinct moment, a spontaneous epiphany. For others, it is a much more gradual process of deciding to change direction. Some lawyers, perhaps many, want to do something else, but just don't quite know what, or how, or both.

The reality, for most lawyers, is that there are not momentous changes accompanied by a grand story. Most people aren't going to end up becoming a federal judge or handling a historic case. Most of us will not clerk for a Chief Justice of the U.S. Supreme Court, become a state Supreme Court Justice, leave the bench, and become a Buddhist monk, like Michael Zimmerman, one of the story contributors in this section. But perhaps most of us have experienced smaller changes that impacted our lives in fundamental, game-changing ways. Moving from a firm where the billable hours or face-time requirements are oppressive or the competitive atmosphere is toxic to a smaller firm where colleagues are supportive could be a life-saver.

And sometimes, it is the smallest case or act of service—like serving a meal in a soup kitchen, as Cait Clarke did—that can have the most profound impact. Andrew McClurg, in his book, *1L of a Ride*, talks about "the real heart and soul of what it means to be a lawyer." "Big cases," he says, "change history, but the smallest and simplest cases often have the biggest impact on ordinary people."

Full Circle: Build a Life in Public Interest Law

CAIT CLARKE

Law students who want to enter public interest work are advised to take related courses and participate in the clinical offerings. Which is what I *didn't* do at Catholic University Law School. No Criminal Justice nor Civil Legal Aid Clinic. I was competitive for glory, at the top of my class and Editor-in-Chief of the Law Review. But I also worked once a week at a soup kitchen because I knew that I would not feel grounded unless I was doing some hands-on work with the poor. That was my internal compass then and it remains so today. But it isn't easy. There's always gravitational pull away from hands-on service.

My draw to public interest began in childhood. I grew up in a very white, very privileged pocket of Northwest D.C. with an African American caregiver named Maxine Fralin. Cliché though it may be, she really was part of our large Irish-Catholic family; it was she who effectively raised me and my five siblings. At night she left our enclave to return to a part of the city I had never seen, Anacostia. I'd ask her about her neighborhood. Mostly she'd shrug off my questions, but occasionally she'd describe the scene: gunfire, violence, drug deals, abandoned buildings. In rare moments she'd even let me see her fears and I began to understand why it was always so important for her to get home before dark.

Knowing and loving Maxine and wanting to find out about her life, I now realize in retrospect, has been the driving force of my legal life. Unlike me, she was largely unprotected from the cruelties and inequities and random violence of the world. Yet she was a beautiful woman with an enormous heart, and showed me that there were so many other beautiful people like her with rich, full lives that were deserving of respect. And, as I took up my profession in public interest law, I grew more passionate that so many, who were equally deserving of legal services and protection, could not access it.

Throughout high school and college I went to Catholic schools and was drawn naturally to people who cared about social justice, the ones who embraced the liberation theology branch of the Church. The nuns who did direct service particularly impressed me. At Villanova I studied at the Business School, majoring in marketing, but I stayed grounded teaching children in inner-city Philadelphia. The high school where I taught embodied the horrors of inner city education: no books to take home; crumbling walls; bars on the windows.

This was the time of MOVE (a Philadelphia-based black liberation group founded by John Africa who preached against technology and promoted communal living). The MOVE movement ended when police bombed its headquarters in a residential neighborhood in 1985, killing eleven people (including five children) and destroying sixty homes in a neighborhood I knew. The overreaction of police in a poor neighborhood had an impact on me.

It took me a few post-grad years in the "real world" to get to law school. When I got there, I knew that service—giving back directly—was a life-thread that kept me grounded. I volunteered in a soup kitchen my first semester where I met a Spanish nun, Sister Rosa Alvarez, who changed my life. Sister Rosa has a powerful presence.

I had heard about the number of homeless women who hung around the D.C. Superior Court and neighboring Chinatown. With a little re-search I found out that several Spanish Carmelite Sisters of Charity had recently opened a women's shelter and weekend soup kitchen for women in an unused rectory down a foreboding alley near the courthouse. When I went there the first time I noticed there were no lines at the door of peo-ple waiting to get in and be fed. Instead, the sisters sat their guests at ta-bles, and places were set with real (not plastic) silverware and napkins; we cleared their plates so they didn't have to get up with trays. In a word, these folks were welcomed with the same civility as one would receive import-ant guests. Which, the sisters taught me, they were. From this experience

I learned that perhaps the most important thing one can give to others is dignity. It was a lesson that would shape my career in the law.

A few words about Sister Rosa Alvarez. When I met her over twenty-five years ago she was a "take charge" woman who never took "no" for an answer—from D.C. City government officials to the highest power players in the Catholic Church. She was literally on a mission to serve the poor. Sister Rosa established Mount Carmel House in D.C. with her sisters and it continues to operate today. Rosa questions hierarchies, and when needed, she challenges power, always in service of the needy and voiceless. She remains a sprightly, feisty spirit in her 80's, now ministering to the immigrant women who work in the chicken processing plants of lower Delaware. She is the best public interest advocate I know. I had entered law school thinking I wanted to be an international lawyer. After working as a summer law clerk at a prestigious Japanese law firm and living in Tokyo, however, I knew this was not right for me.

There was another character who had a huge impact on my public interest career. After law school, I went to Georgetown Law Center for an E. Barrett Prettyman Fellowship. The professor who was responsible for my admission, Bill Greenhalgh, the founder of Georgetown's Criminal Justice Clinic, would have a huge impact on me. The competition for the Fellowship was steep and my credentials on paper—Villanova Business School and Catholic Law School—lacked the Ivy League pedigree of other applicants, and I also did not have any direct criminal defense experience. But, as I was later to learn, Bill saw the spark of service in my resumé and went to bat for me. He noticed that I had worked at the soup kitchen, had written resumés for prisoners, had repeatedly reached out to small communities as a volunteer. He saw that I had experienced the poor and powerless and that I understood service.

Following Georgetown, I moved to Louisiana as a tenure-track teacher at Loyola College of Law in New Orleans. It was a wonderful job and, in retrospect, I sometimes wonder if I might not have been best-served in an academic setting. I was not a traditional law professor. I published articles (still the only credential that the legal academy really counts) and received high marks in all of my teaching evaluations (even winning the "best professor" award from students). In hindsight, I may have "upset" the stately decorum of my colleagues by starting a Street Law program in a few New Orleans public schools and the Ninth Ward Jackson Barracks while taking my students into the prisons to spend time, most notably at the fabled Angola penitentiary.

As is likely apparent, along with "service," the other strong current running through my career is a love of ideas and intellectual activity. This would lead me to Harvard after several years at Loyola, where I again became a student and earned an S.J.D. at the Law School. Without getting lost in the past, let me simply note that I ended up, post-doctorate, at Harvard's Kennedy School of Government in the Program in Criminal Justice Policy and Management. This, in turn, would lead me to the National Legal Aid & Defender Association (NLADA) in Washington, D.C. As a Prettyman Fellow at Georgetown Law Center, teaching in New Orleans and working with Chief Public Defenders from all over the country, I saw an area where my service could have an impact—protecting the right to counsel. At NLADA my "public service compass" focused on leadership development in public defense. With the help of the Open Society Foundation I became the founding director of the National Defender Leadership Institute. It was incredibly rewarding to convene educational seminars all over the country and provide on-site technical assistance to public defense leaders. Service to public defender managers and leaders who struggle against enormous odds each day continues to be my passion.

The "Big Idea" I want to underscore in the unfolding of my career, however, is not the stuff of a *curriculum vitae*. Rather, it is the notion that my life as a lawyer has largely—for better or worse—been an on-going expression of the things I had learned from Maxine and Bill and keep learning from Rosa. Their "truth" is that justice is ultimately best-served by rendering acts of help and respect to people who need them.

That's not always easy or rewarding. My "innocence" in that respect has long since been worn away. Alas, public service and non-profit organizations are subject to the same kinds of ambitions, rivalries, jealousies, and competition for resources as other less self-consciously lofty fields. Lawyers, however, are uniquely qualified to serve. We are trained to listen; we are empowered to act.

I was empowered as a Prettyman Fellow. When a circle of opportunity came around to assist others seeking prestigious fellowships after law school, I agreed to help. I spent four rewarding years as a director at Equal Justice Works where I helped to build the fellowships program, expand AmeriCorps legal fellowships, and start Public Defender Corps by landing federal grants for criminal defense fellowships. My Equal Justice Works team had special energy because, in our own individual quirky ways, we were deeply committed to one common goal: launching the careers of our Fellows as lawyer-leaders. I keep in touch with some Equal Justice Works Fellows and remain honored to lend a helping hand to accelerate their important work.

Public interest work is never-ending. Another circle came back around in my life recently. I was asked to return to NLADA during the organization's Centennial celebration to lead a Public-Private Action initiative. The initiative is aimed at closing the "justice gap." Continued and substantial cutbacks in federal support for legal services, reductions in Interest on Lawyer Trust Accounts (IOLTA), and dwindling private sources of revenue on which public programs rely has resulted in a dangerously widening "justice gap" in our civil and criminal justice systems. People who deserve and need lawyers cannot access them without money. Law firms and corporate lawyers have helped meet some of the needs of low income people by providing *pro bono* representation to clients of legal aid and public defense organizations. Sadly, there are many bottlenecks to ensuring that cases flow steadily to *pro bono* lawyers. I am now working with a Blue Ribbon Commission to substantially increase these public-private partnerships to ensure that justice is not rationed based on ability to pay. Our focus is to launch pilot programs in several states. We are making the most progress in North Carolina serving veterans through a newly formed North Carolina Veterans Pro Bono Network. Although they have served their country with courage, too many of North Carolina's 765,000 veterans are living in poverty, facing homelessness, dealing with post-traumatic stress disorder or traumatic brain injuries, and in great need of civil legal aid and criminal defense help. North Carolina is an example of many people eager to help build a network of lawyers and non-lawyers to substantially expand the nature and scope of public-private partnerships in service to others. I believe that replicating innovative models for volunteerism will impact the access to counsel crisis. As a public interest lawyer working for the rights of the poor across this country it sometimes feels like I keep swinging at windmills, but helping a client or seeing even the smallest impact in a community keeps me swinging away.

In April of 2013 I accepted the position as the Chief of the Defender Services Office at the Administrative Office of the U.S. Courts in Washington, D.C. This office is responsible for the administration of the nation's federal public defense program established by the Criminal Justice Act of 1964. The Defender Services Office (DSO) supports 81 federal defender organizations and approximately 12,000 private criminal defense attorneys throughout the United States in fulfilling its mission to ensure that the right to counsel guaranteed by the Sixth Amendment is enforced on behalf of those who cannot afford to retain counsel.

No one had ever heard of the term "sequestration," let alone thought it would come to pass; but it did, and with a vengeance. When I started as the Chief, the entire Federal Defender program was facing tumultuous times. Not only were there an unprecedented number of retirements of senior people in DSO, but deep budget cuts loomed large for defenders and panel attorneys alike. Federal Defender Organizations were also gearing up for the imposition of a new work measurement study calling for staffing formulas in allocating staff resources across the 81 federal defender organizations. Tensions were high.

Within my first year, the Defender program had been weakened by an unprecedented reduction in the number of federal defense personnel (nearly 300 full-time FDO FTE in FY 2013 plus approximately 165 additional FDO FTE in FY 2014); many work days had been lost (approximately 165,000 hours) in the second half of FY2013 due to furloughs of federal defender employees; and, for the first time in the 50-year history of the program, panel attorney hourly compensation rates had been rolled back. Morale was terribly low.

While the sequestration crisis has abated in 2017, it has taken years to build back some of these defender organizations. I try to analogize the situation to cutting off the engines of a very large ship moving through ocean waters then turning them on again where it takes time to accelerate to full speed in choppy waters. The headwinds of uncertainty about the future budget climate make many Federal Defenders reluctant to staff-up even three years later. Lingering feelings crop up where "Washington, D.C." is the enemy because many defenders had to furlough staff while others had to reduce their staff and these were terribly difficult choices. They are understandably gun-shy to expand head counts that may be similarly jeopardized in future fiscal years. This reluctance was compounded by a work measurement study imposed for the first time and a study of the entire program. Chief Justice Roberts convened a Criminal Justice Act

(CJA) Review Committee that was instructed to study the entire Federal Defender program, addressing such issues as capital habeas representation, information technology needs, diversity, voucher review by judges, and, the most complex question—independence of the federal defense function. This study was long overdue.

When I took the helm of DSO, it had been twenty years since the last comprehensive study even though it was supposed to be conducted every seven years. At the end of 2017 the report of the CJA Review Committee was published and sent to the Executive Committee of the Judicial Conference. The Conference will determine which recommendations in the report will be implemented and which will not. Though the process remains unclear, there is one thing that is very clear: this much-anticipated report will generate significant debate about the Criminal Justice Act, the Federal Defender and panel attorney programs, and what it means to provide effective assistance of counsel under the Sixth Amendment to the Constitution.

Let me conclude with a final personal story that offers a fitting epigram to my tale and perhaps an inspiration to those of you who might be considering following a path not unlike mine.

While I was an S.J.D. student living in Boston, my husband Neil and I began trying to conceive a baby. But as a DES daughter, while I could carry a baby, the egg-donor route was long and difficult. We both came to the conclusion that there were so many children without parents, so we began exploring adoption. We learned quickly that we didn't fit the m.o. for domestic adoption, since we were "older" parents. Since Neil had two daughters from a previous marriage, we thought it would be nice to adopt a boy. The social worker told us how long and emotionally precarious the international adoption process was—unless, of course, we wanted to adopt a Guatemalan boy, which could typically be done within a matter of months due to the low demand since (as the social worker so bluntly stated), "Americans don't like short boys."

Through all of my moves, including time living in Cape Town, South Africa, I kept in touch with Sister Rosa. I heard about how she was working with migrant workers who would arrive to work at chicken plants in Delaware. Some, perhaps many, of the women were raped by the coyotes who smuggled them across the border. As part of her mission, Sister Rosa was making sure these women knew about the possibility of adoption. She had raised money by knocking on doors to start La Esperanza (the Hope), an organization to provide support for immigrant workers in Delaware.

I mentioned to Sister Rosa our desire to adopt. Sister Rosa lamented that she had just made a connection for a Guatemalan woman who was in her seventh month of pregnancy. About a month later, Sister Rosa called me to say that the family who had been planning to adopt this baby was withdrawing and asked if we would be interested. When I arrived home that night to tell Neil, he was just getting ready to pour us each a glass of wine to have with dinner and he asked me, "Red or white?" "Honey," I said, "We have a much more important decision to make."

We decided to embrace life. For the last few days of her pregnancy, there was a horrific snowstorm in D.C., so our son's birth mother, Anna Maria, came to live with us. Anna was of Mayan decent and was an incredibly strong and proud woman (another tale to tell someday). I wondered what she thought when she looked around our Northwest D.C. home and thought about her son's future life. I accompanied her to doctor's visits and was there for William's birth at the hospital in our neighborhood. It turned out to be a C-section, because he was breach and the umbilical cord was wrapped around his neck. When Anna handed William to me, a fairly insensitive social worker asked how she could give her son away. Anna, who was amazingly stoic, replied, "He is of my blood, but he is her son. I know he won't suffer."

So my soup kitchen days of the first semester of law school have brought my life full circle—we have a gifted son whom his grandfather used to watch intensely and say: "What *isn't* he good at?" Neil and I sometimes watch William helping out a child who is sad and then see him do some hip hop move with incredible ease. William has also given us a connection to a Guatemalan community only two hours from Washington, D.C. We now run a safe house in Delaware for women like his birthmother. The house is called Gardenia House, a circle of safety that spun out of those soup kitchen days because Sister Rosa now runs it with us. I realize with our son William, Gardenia House, and my public interest career that those volunteer days would always give me much more than I ever gave for a few hours a week. My days there led to our son coming home to us and to a fulfilling (though challenging) legal career.

Being Prepared for Opportunity's Knock on the Door

THE HONORABLE FERNANDO J. GAITAN, JR.

I grew up in Kansas City, Kansas, at the end of the era of racial segregation. During my senior year, white students began attending our formerly all-black high school. It was not just schools that were segregated in those days. Black people lived only in the black neighborhoods. In a way, that was a blessing for those of us who were of meager means. No one in my family had gone to college. My father dropped out of high school to join the Army. He went from there to working in a meat packing house, just like his father before him. But we lived among teachers, lawyers, bankers, and other professionals who could not live anywhere else in town. African-American communities thrived in those days, as did the many small businesses that served them.

A handful of black attorneys worked in our part of town. When I was in high school, I cleaned some of their offices, including the office of Cordell Meeks, Sr., who later became the first African American district court judge in Kansas. Those lawyers were wonderful role models of professionalism and achievement. They were my first real exposure to the legal profession and they made a lasting impression on me.

Cleaning those offices wasn't my first job. My parents put a big emphasis on work ethic, and so from the time I was a little boy in grade school, I always had some sort of job to do. I shoveled snow in the winter. I mowed grass in the summer. I dug up worms and sold them to fishermen in the neighborhood. Every Friday afternoon, I stood in front of a local bank and sold copies of *The Call*, the African-American newspaper of Kansas City. I bussed tables in the restaurant of a hotel.

When I finished high school, I started taking classes at the local community college but made the mistake of focusing too much on the social side of college life. I played cards, went to parties, and had a lot of fun but didn't study like I should have. My grades showed it, and I ended up dropping out at the beginning of my second semester. Fortunately, I realized that it wasn't too late to change direction. I regrouped and enrolled at another local community college, Donnelly College, the next fall and made studying my top priority. I went to summer school to make up for the year I'd wasted, and I accomplished my goal of graduating on time. Eventually I transferred to a Kansas school, Pittsburg State University, and got my grades up to a respectable B average. My record could have been so much better if I had focused on academics earlier.

By the time I got my diploma, it was May 1970. Society was in turmoil, particularly on college campuses. Racial injustice was still a major issue, as was the Vietnam War. At Kent State University, National Guard troops fired at anti-war protestors, killing four students. Ten days later, police killed two black students at Jackson State College in Mississippi.

As I celebrated my graduation, I thought a lot about the future of the country and the serious issues it faced. But I still did not know what I should be doing with my life. Corporations were looking to integrate their workforces, so there were good job opportunities available to me. I took a job in sales for a Fortune 500 company, which meant a good paycheck, travel, and expense accounts. However, I quit the job after three months: it just wasn't for me. My father thought I was crazy. From his generation's perspective, that sort of job was an unbelievable dream come true. But I knew that it was never going to be something that was fulfilling to me. I didn't know what I wanted to do, but I knew it should be something that would make a difference in the lives of others.

When I quit the job, I returned the company car that I'd been using and called my brothers to pick me up and give me a ride home from the office. The police stopped us to ask what we were doing because it was unusual for blacks to be driving in that part of town. I then realized that although the world had changed a lot, with Supreme Court decisions promising equality and big corporations making a push to hire people they previously would not have considered, some things hadn't changed.

My next job was with Y-Pals, a youth organization co-sponsored by the YMCA and the Young Lawyers section of the Kansas City Metropolitan Bar Association. There I worked closely with young lawyers who volunteered to serve as mentors for troubled juveniles. That experience convinced me that I wanted to go to law school. It was an era when so much social change was happening, particularly in the realm of civil rights, and lawyers were at the forefront of it all. Seeking advice, I went to the lawyers whose offices I had been cleaning not too many years earlier. Talking to them made me even more convinced that law was the right career for me.

First, I needed to get admitted to law school. I signed up to take the LSAT at the last minute, leaving me very little time to study for it. I didn't do as well as I should have, but sent out my law school applications and hoped for the best. I got admitted to a few schools, but none of them offered financial aid, and I couldn't afford to go to school without some help. I eventually heard from the law school at the University of Missouri—Kansas City, which was exciting because it was the hometown school for me. However, the dean of the law school wanted to interview me. He basically tried to discourage me from going to law school, explaining that my grades and my LSAT scores indicated that I was someone who would not succeed. Hearing that just made me even more motivated than before. "Just give me a chance," I said. The dean reluctantly agreed to do so.

I threw myself into my studies. Although 1L students were not supposed to have jobs, I kept my part-time job with Legal Aid in order to survive. When I wasn't at work, I studied day and night. The regimen was grueling. I'd do my research and preparation for class; listen to the lectures; come back and reread the cases; and then go to the hornbooks. After that I'd create an outline. I even made tape recordings of myself reading my outlines, so that I could play them back as I went to sleep. After the first semester, I was proud to find out that I'd made the Dean's List and been invited to join the Law Review staff. I felt like I'd proven to myself, the faculty, and the dean that I had the ability to succeed.

Even in the relatively enlightened and progressive environment of a law school, it was hard not to be aware of racial differences. Most of the other students joined study groups to split up the course material and help each other through it. I'd heard something about study groups but I didn't really know anybody. I hadn't even gotten to meet many of the African-American students there. I remember one experience around the second week of law school. After one class on an interesting topic, people were gathered around talking about what the lecture was about, and what they had read. I didn't know if it was an impromptu study group or their actual study group. Being a little bit bold because I didn't know anybody, I walked over to the group and was going to listen and contribute something. The group just walked away. Their message was clear: I had to do this by myself.

I was not invited to participate in a study group, so I studied alone for the entire first year. I felt that this had a lot to do with race. But once the first year ended, the survivors seemed to pull together regardless of race. We'd been through a grueling experience and it bonded everyone to some extent. The African-American students also supported each other. Minority students eventually formed a chapter of the Black Law Students Association, as well as our own study group, which gave us a place to vent and share mutual concerns. Many nevertheless struggled. Out of thirteen black students enrolled in my 1L class, I was one of only three left by the time we graduated in 1974.

That led to the question of what sort of lawyer I should be. I knew that my ultimate goal would have more to do with public service than financial success, but I didn't know what path I should take. After lengthy discussion with attorneys who were my mentors, I decided to take a job as in-house counsel for the Southwestern Bell Telephone Company. Although that might not sound like the most obvious way to "make a difference" with my law degree, I believed that it was crucial to have minority attorneys doing good work in corporate settings as well as in places like Legal Aid or the Public Defender's Office. My presence at the table in corporate decision making would add a point of view that would otherwise not be considered. I also vowed to do as much work for the community as possible, such as serving on the boards of the Kansas City Science Museum, the National Conference of Christians and Jews, and the De La Salle Alternative School where I later served as Chairman. I was usually the only person from a racial minority group on those boards, and I believed it was an important way to show the majority community a positive image of minority people. It also enabled me to help the corporation use its resources to be a good citizen in the community.

The decisive moment in my legal career came in the summer of 1980, when I attended the annual conference of the National Bar Association, the leading organization for black lawyers. I was just wandering in and out of a lot of different events going on at the conference, and I happened to run across a session featuring a panel discussion about being a judge. The judges there talked about what they did and how meaningful they found it. They dealt with all the subjects that were of most interest to me, like civil rights, consumer rights, economic development, and ways to empower the poor and minorities. They explained how judges play a pivotal role in all sorts of major societal changes. Right then and there, I decided that I would try to become a judge. You never know when you'll have a moment that is a "game changer" like that day was for me.

When I got back to Kansas City, I applied for a vacant position at the local state trial court and wound up getting the job. I presided over a wide range of criminal and civil trials, including a lot of litigation relating to the tragic night in 1981 when more than a hundred people died when sky-walks collapsed during a dance at the Hyatt Regency hotel in Kansas City. The lawyers in that case were of the highest caliber, and it really made me work hard so that I'd be as prepared as they were.

After five years at the trial court level, I went on serve on Missouri's intermediate appellate court and then became a federal district court judge in 1991 and served as Chief Judge of the court for seven years. My road to this judgeship was never about politics; it was about giving back to the community—that was always the passion. My life has come full circle. From my offices at the federal court building, I can see the neighborhood in which I grew up, as well as the Southwestern Bell Telephone building where I worked as a corporate counsel. I have found that there are a lot of ways that one can contribute to society. You just need to be unrelenting in your commitment to make a difference.

Of Bus Rides and Bardos

THE HONORABLE MICHAEL ZIMMERMAN

More than twenty-five years ago, a law clerk of a fellow justice asked me, "How did you plan your career so that it took you so many places and allowed you to end up here so young?" At the time, I was a member of the Utah Supreme Court, a position I had assumed a few years earlier at the age of 40. I recognized that the clerk was flattering me, but also that my trip had been improbably quick. My response was: I didn't plan my career; I had simply taken the first bus that came by, rode it until it stopped, got off and stepped onto the next bus. I got lucky. Those buses had taken me to interesting places. That is essentially the same story I told more than a decade later when I was awarded an honorary doctorate by the University of Utah shortly after I had stepped down from the court and returned to practice.

Writing this piece on the eve of my seventieth birthday, after several more bus rides, I have tried to glean some lessons for lawyers who may want to do something different with their careers, but don't know what to do or how to make that change. I certainly would have liked some guidance in such matters earlier in my career. After thinking it over for quite a while, I am not sure I have much more insight than is summed up by my rather glib bus metaphor used to respond to that young, ambitious law clerk years ago. Perhaps I would have been more honest if I had just said, "I don't know." Yet that fact alone should be comforting to those just starting their careers because it suggests that there is no wrong way to make this journey.

Life is unpredictable. Confluences of events present opportunities, or compel you to find them. A bus shows up and you get on board. When and where you get off is a product of many influences, some knowable and most not. So "luck" may be the only way to describe the route and destination. Let me lay out my story, and perhaps you will find in it something helpful. I am no longer young, so it is not short. If you are impatient—as no doubt I was when I was young—you may skip to the end and simply read my conclusions. However, take my word for it: the trip is over before you know it. And reading of another's journey, and the stops along the way, is just as informative (if not more so) than his retrospective musings about lessons learned. He will be speaking from his perspective, not yours.

STOP 1: FAST CARS AND ODD JOBS

I was born in Chicago and grew up as the oldest of three children in a small town in northwest Cook County, and then in an area of farms farther out in Lake County. When I was fourteen, we moved to what seemed to me the farthest reaches of the planet, Arizona, a state then edging toward a million in population. I finished high school there, and three years of college, attending both the University of Arizona and Arizona State University. Working my way through college, I devoted most of my time and money to cars and hanging out, and what was left to classes. In 1964 I joined the Coast Guard Reserve to get rid of a draft obligation, was discharged for medical reasons, and landed in Salt Lake City, Utah, where my parents had moved several years before. I got a six-day-a-week job as a night clerk and bellhop at a modest hotel. Again, I spent too much time working, too much energy on cars and learning to ski, and too little of either on school. After a particularly dismal semester's performance, something clicked. I recognized that I was going nowhere fast. There was no future in anything I was doing. I decided to stop drifting and put all my attention and energy into finishing college. I cut back on work, parked the car, and knuckled down. A year and a half later, I graduated and applied to law school. A strong LSAT and a good finish to my studies got me admitted to the University of Utah College of Law.

I knew little about law as a career. In fact, I had never met a lawyer. I was drawn to law school because although I had academic interest in political science, history, and philosophy, I didn't want to commit myself to graduate school in a subject that was purely academic. I understood that a law degree might lead to teaching or to practice, so law school would keep my choices open. And I had watched Raymond Burr as Perry Mason. Who wouldn't want to be the unflappable guy who figured everything out?

STOP 2: LAW SCHOOL AND
INTELLECTUAL CHALLENGE

Once in law school, I found I had a real aptitude for it: I enjoyed the rigor and the intellectual jousting, was willing to immerse myself in it virtually every waking hour, and was rewarded for the effort with top grades. I had found an academic home. Law school, and the Utah Law Review in particular, was a wonderfully rigorous educational experience. One of the things I have continually found fascinating about the law is that it constructs a framework within which everything in the world is assigned a place and a set of relationships to every other thing, and lawyers are the unique masters of this framework. Studying law gave me real world power through knowledge. Toward the end of my third year, when my landlord attempted to evict my brother and me from our month-to-month tenancy in a house near the law school on ten days' notice (so he could rent it to someone who would pay more), I told him we had a right to fifteen days' notice, one half of the month-to-month term. He relented, and we stayed there until I graduated. It was a wonderful feeling for someone who had always been an outsider and had never felt empowered. And a side benefit, I learned from fellow students, is that lawyers can earn good money. This was not something I had even considered before applying to law school.

After my second year, I spent a month clerking at a law firm in Phoenix, Arizona doing research on an arcane intellectual property issue. I found the issue interesting, but the law firm environment incredibly foreign. I felt like a duck out of my cultural water. I had no interest in returning. Arriving back in Salt Lake City, I asked my professors what else I could do with my law degree. Some suggested graduate programs in law and some suggested judicial clerkships. More law school sounded like too much of a commitment to academia, so I collected their recommendations and applied for a clerkship, which would keep my options open. I had no commitment to staying in Utah, and was told that the Ninth, the Second, and the D.C. Circuits would be the most interesting. When I received positive responses from two judges on the D.C. Circuit, I flew to Washington to interview just before the 1968 presidential election. Judge Warren E. Burger, then on the D.C. Circuit, offered me a clerkship and I accepted. Needless to say, I was surprised when some six months later he was nominated to be Chief Justice of the United States, and I was asked to ride along to become one of his first clerks on the U.S. Supreme Court. Law school had been a big ride for me. From bellhop to first in my class; from Ayn Rand fan to voting for Eldridge Cleaver. And now the Supreme Court.

STOP 3: CLERKING AND FEELING OUT OF MY COMFORT ZONE

In the summer after graduation, I did my last shift as a night clerk at the hotel, sold my motorcycle, bought an old Volkswagen, and with all my worldly possessions on board, drove to Washington, D.C. Again, I encountered a radically new environment, one unlike any I had experienced. I found a small apartment on Capitol Hill. Some of the buildings nearby were burned out and empty, reminders of the riots that followed the assassination of Martin Luther King, Jr. The city was full of ambitious and seemingly sophisticated young people on their way up, and it was 1969: the politics and culture were roiling. Buses for Woodstock lined Constitution Avenue one weekend and, a few weeks later, 350,000 people filled the Mall to protest the Vietnam War. With snipers standing on the roof of the Capitol, the Chief asked me to drive him home to Virginia past the demonstrators in my beat-up Volkswagen so he wouldn't be recognized.

Then there was the Supreme Court. It was the year of President Nixon's failed nominations of Clement Haynesworth and G. Harold Carswell, followed by the successful nomination of Harry Blackmun, the Chief's old friend from Minnesota. And within the Court, there was total immersion in its work: personal interactions with justices, regular lunchroom games of one-upsmanship (How could a duck from a small western state truly feel comfortable with this Ivy League flock?), working on issues of what seemed to me to be of great importance, watching the dynamics of decision making, and trying to get a sense of what I was going to do next. All this occupied my time and attention. Looking forward, I toyed with getting a broader view of the law in action, of clerking for a trial judge, or working for someone in Congress, or even being a police officer. I didn't know what I wanted to do with this career I had been handed. But eventually I followed the course that the strong legal culture I was encountering held up as appropriate for someone who had been successful in law school, one that was "safe"; I joined a large firm. Rather than stay in D.C., I accepted a position with O'Melveny & Myers in Los Angeles, a firm where the editor-in-chief of the Utah Law Review the year ahead of me had gone to practice. In L.A., my years of obsession with cars and hot-rodding would fit with the city's culture. And it was in the West, where I felt more comfortable than on the East Coast.

STOP 4: BIG LAW AND MORTALITY

In Los Angeles, I gradually acclimated to being in a large law firm—at that time, O'Melveny & Myers was California's largest law firm, at about 140 lawyers. I learned to wear suits, to go to cocktail parties, and to be an urban dweller (which for me meant driving appropriately fast cars). I found the members of my incoming class at O'Melveny smart, from diverse backgrounds, less self-important than the Supreme Court law clerks, and most of us were on equally unfamiliar ground. The firm had a friendly atmosphere. The work was challenging and immensely broadening. I elected to join the litigation department, where I found myself focused on both trial and appellate matters, and on antitrust. The firm seldom staffed a matter with more than three lawyers, so there was plenty of responsibility. I had the good fortune to participate in a half-dozen trials in my six years there, and to be involved in numerous appeals, including two before the U.S. Supreme Court; in one I wrote the successful petition for certiorari. I enjoyed the subject matter and the increasing levels of responsibility. I was able to dip my toe in politics by assisting people in the firm who were movers and shakers in local and national Democratic affairs. And I met a woman in the summer program at the firm who was attending the University of Southern California's law school. She hailed originally from a small town in Idaho and had come to California after college with no connections and had made her way, first in the entertainment field, then in graduate school, and finally at law school. We felt an affinity as outsiders. We explored the city and the law while she moved from law school to a Ninth Circuit clerkship to the federal public defenders' office to being selected for a Douglas clerkship on the U.S. Supreme Court, one she did not fulfill because of his retirement.

From a career perspective, things looked good. But during my time at O'Melveny, my eclectic group of incoming peers thinned out as people found that large firm practice was not for them. To my eyes, there seemed to be a greying of the class as people moved up in the firm. I began to question whether this is what I wanted in the long run, including the implicit cultural emphasis on money as a definition of success. The life felt vaguely foreign and confining. And my domestic relationship deteriorated, leading to our separation.

Mortality also came knocking. During our time together, my partner started having grand mal seizures, at first diagnosed as epilepsy. Shortly after we had separated, she had surgery and a brain tumor was discovered, leading to a terminal diagnosis. Around the same time, I received an invitation to interview at the University of Utah law school. I had been encouraged to think of teaching by my law professors when in school, but the prospect had grown less appealing over time. I flew to Salt Lake for two days of interviews in January of 1976 to confirm for myself that I was not interested. I stayed with my parents, who had moved back to Salt Lake after my father's career had taken him on a coast-to-coast odyssey. On the second day, he was putting on his leather car coat to go to work and remarked that it would last him "the rest of my life." Unfortunately, it did. An aneurysm in his aorta burst at work that day and he died immediately, at age 61. A man I still cannot see clearly, who seems to have been defined by his peripatetic search for the right job.

I returned to Los Angeles with an altered sense of priorities. Evaluating what I should do to make a "success" of my career opportunities against the background of my father's death and my ex-partner's cancer made me question how hard I should work to fit what I saw as the legal culture's model. I received an offer from the law school, considered it a while, and then took it. I returned to Utah, to a faculty with which I was familiar, and to a larger community which I knew only peripherally, to try out teaching, and to be where I could support my mother, and be near my brother and sister. It seemed the better choice, one more congruent with who I was, rather than what I was.

STOP 5: ACADEMIA AND OFF
THE BEATEN PATH

In my mind, this move closed off access to the elite track onto which law school success had launched me, a track available to only a very few of my classmates. I felt as though I had switched off a culturally determined autopilot—the track of big firm law in a big city. I was unsure about what was next. I was going to try academia, the intellectual life, to see if it could be satisfying. And I looked forward to a simpler way of living. In the long run, Utah turned out to be a place that offered me opportunity for broad involvement in the community.

Within a few months of arriving, I was introduced to Lynne Mariani, a warm woman from an Italian-American family; a Utah native who had majored in Art History at Stanford and was now working in advertising. Two years later, after she did a stint in Washington, D.C., and my skiing improved enough to permit me to keep up with her, we married.

After several years teaching at the law school—securities regulation, antitrust, and complex civil litigation—it became apparent that it was not for me. I enjoyed the classroom, and teaching gave me the opportunity to take a new perspective on areas of the law in which I had practiced, and to see their deficiencies in light of my experience as a practitioner. But the pace was too slow, the law school was isolating, the lack of engagement with real-world problems sapped my enthusiasm, and the prospect of writing one more article on some marginal issue in the law purely for reasons of tenure was deadening. A good law student is not necessarily a happy academic. I liked problem solving, and dealing with the people who had those problems and the decision-makers who addressed them more than I liked intellectualizing about them.

I was casting about for what to do next, contemplating leaving Utah and moving to join one of my friends from Los Angeles in practice in Oklahoma, or even returning to L.A. Then one of my former professors who had also been a mentor told me that the recently elected governor, Scott M. Matheson, was looking for someone to be his personal counsel. Although the Utah constitution made the Attorney General the lawyer for the governor, he was of another party and Governor Matheson, a fine lawyer in his own right, was already clashing with the A.G. So a breakfast was arranged between me and the Governor, a person I had never met. We breakfasted informally, alone. (It can happen like that in a small state.) We hit it off instantly and talked for several hours. He offered me the position, and I took it.

STOP 6: SOLO PRACTICE AND
ADVISING THE GOVERNOR

As it turned out, the A.G. prevented me from being the governor's full-time counsel, so I opened a solo practice, sharing an office with my recently graduated brother's small law firm, and spending 60 to 70 percent of my time the next two years working for the governor for $10,000 a year as "Deputy State Planning Coordinator," his counsel in disguise. It was an exciting job in exciting times. I helped investigate the extent of fallout in Utah from nuclear testing in Nevada in the 1950s, pursued questions relating to nerve gas testing at an Army installation in Utah's west desert, helped write veto messages, consulted on policy questions, and did any number of jobs for him. And I got to observe and participate in the political and administrative machinations within the Governor's office, as well as be part of its interface with the legislature, the administrative arms of the executive branch, the courts, and the federal government.

At the same time, being a solo practitioner was a bit scary, but I got a few jobs from lawyers at O'Melveny, and began to pick up small pieces of work from other lawyers in Salt Lake City. We kept our personal expenses low, and I furnished my office with only a desk, credenza, chair, and a typewriter for a part-time secretary to use. The control I had over my time permitted my wife and me to spend many long weekends in Southern Utah, hiking and camping, and in the winter, I continued to work on my skiing, although I never skied as well as she did.

STOP 7: BACK TO LITIGATION AND FIRM LIFE

After two years, I told the Governor I needed to find a firm job. I missed the camaraderie of working with other lawyers, and the need for a stable income became important as we contemplated starting a family. This step would cut down on my availability to him, but I did envision remaining free to help at some level. He suggested I consider a smallish firm headed by his former campaign manager who was a very well respected trial lawyer. I was not interested in going to one of Salt Lake City's larger firms, and didn't have much feel for the job market. So I followed his advice. Although as a result I had far less time to work for him than I had hoped, I continued to find my involvement with the Governor, and with public policy issues, the most pleasant part of my work life.

The demands of litigation practice at my new firm were intense. The first year, I spent three all-nighters, two in a row. Lynne occasionally brought me dinner at the office so that we could spend time together. So much for the idea of laid back small city practice. I became deeply involved in firm management, helping the firm grow from less than twenty to more than forty in four years. The strain on the firm's culture and infrastructure was high, and it resulted in fairly tempestuous relations among the partners. It was emotionally draining.

In 1984, after spending four years working very hard in my practice, I was feeling burned out. Long hours, the contention of discovery and trial practice, and personal clashes within the firm over money and administrative matters left me wondering whether it was worth it. I experienced migraine headaches for the first time since my father's death. The income sustained Lynne and me in our new home, and we had one daughter and another on the way, but I missed the sense of purpose, and of engagement with public policy matters that I found in the Governor's office. I started to look around for other opportunities, some situation in which I would not spend as much energy struggling with my partners as I did struggling with opponents.

STOP 8: THE SUPREME COURT

Fortuitously, at that point a member of the Utah Supreme Court, Dallin H. Oaks, was called by the Latter Day Saint Church to be one of its Apostles, creating a vacancy on the court. In his seven years in office, Governor Matheson had filled all five of the positions on the Utah Supreme Court and it had gone from being what was generally considered a pedestrian court to one with real promise. Matheson's second term as governor was drawing to a close. A friend who was close to the Governor called, encouraging me to apply for Justice Oaks' position. Lynne and I discussed it at length. The money would be much less than I was making. As one justice's wife told Lynne, "It is not just a matter of giving up a few magazine subscriptions." But Utah had no intermediate appellate court, and likely would gain one in the near future. I had always thought of the possibility of judging toward the end of my career. Yet this was a rare opportunity for me to go directly to the Supreme Court, perhaps much earlier than I might have wanted, but then there were the realities: Matheson was a Democrat, and the prospects were not good for the election of another in the near future as Utah was becoming more and more Republican. (No Democrat has held the governor's job since 1985.) If I wanted a turn at being an appellate judge, this was the time. So I applied, and was selected, and we tightened our belts.

At forty, I was a Utah Supreme Court Justice, eight years after I had moved to Utah from L.A. It was another shift in my career, and another moment when a new perspective on the law's universe was made available to me. It did have continuity with my work for the Governor in the sense that I would have the opportunity to be involved in the formulation of public policy, albeit in a judicial context. And it was an opportune time. Utah had no intermediate appellate court so the decisional common law was relatively sparse. Many issues had never been addressed by the supreme court, or only at long intervals. And Utah was a heavily common law state, with a part-time legislature that met in general session every two years. In addition, a constitutional amendment was going to the voters in the 1984 election that would entirely revise the judicial article and likely usher in broad changes. This confluence of circumstances made it an exciting time to be on that court.

The succeeding sixteen years were a post-graduate education in the substance and processes of the law and of its administration. As the sole appellate court until the establishment of the Utah Court of Appeals in 1987, we addressed every area of the law, many of which I knew little about, from death penalty appeals to workers' compensation awards to divorce decrees. Then after 1987, we had to develop a structural relationship with an intermediate appellate court. Finally, the passage of the 1984 amendment had unified the Utah judiciary, made it largely self-administered, and designated the Chief Justice as the chief administrative officer of the whole system. It also opened the way for the establishment of a Utah Judicial Council composed of elected members of the various levels of court. The Council was to govern the judiciary, formulate its policies and its budget, and present them to the legislature. And the amendment presaged a major reorganization of the trial courts, which had been moved from county to state control. I had the opportunity to participate in all of this first as a member of the newly organized Judicial Council and later, as Chief Justice. The opportunity to work on the administrative and political issues inherent in the creation of a unified and administratively autonomous state court system was deeply satisfying.

On the more traditional judging side of the job, learning how to participate in collegial decision making with four people of quite different backgrounds and views was a great education. It was personal politics with a small "p": Intimate, subtle, often arms' length, sometimes not, and occasionally heated. Yet always engaged in with an eye to the fact that the same people would return to the same table to decide the next case. It thoroughly transformed my views on judicial decision making. When I left the court after sixteen years, I saw the law's framework, and the processes by which that framework is incrementally revised and refined, from an entirely different perspective. I was at once far less attached to the supposition that the substance of the law is settled and far more attached to the idea that a lawyer's art is in framing perspectives for decision makers.

STOP 9:
ZEN AND THE RETURN OF THE BIG LAW FIRM—
WITH A FEW LESSONS LEARNED

I left the Utah Supreme Court in 2000. The reasons were an amalgam of professional and personal. Having served on the Utah Judicial Council, and as the Chief Justice, I had wonderful opportunities to be involved in the restructuring of the courts and their administration, and in the interaction of the judiciary with other branches of government. But after stepping down as Chief Justice in 1998, the prospect of simply judging for another twenty years wasn't enough. Also, I felt that as a judge, I had lost my freshness, my capacity to be incensed at the way the system often is blind to considerations that should be important but which the law cannot neatly quantify, and at the law's tendency to put efficiency and finality ahead of fairness. Also, I sensed that I had become too invested in my own jurisprudence.

The first years I was on the court, I would try to figure out what the Utah law was by probing the lines of precedent far into the past, and then write an opinion that wove the precedent and policy with candor in a way that, if possible, produced a result that made sense in today's environment. But after a while, when the issue was one that I had visited earlier, or one that implicated an extension of an issue I had written on, I would devote more of my attention to weaving the current case into the growing tapestry of my own jurisprudence. By the last years of my tenure, I found myself deeply embedded in patterned struggles with colleagues. It seemed each of us had threads in our own jurisprudential tapestries that ran counter to threads in those of the others. Perhaps this sort of hardening is inevitable on a court where there were no new faces for the first ten years, and only one change in the next six. However, the bottom line is that I felt I was seeing the world from deeply invested positions. It was time for fresh eyes.

I firmly believed then, and believe now, that judges serve too long. The public deserves law that evolves to meet today's conditions by being seen afresh, not law that is the byproduct of the inevitable ossification of the law's interpretive organs. There is no reason that the law's timetable should mimic that of men's lives. New people need to take the bench and old leave. I could see the prospect of my getting stale, and I really did not want to become a judge who forgets that the judgeship and the person holding it are not separate, an ailment I think quite common.

There were also very real personal considerations in my decision to leave. By 1993, Lynne and I had three daughters, 11, 8, and 4, and we were pre-occupied with all that this entails. Lynne was a very devoted mother. Then, at age 41, she was diagnosed with terminal metastasized melanoma. In the year that followed, we rode the roller coaster of chemotherapy treatments, and the consequent physical exhaustion and depression. Early on, it was suggested that we attend a three-day workshop put on by a local hospital. The subject was meditation for the relief of pain and stress. We were told that Lynne in particular, and I more generally, could anticipate experiencing distress during the course of her illness that medication could not cure. Jon Kabat-Zinn, a Ph.D. from the University of Massachusetts in Worcester, was the instructor. He taught what amounts to a secularized form of Buddhist meditation described as "Mindfulness Based Stress Reduction." Lynne did not resonate with the class, but I really found it a revelation. The concentrated engagement with the breath, with internal bodily sensations, with the present moment, was fascinating, and calming. It opened a window for me that seemed new and important. I had done extensive reading in world religions as our daughters grew and Lynne and I tried to decide what training to give them. That reading had piqued my interest in Buddhism generally: I was attracted by its non-theologic approach.

I followed up the Kabat-Zinn program by reading several books on Buddhism and meditation, but didn't actually undertake the practice seriously until around the time that I was sworn in as Chief Justice, in January of 1994. Lynne was present for my swearing in, and put on a brave face, but she was failing and died within the month. I was utterly without resources. The job of Chief Justice, which Lynne encouraged me to pursue, required me to shoulder additional administrative responsibilities, something that I had looked forward to, but it would take more time from my domestic life. I was emotionally bereft, grieving, unsure of my ability to competently raise three young girls on my own, and feeling trapped. Nothing seemed to help; not exercise, not a drink in the evening, not conversations with friends, not the antidepressants I had tried. So I began to sit on the front steps occasionally in the early morning, before the girls were up, and meditate. I found it calmed me, opened a small window where I was in the present moment only, not in the past, regretting and grieving, or in the future, fearing what was to come. Just being spaciously in the present, where nothing has to be different and everything is deeply alive.

Serendipitously, less than a year after Lynne's death, the court administrator hired a woman to run our new court annexed alternative dispute resolution program. That woman, Diane Hamilton, turned out to be a meditator. She was from a small Utah town, had been Miss Rodeo Utah, but was drawn to contemplating deeper matters as a consequence of the deaths of seven friends in one year during high school. She studied English and Philosophy at the University of Utah and later attended Naropa Institute, a Buddhist school in Boulder, Colorado, earning a Master's in Contemplative Psychology. She had married an artist and lived in New York and Seattle, where she trained as a mediator. When we met, she was divorced and the mother of one child, a boy with Down syndrome the same age as my youngest daughter.

I began to discuss meditation and Buddhism with Diane. She suggested more readings for me, and I found in them a deep resonance with my experience and my evolving perspective on life and death. Diane told me that there was a Zen center near my house, and in early 1997, I attended an introductory class with two college students. The instructor, a monk from Poland, told us that in Buddhism, "there is no hope," only the present moment. The next week the college students did not return, but I was hooked. I took Zen vows shortly after I stepped down as Chief Justice, and, in late 1998, Diane and I were married. We shared a commitment to Zen practice, we each had children who needed a two-parent family, and we were both deeply involved in promoting mediation and other forms of alternative dispute resolution in the legal community and beyond. While I remained a justice I did not speak openly of my Zen practice, thinking that it would be seen as too odd for the only non-Mormon on the Utah Supreme Court to be a Buddhist convert. Today, that concern seems strange to me. My practice is often one of the first things I am asked about when I meet someone, and not with disapproval.

My leaving the court fit with my new marriage, with our mutual interest in ADR, and with the aging of my children. My oldest started college in 2000, and the prospect of putting children through school on a judge's salary was daunting. I looked forward to the prospect of involving myself in providing alternative dispute resolution services, in practicing law again, and I wanted to deepen my Zen practice without feeling any public inhibition.

In the years that followed, Diane and I both became quite involved in Zen. We received ordination in 2003, and in 2006 first Diane and then I became transmitted Zen teachers. We remained at the local Zen center until first Diane and then I left to teach on our own. We began offering retreats at our home in southern Utah in 2007, and in 2011 opened our own center in Salt Lake City, where I offer morning sittings five days a week and Diane teaches regularly there as well as nationally and internationally. The turn to Zen has been a fundamental shift in my life and has brought a deep congruence to my philosophical, scientific, religious, and psychological perspectives.

I do not know whether it is the Zen practice, or the experience on the court, or my maturation, or all of the above, that has made my return to law practice such a positive experience. When I left in 1984, the stress, the contentiousness, was toxic for me. I wondered if it was possible to practice law without either being trapped by the drive to make money, or hardened by the often nasty character of the interactions among lawyers, both between and within law firms. Joining the Salt Lake office of Snell & Wilmer, a multi-state law firm headed by a long-time friend (ironically a much larger incarnation of the same Phoenix firm I had clerked for in law school) I found practice no longer toxic. On the administrative front, firm management was handled out of Phoenix and the leadership was far more enlightened than I had experienced in my last practice situation. This also largely eliminated the administrative burden on the Salt Lake partners. In addition, we had a black-box compensation system, which meant the partners had one less thing to fight about—money. I was free to devote myself to developing my practice.

On a personal level, I found that I had developed the capacity to take a distancing perspective on the contentiousness of lawyers that permitted me to remain relatively calm while fully engaged. Moreover, holding that perspective actually seemed to mute the contentiousness in my interactions with other lawyers, and theirs with me. At the same time, I directed part of my practice toward mediation and arbitration, which gave me a sense of being part of the solution, not part of the problem.

Since leaving the court I have come to see the dysfunctional interaction among litigation lawyers as self-imposed suffering not necessary to achieve client aims, and not inherent in the adversary system. It seems to be principally a product of lawyer culture, a product of individual lawyers and even law firms becoming trapped in a story about what a lawyer is, or about who they think they have to be personally. A caricature of what it means to be a lawyer.

STOP 10: GOING SMALL, AGAIN

Two years ago, after eleven years with Snell, I made yet another change. As our last daughter graduated from college, and as I considered my future, the prospect was uncomfortable. Realistically, I could look forward to a gradual slowing of my practice in a large multi-state profit-maximizing law firm, one in which I knew a large majority of my partners only by name, at best: In effect, gradual retirement from a large business. I would be free to spend more time on Zen teaching and practice, but I didn't feel ready to give up the law. At that point, another possibility that I had long considered ripened—starting a small, exclusively appellate firm.

A lawyer with whom I worked almost constantly at Snell and had mentored closely, someone I felt had unique talents as an appellate lawyer, was up for partner. Despite assurances, I discovered that he was likely to be a victim that year of the large firm partnership numbers game. At the same time, he had come to realize that even as a partner, the numbers game would never favor a service partner, which is what a lawyer who only does appeals usually is to a large firm, and that is all he wanted to do. He felt that his future had become clear, and it lay elsewhere. I felt a sense of loyalty to him and that there was something unique in our working relationship. We began to talk of starting something on our own. Shortly afterwards, I was approached by another talented lawyer, a woman who had impressed me with her advocacy when I was on the supreme court and who was tiring of doing appeals for the Salt Lake Legal Defenders. She had heard I was considering my own venture and said she would like to join us. With the encouragement of the two of them, I decided to take the leap and the three of us formed Utah's first appellate boutique.

Taking a step into the void, not sure that there was a market for this new venture, gave me plenty of sleepless nights. But the weekend before we opened, I received a call from a lawyer asking us to handle an appeal from a $60 million dollar adverse jury verdict. We had our first case and the prospect of being able to pay our bills. Within two years, we had eight lawyers in a firm committed to profit-making, but not profit-maximization, and to spending at least 20 percent of our firm's billable time on pro bono matters. Despite predictions of our early demise, it is working. Our primary client source is other lawyers, and we are involved both in high profile civil matters and pro bono cases that appeal to our sense of justice. We are all committed to building a firm culture compatible with the enjoyment of life as a lawyer and as a human being. It feels as though I am melding my life lessons and Zen insights with my law career, not just in my person, but in an organization. It is deeply satisfying.

This is the end of my tale, the current stop in my travels.

THOUGHTS ON THE RIDE

So, what lessons do I draw from all of this? What would I say to someone who wants to do something different and just doesn't know what or how or when, someone worried about making a "wrong" choice?

As for the "what"—what to do as a lawyer who feels a need for a change—I notice that, from one perspective, many of the things I have done are not particularly unusual by the standards of the lawyer culture. All the buses I took happened to be going places the larger lawyer community would suggest were appropriate, except perhaps for Zen, for leaving the court, and for the fact that I made it much more of a meander than a goal-directed trip. I also notice that none of these buses left me where no other bus was likely to come by. So my experience is that the law actually is not a narrow path, but a very broad thoroughfare. The buses run in a number of directions without encountering dead ends, so don't worry about wrecking your career. There is far more tolerance for experimentation and change in the law's universe than our peers and law school advisors tell us when we are starting out. And there is no shortage of satisfying work, of opportunities for intellectual challenge and for the exercise of judgment and moral wisdom. Of course, I really didn't just hop on whatever bus came along. I was careful to appraise the likelihood that when the bus stopped, there would be some opportunity available, even if I couldn't know what it might be. Taking a risk does not mean being foolish. Luck is important, but foresight is a safety net.

As for the "how" or "when" to make a change, that seems perhaps a harder question. Lawyers are not risk takers when it comes to careers. We like power and certainty and control. And we are very likely to think that "success" is a narrow path and be cautious. For example, in the time it took me to go through law school and move into clerking, I had been pretty strongly acculturated to view big firm, big city law as something I "should" do because I could do it. It was harder to get into, so it must be better. The competitive, achievement orientation of law school carries over strongly into the bar. Even though I was uncomfortable with the choices I had after clerking, and felt some impulse to experiment, I did not. The easiest approved path was the one I took, or I should say the easiest path approved by my law school professors and my achieving law school peers and my fellow Supreme Court law clerks is the one I took. Once that choice was made, I was with others who had made the same choice, we all confirming each other in that choice.

Was my initial choice an error in retrospect? I would say that O'Melveny was a very valuable apprenticeship, one that permitted me to be exposed to very good lawyers and very good lawyer craft, and to receive very good mentoring. When we are starting out in the law, we really have no idea what we need by way of training, but we do know that we don't really know much about the practice. So listening carefully with a measure of skepticism to the culture's suggestions may be wise. For me, those years are the bedrock of my practice training. I still ask myself what one or another of my mentors there would do when faced with a difficult choice.

Leaving that situation was difficult. But for a confluence of personal factors, for two almost simultaneous and very real encounters with our shared morality, I might not have done it. Once in a subset of the legal practice, there is a strong tendency to buy into the values of that sector's culture, and to feel somehow wrong for considering leaving. So how would I advise someone in that situation, in their first post-law school job finding themselves increasingly out of sync with where it is going? That first job is no more likely to be the bus you want to ride for your whole career than in any other. Therefore, to decide to leave is no sign of failure. It just means you have concluded that who you are now is not congruent with that small part of the larger world of practice in which you now engaged, nothing more.

How do you decide whether to move, or when? I think this is where listening to yourself, and not to the lawyer culture within which you are immersed, is critical. Considering moving jobs or areas of specialization because we are dissatisfied exposes us to our felt sense of vulnerability and raises our level of anxiety. Frankly, we need to sit with that anxiety, see it for what it is—a fear of not belonging, of not being seen as valuable, and also a fear of the unknown.

Here, a concept from Tibetan Buddhism, the "bardo," is useful. A bardo is the gap, the transition between one place and another, one thing and another—between one life and another. The teachings in that tradition say that bardos are places where one can easily lose one's way. A bardo is definitionally an anxious place: There are no reliable reference points for a transition that has not been made consciously before. Therefore, there is a tendency to grasp for what is familiar, whatever will relieve the anxiety of "not knowing." But the teaching is that one in a bardo needs to trust in the passage, in the "not knowing," and let their internal compass guide them. In Zen we say that not knowing is liberating, not threatening, because if we look hard, we see that nothing in the future is really known or controllable. In the context of making a decision to change your current direction, you need to trust in your sense of self, your self-awareness in this moment. Who am I at this moment, and does the contemplated choice give that person energy, excite with possibility? Don't decide from the perspective of some hypothetical lawyer on a hypothetical "success" track.

Each career move, indeed life move, is addressed the same way, always quietly inquiring of the person who you have become both as a human being and lawyer since you embarked on your present course. I take as an article of faith born of experience that we grow and evolve as we learn, and that the person you are today is not the person you were five years ago, or twenty-five, and not the person you will be in five or twenty-five years more. When we have an opportunity to do something new, we need to appraise that opportunity not from the perspective of the one who at some point in the past took the path we are now on, but from the perspective of the person we are now and who faces that opportunity now.

As you ride whatever bus you last boarded, keep your heart and head alert to who you are becoming. Watch for opportunities that feel strongly congruent with that evolving person, and that promise growth and change. Then have the courage and confidence to get off your bus and take the next one toward that always unknown destination.

Part VIII
Making a Life in the Law

Despite the demanding nature of law practice and the stress of billable hours, most of the 1.3 million lawyers in this country say they are happy. Relative to other occupations, we're roughly in the middle of the pack in career satisfaction. Now, lawyers don't like to be in the middle of the pack for much of anything—they tend to like decisive victories: let us come out on top or at least let us win the race to the bottom. But the picture is much more nuanced than that.

In a survey of University of Virginia law graduates, about 80 percent of those responding were satisfied (35 percent "extremely" satisfied) with their choice to become a lawyer. Lawyers like the intellectual stimulation their jobs provide. They like fighting for people's rights and helping underdogs. They find themselves in a state of contentment when they are trying to solve a real-world problem or write a brief. They feel the electricity of an adrenaline rush in the courtroom.

Lawyers' career satisfaction ratings depend on their individual jobs. According to numerous surveys, among the least happy lawyers are associates who work for large law firms. More than one-third of BigLaw associates leave by the third year. Attorneys do suffer higher rates of drug and alcohol abuse and depression than many other professionals. On the other hand, about 70 percent of American lawyers who work in private practice are in solo and small firms; these lawyers, as well as those who are in government and public service jobs, report much higher levels of job satisfaction.

The most satisfied lawyers are those whose work aligns with their values, who work with people they like and trust, and who have found a measure of work-life balance. These are the lawyers who have discovered that it is a myth that a high-paying law job leads to happiness.

The lawyers who wrote stories for this chapter write about turning inward and turning outward. Judge Donn Kessler writes about how to find compassion in what might be considered a somewhat antagonistic profession. His advice is reminiscent of Henry Wadsworth Longfellow's: "If you knew the secret history of those you would like to punish, you would find a sorrow and suffering enough to disarm your hostility." He also writes about mindfulness—showing up in the present moment, observing without judging, and paying attention to the people around you. These are not only lessons in compassion about other people, but also lessons in self-compassion and ultimately happiness, because a nonjudgmental approach can be applied internally as well. At the end of the day, the lawyers who are the most satisfied, who have made a good life for themselves in law, are lawyers who developed resilience—the ability to put things in perspective and to bounce back after disappointment.

When lawyers turn their talents to the service of other people, they find deep satisfaction. Several of the writers in this chapter, Pamela Bridgewater, Stephen Carter, and Adrien Wing, became law professors. Interestingly, they wrote less about talking—which is the typical vision of a lawyer—and more about listening. They wrote about creating atmospheres for students to be treated fairly and to prompt student collaboration, as the students are on their way to becoming lawyers, and the importance of weaving in and exposing students to global issues of equality.

The Infinite Alchemy: A First Year Journey in Three Acts Spanning Three Decades

PAMELA BRIDGEWATER

ACT I

"You will read so much your eyes will bleed," was the first bit of wholly unhelpful advice I received from lawyers who were friends of the family the summer before my first year of law school. Another family friend offered the slightly more useful advisory, "Write down everything, even when the professor clears his throat—write it down because even the pauses are important." The following exchange took place between me and yet another lawyer friend:

JAMES: Pamela, how many dumb lawyers do you know?

ME: At least one.

JAMES: No, seriously, you know so many lawyers and if they can do it surely you can.

This was perfectly calculated[153] to propel me confidently into the first semester of my first year of law school. Yet, it did not prepare me for what happened in my first class on the first day of the first semester of my first year of law school. At the front of the auditorium-like classroom sat a

---

153. This lawyer friend is also my brother, Judge James Ruth. He meant no disrespect to his colleagues, I am sure. He was simply boosting the ego of his little sister.

white-haired, white-faced, genteel southern man. He wore a blue and white seersucker suit. He wore a powder blue bow tie. His hat with a powder blue ribbon sat on the corner of the desk. I remember appreciating his Matlock drawl.

After silently sizing up the room, he spoke. His voice was authoritative yet soft, like a grandfather. He donned a southern accent dripping with molasses. He intentionally betrayed his formal education with gratuitous uses of the word (if it is one) "Y'all" and by rounding off all words ending in "ing." He introduced himself and gave us permission to just call him Professor if we preferred such informalities. He said that in years past he would have asked us to introduce ourselves to him but he had abandoned the practice some years ago because the names got harder to pronounce. He ended his introductory comments with, "Well, what can you say, my job was a whole lot easier when the students were all white, male, and ugly."

Taking the slightly useful advice of my family friend, I wrote all of this down.

The remainder of my first year, indeed my law school career, was pretty much a traumatic blur. I spent the rest of the year in the panic mode in which most first-year students find themselves—running as fast as we could without any hint as to the destination. I also spent quite a bit of time unsuccessfully fighting back tears because of some perfectly pitched insult or slight. For example, when I explained to one of my professors that his statement about people in Plaquemine Parish, Louisiana being ignorant and poor was problematic if not racist, he was offended. When I further explained that my family was from that town and I knew that the racial make-up was predominately black and poor which, to my knowledge, did not equal ignorant, he said that I was supersensitive because I knew the facts.

I wrote this down. I also wrote the First Amendment hypo featuring use of the N-word. I wrote it all down—even the pauses.

ACT II

My eyes did not bleed but my heart broke. It was during the fall of my second year that I tuned back in to law school. I have Patricia William's amazing autobiographical essay, *The Alchemy of Race and Rights*,[154]

---

154. PATRICIA J. WILLIAMS, THE ALCHEMY OF RACE AND RIGHTS: DIARY OF A LAW PROFESSOR (1991).

to thank for this. There is no way to sufficiently describe the importance of this book to law students from historically marginalized groups. She performed a miracle and an exorcism in the first few lines of her book by simply stating: "[S]ubject positioning is everything."[155] I could relate to and rely on her because her voice was not only the authoritative voice of a law professor (the only people law students care about) and of a lawyer (the professionals law students aspire to become), but also of a great-granddaughter of a slave and a slave owner. As a contract law professor, she discusses the contract for the sale of her great-grandmother. She gave me tools to revisit property law and understand it as it related to the sale of bodies—bodies that looked like mine. Professor Williams provided my generation of outsider law students with analytical, emotional, and linguistic tools with which to interpret, critique, and reconcile our relationships and experiences inside the institutions of legal education, law practice and legal history.

One of the particularly meaningful lessons I learned from *The Alchemy of Race and Rights* was Professor Williams' description of how she attempted to help a distraught first-year student who complained about racial stereotypes used in a final exam question. In the story, "Crimes Without Passion,"[156] Professor Williams describes her efforts to help the student. First, she listened to the student. She then spoke with the colleague who wrote the exam. She also researched other exams at her school and others. She wrote a memo to her colleagues inviting them to consider the utility and implications of race, gender, and sexuality-based stereotypes in their fact patterns. Her efforts made her vulnerable to wrath of well-meaning liberals in legal education. She was accused of humiliating her colleagues. Frightened yet undeterred by their responses, she continued to reflect on her students' experiences and to assist them in navigating the choppy waters of law school. In doing so, she shared a beautiful and painful example of another "outsider" episode involving her sister—the only black student in her fourth grade class. When her sister's teacher left the room, all of her classmates tore up the Valentine's cards she gave them and dumped them on her desk. Professor Williams used this memory to reflect on the various responses outsiders can have to traumatic experiences on the inside.

---

155. *Id.* at 3.
156. *Id.* at 80.

This story served as a remedy for much of my first-year trauma. It also propped me up and propelled me for the remainder of my law school career and beyond.

ACT III

Fast forward. I became a full-fledged law professor in 1997. Since then I have played an integral part in many students' first-year experience. What most people do not know is that these years as a law professor have provided insight on my own legal education. In fact, it has continued my legal education in such a way that I often feel like that frightened, silenced young woman facing that elderly man in the seersucker suit, or that fierce young woman facing down her professor with anger and facts, or that insightful, enriched, and empowered young woman reading, relating to, and relying on the written word, narrative and theory to shape my understanding. Of the many "alchemical" moments since starting law teaching, one recent episode really stands out as a beautiful and painful example—much like that of Williams' sister's Valentine's day story—of the outsider resilience to traumatic experiences on the inside.

My story starts eerily similar to Williams' in "Crimes Without Passion." A student knocked on my door. Three students entered. They, three women of color who are smart and engaged, were my favorite people at the Law School. It was the summer following their first year and since I did not teach them during their first year I was hoping they were coming by to register for my class in the fall. I could soon tell that their visit was not a happy one. Two of the women were near tears and the one who was most composed explained the cause of their consternation. They had just received an e-mail from one of their professors from the second semester of their first year. In his e-mail to the three students, the professor said that although their evaluations of the course were anonymous, he suspected that two of the students wrote the most angry, critical evaluations he had ever received in his two years of teaching. The spokeswoman's voice cracked and she handed me the e-mail. The professor apologized for e-mailing all three of them when there were only two extremely negative evaluations of him, but "based on class dynamics" he thought that each of the students shared some of the same criticisms. He offered to speak with them individually or as a group—not to justify but to explain his approach and the content of the course.

I wish I had been able to stop my mind from traveling back to my first year. I wish I could have reached for my trusty copy of *The Alchemy of Race and Rights* and followed Professor Williams' roadmap. It was right there on my bookshelf, within arm's reach had my mind been with me in the office and not in that auditorium seat or in that offended and offensive professor's office. When my mind returned to the moment, I apologized to the students because they had been wronged and I felt it was important to recognize that from the start. I told them that the Law School has an anonymous evaluation system and that in my opinion their expectation of anonymity had been violated. I also asked them for some time for me to come up with an idea of how I could help. In the meantime, I gave them my copy of *The Alchemy of Race and Rights*.

A few days later, I got back in touch with the students. They shared with me their plan to help themselves. These first-year students had already regained their poise and decided on their collective position on the matter. They had prepared a group letter to the Dean. It was stunning in its eloquence. From the very first sentence, I knew that they had read *The Alchemy of Race and Rights*. It started: "_____ is a professor and we are students." These young women—smart and clear—understood Williams' point about subject positioning being everything. They went on to say, "We feel intimidated, attacked and unjustly accused by a person who is not only in a position of power over us, but also someone who is supposed to be invested in teaching us skills we need in order to be good lawyers. He has made it unsafe for us to express ourselves in the future in both class discussions and in course evaluations. That is unacceptable. We are all very busy, but we know that we cannot allow this action to silence us. We understand that it would be a grave injustice to both the women of color who have come before us and those who will follow."

I was moved to tears. I had not planned to give them any advice that would have been as perfect as their letter. I was proud beyond measure and humbled by their eloquence and strength. These were first-year students who had taken me back to my first year of law school and carried me from that place of silence and hurt to the present to lead me in their wisdom and strength. Here I was, the professor of law, being taught such an important lesson by first-year law students.

This story took twists and turns like those in "Crimes Without Passion." Just as in Williams' story, there were conversations with colleagues, defensiveness, disappointments, accusations, vulnerabilities—exposed and exploited, institutional disregard. I wish I could have been witness to a better result for these students and myself—yet instead they became victims of the same institutional impotence that plagued Patricia Williams and her student. In many ways it was worse because we all had a blueprint to validate their experiences. Yet, the story ended in much the same way: I, a law professor proud and accomplished, while in my office listening to my students' letter in a swell of unscholarly emotions, was humbled by the truth and grateful for the lessons taught to me by these wise and wonderful 1Ls.[157]

---

157. This essay is dedicated to them.

Last Reunion

STEPHEN L. CARTER[158]

By the time Jake Rodden got around to telling us about the murder, Doreen Shipley was half drunk and Walt Feinman was telling the same bad jokes that got him no laughs five years ago. Given the way things worked out, I would come to wonder whether Jake had planned the whole evening, or just allowed events to unfold according to their own course. Doreen told me later that she was pretty sure he had calculated the entire conversation, because he had that kind of mind. But she had always had a thing for Jake. Everybody knew that they had been an item back in law school, notwithstanding that he was a married man. Now, at our twentieth reunion dinner, she was gazing at him with the same doe-eyed tenderness that we all remembered from the days when he broke her heart.

"Maybe you heard the one about the man who walks into the hotel lobby with a little robot," began Walt, and everybody turned away in order to tune him out. We were in the main campus banquet hall, fifty or sixty strong, seated beneath the disapproving gazes of the dead white males who had founded the university and built it into an Ivy League powerhouse, most of us preening desperately, for a reunion presents an opportunity to impress your classmates by pretending to be more successful than you really are. Because I teach at our alma mater, they all seem to think I am something special. Actually, my career has been rather ordinary, but col-

---

lege graduates tend to think like students, who secretly believe all their professors to be geniuses.

There were five of us at the table, Walt and Doreen and Jake and I, and a squirrely little man named McMasters, whom none of us quite remembered. He kept his head down and ate slowly, with the deliberation of the prisoner. Most of us were dressed in some variety of business casual, but McMasters wore a dark suit and white shirt and dark tie. He looked like an undertaker, or a Secret Service agent, or maybe just the friendless nerd he evidently wanted to be. The rest of us were laughing about shared history we secretly regretted, or cooing over photos of Jake's new baby, but McMasters never said a word: or not until later.

Well, it was Doreen who cast a pall over the conversation by bringing up Cassie Carmichael.

The thing was artfully done. She waited until dessert, a soggy tiramisu, sequel to our choice of entrees—unappetizingly small chunks of underdone chicken or overdone beef, drowned in unsavory sauces—university dining at its finest. A chilly October rain strafed the windows.

"So, what's going on with Cassie?" Doreen asked, touching Jake on the forearm. "Are there any breaks we should know about?"

You should understand that Doreen meant by this to zing her ex-boyfriend, putting him in a position where any answer would sound foolish. Cassie was another classmate, a partner in one of the big Washington firms. She had vanished three weeks ago, and the press was primed for a scandal: Cassie's practice was white collar crime, and her clients were a who's-who of fallen Wall Street titans. Jake was the public prosecutor for the District of Columbia. The investigation fell within his ambit. We had all seen him on the evening news.

Doreen's zinger missed its target. Jake seemed more amused than annoyed. He was big and bluff and tawny-haired, with an eternal boyishness that had evolved over the years into a lazy charm. Jake was never a classroom star, but, by the end of first semester of law school, Jake was on breezy first-name terms with half of his professors. I had always found Jake fascinating, more as specimen, I suppose, than as friend. Doreen had probably loved him. Walt, nowadays a venture capitalist, had never warmed to him.

Now, here he was again: thanks to Doreen's question, the center of attention. Jake was, as I said, the public prosecutor of the city of Washington, D.C., and the fact that the office was elected created a certain awe in the rest of us. We might have fine resumés, but none of us had ever been elected to anything.

"We're pursuing fruitful lines of inquiry," Jake said, with his shy, camera-ready smile. "My people are working around the clock."

My people: I liked that. Last month, Jake had arranged for me to come down and talk to his people, the sort of boondoggle that those in public life can hand out while dumping on those in the private sector who do the same thing. All the hundreds of alumni in the Washington area had been invited. A dozen or so had even showed up.

"That's all you can tell us?" said Doreen. "The same thing you tell the press."

"We're your friends," Walt lied. Walt had also been one of three candidates, all among the most brilliant in the class, whom Jake had somehow defeated for editor-in-chief of the law review. Lawyers are small-minded: we don't forget things like that. "You can tell us the truth."

"We'll keep your secrets," Doreen added, with heavy innuendo.

Jake toyed with his wineglass. He was enjoying himself. "Well, I suppose I could tell you about one break we've had."

"How big?" asked Doreen, now eager.

"We found her body."

Grim silence, as all of us took a moment to remember Cassie: her earnestness, her sweetness, her scholarly bent, the way nobody ever saw her without her stack of books under her arm, or with a man. None of us knew what to say. The pall of Cassie's mysterious disappearance already hung heavily over the reunion, but most people retained some hope that she might turn up. Now here was Jake, the prosecutor, announcing in his dulcet tones that her body had been found.

None of us knew what to say.

Walt, suddenly sober, was first to venture a question: "When?"

"Two days ago. We just made a positive identification this morning. We'll announce to the media tomorrow."

"How did she die?" asked Doreen.

"Murder," said Jake. One of his fists clenched. It was different, I supposed, investigating the violent death of someone you knew. "She was bludgeoned to death. We found her in Rock Creek Park."

"Bludgeoned," I echoed, faintly, as my mind's eye gathered images of blood spatter and smeary brains.

"But we were already making progress," Jake continued. "We might even be on the verge of an arrest."

"Who?" asked Doreen, always a gossip.

"How?" said Walt.

Jake waved a hand in a pretense of modesty. "You don't need to hear the boring details of police procedure. You can read all about it in the papers in a day or two."

"That soon?" Doreen persisted. She touched his arm. "Come on. Tell us who it is. Give us a hint, at least."

*　　*　　*

Jake had us in the palm of his hand now, and that was where he liked to keep his audiences: helpless in his grip. He kept pretending to a reluctance utterly feigned. It was plain by now that he intended to tell us the whole story. And so he did, an agonizingly detailed précis of exacting and extensive police work. Jake told wonderful stories. He had the gift. Every time we seemed to be losing interest, he would toss out a nugget of pure gold.

And then he told us about the big break.

"When we dumped Cassie's cell phone records," he said, "we came up with something a little bit weird."

"What was that?" asked Doreen, fascinated in spite of herself.

Jake gave her a glance. "Turned out, Cassie had made seven calls in a week to a number at my office. A lawyer, pretty junior. A man named Sheehan. The last call was the day before the disappearance." He sloshed his dessert around but never lifted the spoon to his mouth. "We couldn't find a connection between them. Tony Sheehan went to law school here, but sixteen years after us. They didn't have mutual friends. Sheehan was a married man, but we thought, maybe an affair. That would explain why Cassie never called him at home. The calls were all pretty short—I think the longest was about two minutes—so they could have been arranging to meet."

"You must have interviewed Mr. Sheehan," said Walt, desperate not to be left out.

"We tried. Only it turned out that Sheehan was on a cruise with his wife. Ship departed a few days before Cassie vanished. And here's the interesting part. The calls kept coming after Sheehan left on vacation." Jake sipped his drink. "Somebody else was answering that phone."

Doreen's look of interest had turned feral. I suspect she was thinking what I was thinking: this would be the perfect moment for the detective to disclose that he was the killer.

Alas, what Jake told us was more prosaic.

"Turned out that Cassie was talking to Sheehan's assistant. Woman by the name of Ochoa. Not to Tony Sheehan at all."

I ventured an objection: "Didn't his assistant have her own line?"

"Sure. But at the prosecutor's office we still do things the old-fashioned way. Believe it or not, secretaries still answer the phones for their bosses."

Doreen again: "Okay. So why was Cassie talking to the assistant? Were they friends from school or something?"

Jake shook his head. "As far as we can tell, they'd never laid eyes on each other. Ochoa told us, until Cassie started calling the office, they'd never spoken to each other either. Never even heard of each other."

That chilly dread returned. This was going to end badly. I could sense it. I wonder whether the others could.

Walt rose to the occasion. "Okay. Tell us why she was calling."

Suddenly Jake smiled. Smiled like the man who held the winning hand, and was telling the best joke. The only trouble was, the smile fell several miles short of his eyes. He looked like a happy executioner.

"Because Sheehan and his assistant handle special events for our office. One of the burdens of being a junior lawyer." He pointed across the table. "She was calling to find out when your talk was."

I tapped my own chest. "My talk?"

Jake nodded. "Every day or two, she'd call. Just to confirm the time again. To make sure you hadn't canceled. Ochoa said she sounded pretty neurotic—"

I tuned out for a moment, remembering now. Jake had issued the invitation for my visit but Tony Sheehan had made the arrangements. He had treated me with exaggerated deference, as if I were still his professor. And he had called just before he left on vacation, to tell me that I seemed to have a stalker, a woman who kept calling to make sure that the talk had not been canceled. He did not recall the name but said he would get it if I wanted it. I told him not to worry about it. Tony asked, joking, if I wasn't afraid she would try to gun me down. I laughed, and told him I'm not a celebrity, just a law professor.

We let it go at that.

"But Cassie didn't come to my talk," I objected now. "Why would she call so many times if she wasn't planning to attend?"

"That's the point," said Jake. "We think she was planning to attend."

Once more, Doreen was ahead of the rest of us. "You're saying she disappeared a night earlier than everybody thinks. Tuesday. Not Wednesday."

Jake nodded. "We assumed Wednesday, because that was when the report came in. But your talk was Tuesday. She was seen on Monday morning. She called Sheehan's office on Monday afternoon. Sometime between Monday afternoon and Tuesday evening, Cassie disappeared."

Walt grinned savagely. At me. "Maybe *you* made her disappear"—a joke I did not consider particularly funny with a prosecutor sitting at the table.

Doreen laughed. So did squirrely McMasters. Jake did not. "We considered that angle." Addressing me, not Walt. "We knew you'd been in the city since Sunday."

"I came down for the Redskins game," I said.

"Right. Stayed at the Marriott. You had meetings on Monday, but you were free on Tuesday. The two of you could have met up."

"We didn't."

Jake nodded, but only in confirmation of his own logic. "Why did she keep calling? She seemed awfully anxious to see you. Maybe you were planning to have a drink after your talk. Go to your hotel, maybe."

I sat up very straight. "I'm a married man."

Jake shrugged. "If we were willing to suspect Cassie of an affair with Tony Sheehan, there's no reason we couldn't suspect her of an affair with you."

"But we weren't having an affair."

"The point is, the two of you could have met up on Tuesday."

The table went very still. For the first time all night, I had the full attention of my classmates. I cannot say that I liked it.

"On Tuesday," I said, carefully, "I went to the National Gallery of Art in the morning. I like to look at Monet's renderings of the cathedral at Rouen. I visited my sister in Bethesda in the afternoon. I had dinner with friends." I fought the urge to lick my lips. Here I was, at my own reunion, under interrogation by a man I considered a friend. "There wasn't really time for me to meet up with Cassie."

Four heads, including my own, swiveled back to look at Jake, waiting for the riposte we all knew was coming.

"The last reported sighting of Cassie was Tuesday morning," he said, tone now courtroom brisk. "A cab driver. We didn't release this detail to the media. The driver dropped her at the outdoor café a block from the National Gallery of Art. Where you just told us you spent Tuesday morning."

Again I was the center of attention. I felt as if breathing itself was a sin. "At the gallery. Not the café."

"Video monitors have you entering the gallery at 9:42 and leaving at 10:05. Cassie was dropped off at ten sharp."

"That doesn't have anything to do with me."

"It fits together. You met Cassie at the café. You had an argument. Maybe you wouldn't leave your wife for her. Maybe she threatened to tell. Maybe she was doing the breaking up. Either way, you could have had a fight. You could have gone somewhere private, killed her, disposed of the body."

"That's absurd." I was trembling. I glanced around at the other faces. Plainly, they expected some stronger denial. "I drove from the National Gallery straight to my sister's."

"Where the doorman logged you in at 3:30. That's five hours after you left the museum. Plenty of time to do whatever you did."

Jake was on his feet. Somehow we all were. Clever of him to leave this moment until the room was deserted. Kind, too. He pointed at the squirrely man none of us quite remembered.

"Mr. McMasters here isn't a classmate. He's a detective on the Washington, D.C., force. The campus police are outside. You're going to have to come with us."

*   *   *

The detective put a hand on my arm. I shook it off.

"Wait," I said. "I'm being set up."

"So was Oswald."

I gestured at Doreen. "You're my lawyer now. Represent me."

Her eyes went wide. She covered her mouth, then uncovered it again. She shook her head. "I can't. I'm sorry. I'm a securities lawyer, remember?"

"You're the only private practitioner in the room. The only one who's sober, anyway. Please, Doreen."

She bit her lip, said nothing, nodded reluctantly. "Are you arresting my client?" she asked the floor.

"Yes," said Jake.

"On what charge?"

"The murder of Cassandra Carmichael." This time I was unable to shake off the detective's hand, maybe because of the other cops in the room, helpfully cuffing my wrists behind me. The handful of classmates still in the room gave us a wide berth.

"Wait," I said again, surprised to find tears welling. I had always imagined this moment, the humiliation, even the fury, but I had never considered the tears. "This is a mistake."

Jake ignored me. He was talking shop with my lawyer. They would take me to the city jail, he said, and have me before a judge in the morning for extradition to Washington. I would be arraigned the day after tomorrow.

Doreen shook her head. "No," she said. "He won't."

Jake's eyebrows lifted. "I'm sorry?"

"You won't be taking my client to jail, or back to Washington. As a matter of fact, you'll be releasing him. Right now."

"Why would I do that?"

"A moment," she said, and drew Jake over to a corner. All of us tried to listen in, but they were old pros. They kept their backs turned, and their voices low. As Doreen spoke, Jake's straight back began to bend, first a little, then a lot, the sign of a man in terrible pain. Doreen put a hand on his shoulder, whispered reassuringly. Jake shook his head. She kept on whispering. Jake finally nodded. He turned, made some kind of sign to McMasters.

The cuffs came off.

Jake gave me a look that said this wasn't over. Doreen crossed her arms and glared at him. A moment later, the prosecutor and the cops were gone.

"What was that all about?" I asked.

"Later," she said, taking my arm firmly, leading me down the stairs and out onto the campus. For a few minutes, we passed silently through the chilly Gothic shadows. A freezing mist obscured the details.

"This is going to make the papers," Doreen said. "I always try to make sure my clients know that. You weren't arrested, they backed off and changed their mind, but people will talk. The reporters will have the story by tomorrow, your colleagues and students will read it on the Web, your family—"

"Just tell me what happened in there."

"You dodged a bullet."

"I know." In the frigid dark, each streetlamp was its own yellow island of safety. We moved from one to the next, into the brightness then out again. "I want to know how."

Doreen seemed to smile. Not happily. "Cassie and I were friends. Back in law school, we both had trouble with Jake. You didn't know that, did you?" She did not wait for my answer, because we both knew she was telling secrets. "I was pretty blatant. Everybody knew about me and Jake. But nobody knew about Jake and Cassie. They were discreet."

"All this while Jake was married."

"Yes. But he was obsessed with Cassie. Here she was, a serious student, managing editor of the law review, trying to stay away from guys because they can wreck your career, but Jake chased her. Secretly, yes, but—well, let's say, ardently."

"I had no idea."

"Nobody did." She laughed, the sound tiny and bitter in the fog. "They had a fling. That was how we got to be friends. Cassie and I. Jake dumped me, I followed him, I saw them together, and, like silly girls everywhere, I blamed her and not him. But Cassie dumped him, and we got to be friends." A pause. "Lifelong friends."

Doreen lapsed into silence. Probably she was crying. For once I showed the wit not to interrupt.

"Cassie called me the night before she disappeared," said Doreen. "She said she was going to meet her lover in the morning. To break up with him." A beat. "Her married lover."

I slowed down. "You told the police."

"Of course I did. That's what got them on to you. They figured she met her lover, they broke up, he killed her. When they saw the tapes from the Gallery—well, you see the rest."

And I did: right down to why Doreen seemed unhappy about representing me, even briefly.

"I love my wife," I said. "I wasn't having an affair with Cassie."

"Maybe you were. Maybe you weren't. It had to be either you or Jake."

I asked what had to be asked.

"Did Cassie ever tell you which of us it was?"

For the first time that night, Doreen looked me in the eyes. Her dark, handsome face was wet, from tears or the cold or both.

"We were friends," said Doreen. "Of course she told me."
She kissed my cheek, and vanished in the fog.

THE END

Author's Note: This story was written in honor of Scott Turow. I should add for the benefit of readers that the Office of Public Prosecutor of Washington, D.C., does not exist. Crimes in the city are prosecuted by the United States Attorney for the District of Columbia.

Finding Inner Peace and Happiness
in the Law

THE HONORABLE DONN KESSLER

I began practicing law in 1975 and have been sitting on the appellate bench since 2003. One thing that strikes me is that law has increasingly become a toxic profession from the excesses of the adversarial processes, potentially dissatisfied clients, and the changing emphasis from high ideals to bottom-line profits. Despite the dangers that lurk in the practice, I have focused on three themes that have helped me find more inner peace and happiness in the law: compassion for myself and others, mindfulness, and recognition of the importance of the journey. While there are other tips and practices which might help you deal with the stresses of law,[159] my emphasis is on finding inner peace. In the remainder of this essay, I will use anecdotes to show you how I have attempted and am still attempting to find that inner harmony.

---

159. An excellent source of those external practices is NANCY LEVIT & DOUGLAS O. LINDER, THE HAPPY LAWYER: MAKING A GOOD LIFE IN THE LAW (2010). There, the authors discuss short-, mid-, and long-term goals in dealing with the toxicity of the law, most notably figuring out what type of practice matches your personality, interests, and values, and ensuring that you are working at some place where you feel valued and enjoy your work and where you share similar values with your peers. Almost all of the tips and ideas in the book rang true for me.

EARLY LESSONS

I graduated from Yale Law School in 1975. Probably like most law students, I found that while law school gave me methods to deal with the substantive issues of law, I learned almost no tips on how to deal with the stresses of law or simple practical problems I would face. Luckily, I learned some early lessons in compassion, mindfulness, and the importance of the journey rather than the result in a nurturing yet professional environment with the Hawaii Attorney General's Office.

Yes, you heard it correctly. The "dream job" after law school—a deputy Attorney General in Paradise. And in many ways it was. I was interested in cross-cultural relations and was a beach child—loving the ocean and being able to read and think with the sound of the surf and soothing tradewinds. But I was lucky that the Attorney General's Office was more than I could have ever hoped for professionally—nurturing and staffed with dedicated and intelligent lawyers.

My first lesson was in compassion. I was representing several state agencies and had never learned how to keep a calendar for deadlines. Pretty simple, right? But something I was never taught in law school. About a year into working for the state, my supervisor came in. He explained that he had just received a call from the clerk for the Hawaii Supreme Court and they were wondering if we were going to file an answering brief on an appeal. I had been assigned to the case and knew it was proceeding, but had never created a tickler for the deadline (especially in the days before computerized calendars and systematized reminders). In another environment, the supervisor could have been justified in simply firing me. Instead, he explained how I should keep a calendar and reassured me there was no harm done because we could get a reasonable extension. Lesson learned. Not just in keeping a calendar, which was simple enough, but in treating others with compassion and fairness, putting yourself in their shoes and helping them learn and grow. It was also a lesson in self-compassion. Rather than denigrating myself over a simple error, I simply focused on the present and made sure in the future to keep that calendar updated. Even in this day of computerized scheduling, I always keep a paper calendar too. (After all, you never know when that computer will crash.) The other lesson I learned was the importance of the journey rather than the result. I cannot even remember what the case was about or the result (although

I assume we prevailed). What I did take away was the importance of the journey—how to treat myself and others.

The second incident was in mindfulness and again, the journey. In this sense I use the term mindfulness as used by people like Charles Halpern and Shauna Shapiro—an abiding in the present moment, observing an issue or event without reflection or judgment.[160] One of my assignments was to help represent the Lieutenant Governor's Office, which office was the chief election official. We had a constitutional challenge to the requirement for persons to have sufficient signatures to be placed on the ballot. The trial judge had denied the plaintiff a temporary restraining order, and given the importance of resolving the issue well before the election, we entered into stipulated facts with the plaintiff after conferring and obtaining the agreement of our client. The stage was then set for writing the brief and preparing for oral argument before the Hawaii Supreme Court.

We had four attorneys working on the case—two of them slightly senior to me, one junior to me, and me as the lead attorney. We spent multiple weekends and evenings in the office (weekends without the beach), jointly focusing on every issue and nuance of issues, including tracking down the results of cases on remand in other jurisdictions. We spent hours upon hours moot courting the issues until the big day—my first argument before the Hawaii Supreme Court with a team of dedicated peers supporting the effort. We ultimately won the case, but that is not the lesson I took away from it. Rather it was mindfulness and the journey. Instead of simply intellectualizing the issues, we tried to see a bigger picture—back then we probably called it "thinking outside the box." Now, I would call it "mindfulness"—being focused on the present and observing something without prejudgment in as objective a way from different perspectives as possible. What would the justices be interested in both from precedent and the policies behind the statute?

I remember one question in particular. The justices wanted to know what had happened after a remand from a California appellate decision

---

160. *See* Shauna Shapiro & Linda E. Carlson, The Art and Science of Mindfulness: Integrating Mindfulness into Psychology and the Helping Professions (Am. Psychol. Ass'n 2009); Center for the Contemplative Mind in Society, The Law Program, http://www.contemplativemind.org/archives/law. For more on mindfulness, I highly recommend the videos found at "The MindfulLawyerConference.org".

on a similar statute. By staying focused on what issues the justices might be interested in, we had anticipated that question and had tracked down the California trial court and appellate court's unpublished decision on remand. We could cite it to them chapter and verse. I remember two of the justices looking at each other and being pleased with our preparation.

The other lesson was the journey. Whether we won or lost, it was a team effort and even before the ultimate decision, all four of us celebrated over our team effort and the learning experience.

PRIVATE PRACTICE AND LESSONS IN INNER HARMONY

After almost three years in Hawaii, I decided to move back to the Mainland. Some called it rock fever. I attribute it to being young and naïve. But I moved back and after a year with another public agency in Virginia, I decided to join a private firm. Given that I was earning less money than the secretaries at the public agency, I thought it was a no brainer. And it probably was from a professional and financial perspective.

But there is no free lunch. While the firm I joined was highly professional and it was still the days when the atmosphere was if you do a good job, the business will come and you can stay for life, there were prices to pay: being thrown into court with little time to prepare, even victorious clients being upset over bills, over-reaching and excessive aggression by opposing counsel (oh, the testosterone levels), and even some lawyers in my own firm being less than nurturing.

These toxic aspects of the legal profession only increased as the business of law changed. After joining a large firm in Phoenix and watching salary inflation set in (thanks, Wall Street firms), there was an ever increasing emphasis put on the bottom line rather than simply doing a good job. An attitude prevailed of "Don't tell me what you did yesterday or even today—what can you do for me tomorrow so I can buy a new car or take an expensive trip." Monthly runs compared my share of the overhead (even though I had almost no say in that overhead) with my billing runs (over which I had little control of how much had to be cut to satisfy a client and no control over whether we got paid). The expectation was that young associates would focus on bringing in business rather than improving their professional skills.

Naturally, I found my anxiety levels increasing because some aspects of that bottom line practice did not meet up with my primary interest—the intellectual issues of the law and honing my professional writing and advocacy skills. So, besides doing more public service work and ultimately reflecting and going back to public service, how did I deal with those issues? Once again, finding compassion, being mindful, and remembering the importance of the journey. Let me tell you three tales.

The first set of incidents was simply having to sit in partnership meetings where people complained about why they should earn more money or why they should have a corner office. At times, it was lawyers liking to hear themselves talk. I found my frustration and boredom levels rising. Suddenly, instead of listening and looking at partner X talk about why she or he should have the corner office, I imagined what the partner looked like as an elementary school child—say nine or ten years old. It was absolutely amazing. Not only did this imaginary journey relieve my frustration level, but I could suddenly have more compassion for the other partners—so that was what they were like when they were more innocent and open. That was how their basic personality was formed. And, believe it or not, I still do that. Not only in judges' meetings (where the other judges are much more reasonable and open), but sometimes in thinking about the counsel at an oral argument. Try it sometime; it is almost addictive. It not only increases compassion for others, but also for you. What was I like as a ten year old?

The second incident was a lesson in compassion, mindfulness, and the journey, all at once. I was hired to represent plaintiffs in a small airplane crash case who had successfully sued one of the defendants in the trial court to the tune of a multi-million dollar judgment. (No one was killed, but there were serious injuries). Needless to say, the defendant and its insurer appealed. The opposing counsel, a good attorney but not an appellate attorney like me, called me and asked for an extension of time so he could get his opening brief cut down to the maximum page length. Little did he know that the appellate court had recently eliminated page lengths for briefs and moved to word count. Now, I could have simply said, "Sure, I will stipulate to your filing a 35-page brief," and then watched him step into the buzz saw. But why? How would I have wanted to be treated? So I explained the rule change to him and stipulated to the additional time. Compassion without sacrificing the interests of my client.

In that same case came a lesson in mindfulness. I started reading the opening brief. The first and main argument was that the court erred in giving a jury instruction on one of the plaintiffs' theories. The insurer argued that an erroneous instruction had to be reviewed de novo, which would be to the insurer's advantage. Without stepping back from the issue, I could have simply argued why the instruction was not legally erroneous. However, the more I actually stepped back from the brief and thought about it and the issue in a nonjudgmental way, the more I realized the insurer was not arguing that the instruction was legally erroneous (it was not), but that it was not supported by the evidence. The standard of review for that was much more deferential to the trial court, as I argued in my brief. At oral argument, the first line of questioning for the insurer was the standard of review. Two weeks after oral argument, we received the decision affirming and noting that the attack was not on the legal correctness of how the instruction was worded, but whether there was evidence to support the instruction. Several weeks later my clients received their check satisfying the judgment. It was that mindful, nonjudgmental ability to step back and examine the arguments objectively that helped foster that success in the appeal.

The third incident is my favorite because it shows what compassion and mindfulness can do. By this time, I was a new judge. One of our duties is to hear unemployment appeals, most often from claimants for unemployment compensation who are representing themselves. In Arizona, these are discretionary appeals which we can simply decline. One of my first such appeals was from a woman employee who was a foreign national legally in the United States. When her papers were approaching their expiration date, she timely submitted her renewal application after having worked legally in the country for years. Due to a government delay, her papers expired while the application was pending. And as luck would have it, she then lost her job and sought unemployment compensation. The total claim was not a lot to you or me, but to this blue collar worker, it was important. The agency denied her claim on the theory that until she ultimately received her renewed papers, she was not eligible to work in the country and therefore not eligible for unemployment compensation.

If my law clerk and I had simply followed that logic, we would have recommended declining jurisdiction. But we stepped back from the issue and simply thought about it from different perspectives. This could not be the law or the law is a ass.[161] There must be some federal policy that would have allowed this woman to obtain work while she was waiting for her papers to be renewed and thus be eligible for compensation. Our moderate research found nothing. So we thought, "There must be a government policy on the net dealing with this." So, we went to the federal agency website and started looking for any leads. Ultimately, we opened up an employers' manual and . . . voila, there it was. In exactly this situation, an employer who wanted to hire the applicant could apply for a waiver and temporary papers until the renewal came in.

Now, what to do with our new-found knowledge? The normal course would have been to accept the appeal and allow briefs to be filed. Of course, neither the pro per claimant nor the state would have been alerted to this policy. Time for more stepping outside the box. Why not issue an order to show cause why we should not reverse, citing the regulation and policy, and ask the state to respond. It had never been done before but there was no rule against it. The panel liked the idea and the show cause order went out. Two weeks later, the state filed a confession of error and asked us to vacate the decision and remand to allow the woman to be paid. Satisfaction from a professional and personal level.

TAKING IT TO THE NEXT STEP—THE SEARCH FOR JOYOUSNESS

All of these lessons are great for the practice of law. But what about a deeper sense of harmony and peace in everyday life (as we know it)? One more anecdote, because it is relevant to finding a sense of joy and I love this one. After reading Julian Jaynes' *The Origins of Consciousness in the Breakdown of the Bicameral Mind*,[162] I started realizing that many things that appear real are only real based on our mental perspective and it was important to try to get out of that perspective.[163] With the encouragement

---

161. *See* JAMES.E. CLAPP ET AL., LAWTALK: THE UNKNOWN STORIES BEHIND FAMILIAR LEGAL EXPRESSIONS 153-56 (2011) (discussing the origins of the phrase "the law is a ass," tracing it back to an obscure 17th century English play *Revenge for Honour* as well as to Charles Dickens' more famous use of the phrase in *Oliver Twist*).

162. JULIAN JAYNES, THE ORIGINS OF CONSCIOUSNESS IN THE BREAKDOWN OF THE BICAMERAL MIND (1976).

163. One of Jaynes' theories is that early humans really did hear voices. But the voices were one hemisphere of the brain sending signals to the other hemisphere. Without anyone

of my wife, a practicing clinical psychologist, I started reading more about Buddhism and meditation, attending retreats and practicing meditation on a regular basis.

One episode of both the intellectual and metaphysical haunts me still. I have decided that every year (as long as I can afford it), I will take a week and go to Hawaii to refresh my batteries. More often than not, my wife does not go. I meditate, swim, practice yoga, and reflect. I rent a small cottage on the windward side of Oahu that is not near any tourist spots but is right on the ocean. A simple, but comfortable house where I can read, meditate, watch the sun rise and feel the wind and breathe fresh air. Okay, being one with everything around me, as trite as that might sound.

On one trip, I arrived and it had just rained. I parked my car by the small grocery near the house and in a puddle was a bird bathing itself. Not just bathing, but if birds can be joyous, this bird was. Splashing in the puddle, feeling the water on its head and back. A wonderful, quiet moment of joy.

But it gets better. The next day I went to a yoga co-op about forty minutes away from the cottage just outside of Haleiwa on the north shore of Oahu. I was the oldest person in the class (by at least a decade) and we did some flow and restoration poses. For those of you who know yoga, imagine holding pigeon pose for five minutes. Well, at first the stretches were pretty intense, but then I started seeing in my mind's eye that joyous bird. Then my mind went from the moment to seeing my first grandson (who was about eighteen months old at that point) and was a joyous child, to finding almost everything (including me) hilarious and great to laugh at. I start thinking, when do we lose that joyousness? After yoga, I went back to the cottage (to recover) and happened to be reading a book by a psychiatrist talking about the interface between Buddhism and clinical psychiatry.[164] Suddenly, without any forewarning, I turned the page and he posed the question, "When do we first lose that simple joyousness we had as a child?" Coincidence? Maybe, but I have my doubts. While the author had what to my layman's mind was a reasonable psychological answer, I

---

else around and not recognizing the inner voice or sense of self, early humans concluded they were hearing from gods. As the cross-hemispheric signals declined, a sense of self increased, but humans kept looking for that god.

164. MARK EPSTEIN, THOUGHTS WITHOUT A THINKER (Basic Books 1995).

was more interested in identifying that loss and finding ways to recover it. I have even had the nerve to ask my wife, my colleagues, and friends to think about when and why they lost that sense of childlike joy.

Where this has led me is to consciously take the time to just be joyous in the present moment with a nonreflective, nonjudgmental sense of wonder. Maybe it is the face or laughter of my first grandson (now four) listening to the Gummy Bear song. Or my second grandson following his brother around. Maybe it is watching my wife's eyes and hearing her voice as she thinks out loud about her life and practice. Maybe it is feeling a rare cool breeze or experiencing a cloudy day in Phoenix. Maybe it is sitting with a number of other lawyers interested in meditation and the mindfulness movement and simply exalting in their insights. Or maybe it is watching a lawyer argue before me and wondering what the lawyer was like as a nine-year old. Try it sometime. It may be refreshing and bring a sense of joy into your life.

One L Redux

ADRIEN KATHERINE WING

As I write, I sit where it all began—the library of Stanford Law School. It was the fall of 1979 when I came to this building for the first time. I was excited and nervous like any first year law student, but felt that I was ready for the challenge. After all, I had had a fine education growing up, starting with six years in college preparatory school. I had attended the Mary Beard School for Girls in Orange, New Jersey, for three years, and then graduated with honors from Newark Academy in Livingston. I had swept through Princeton, graduating *magna cum laude* in Political Science with a certificate of concentration in "Afro-American Studies," now called African American Studies. I had doubled up my course load and graduated with a Master's degree in African Studies from UCLA in one year—earning all As, even while learning a new language, Swahili.

I knew how to flourish in difficult conditions. At Newark Academy, I was one of the first forty-nine girls in a 200 year-old boys' school. I was one of the few black Americans. At Princeton, I was also in one of the early classes of women and black Americans. My peers were drawn substantially from the same kinds of people who attended Newark Academy. I was able to excel despite my double minority status as a black and a female. I was used to white people not knowing what to make of me. On the other hand, since I was surrounded by them, and immersed in their culture and values all the time, I understood them very well, especially WASP, Italian, and Jewish elites.

I felt that many whites of whatever background looked down on people like me. Some were overtly racist. Some were unconsciously condescending. After all, in their eyes, I was from a stereotypic black single parent family. I grew up in Orange, a poor suburb near Newark, which was a broken city known for racial riots and high crime. My mother, however, was not a stereotypic "welfare queen." Katherine Pruitt Wing was a high school teacher, and all her siblings were educators. While we did not own stock, take fancy vacations, or have lawyers in our family, my mom sacrificed everything so I could become a third generation college graduate. This was a rare achievement for any family—black or white. My late father, John E. Wing, Jr., had been a Phi Beta Kappa alumnus of UCLA, and had graduated second in his class at N.Y.U. Medical School.

I had read *One L* as part of my preparation for law school. I gobbled it up in a day. It scared me, but I was also grateful to author Scott Turow for bringing the law school world to life, especially for those of us without prior exposure. I had heard that Stanford Law was much more laid back than Harvard Law, where I had also been admitted. As a native Californian, it seemed clear that sun and Napa Valley were a better option than cold haughty Cambridge, Massachusetts. The *One L* description of 140 students per section was not the way I wanted to learn.

At Stanford, I was part of an experimental curriculum B, designed by Paul Brest and other faculty.[165] We were to do simulations of cases. We were to take Law and Economics in the first year. We were to bond together in new ways. Additionally, I was part of the largest number of blacks in Stanford Law's history. There were fourteen of us in the 1L group! The prior class only had five. It was all so exhilarating! I couldn't wait to crack open my beautiful heavy new books and try to decipher the arcane language. My preparation had even included three years of junior high school Latin.

Little would anyone in my Stanford class of '82 imagine, and little would I imagine that I, Adrien Wing, of east coast and west coast, would end up with five sons in Iowa, of all places. Little would anyone imagine that I would be a law professor for thirty years in Iowa. Little would anyone imagine that I would become known for gender theory and for Middle

---

165. *See* Laura O'Hara, *Chronology of Stanford Law School, 1885-2005*, at 16 (2005), https://www-cdn.law.stanford.edu/wp-content/uploads/2015/05/by_OHara_Chronology_of_Stanford_Law_School_1885-2005.pdf.

East affairs—two subjects I knew nothing about in 1979. As a matter of fact, I am here now at Stanford to do a talk on Muslim women's rights for the Black Law Students Association (BLSA). Posters with my picture were plastered all over the building. I wondered what the predominantly white male alums that were there for reunions thought of these posters? Muslim women were not a subject of discussion back in my law school days. Someone who looked like me would not have been a speaker back then.

As I sit in this library again and think back to my 1L year, I would like to be able to tell you that I thrived—that I loved it—that it was the culmination of my wonderful educational experiences. Unfortunately, it would be a lie. I hated law school. I hated it—unlike any other level of education I had undergone. Stanford Law in 1979 was more like Harvard *One L* than I had thought it would be. At that stage, I was not sure what was wrong. I was confused. I was traumatized. I was numb. All my life, I had been a talker. I was never short for words in any level of schooling. Suddenly, I was mute. I was speechless—dreading, fearing that I would be called on and expected to perform in a game where I did not understand the rules. If I were found wanting, it might be that the white males would think all people of my race or gender were lacking. If one of them failed to handle the grilling, it would just be regarded as his personal failure.

It would not be until my 2L and 3L years that I would truly find my voice again. I enjoyed taking courses I could select such as Law in Radically Different Cultures. I would later teach this course at Iowa. I joined the *Stanford Journal of International Law* and the International Law Society. I did an externship at the United Nations and clerked for a Beverly Hills entertainment law firm the first summer, and an international law firm in New York the second summer. As head of the Southern African Task Force for National Black American Law Students Association (BALSA), the previous name of BLSA, I even got to go to Angola, and later Tanzania and Zimbabwe. I was involved with the campus-wide anti-apartheid efforts and would later win the Stanford African Student Association Prize.

That first year, I was excited to learn that I would have female professors. I think that there were only two in the law school. One was a new prof named Deborah Rhode. She had even clerked for Supreme Court Justice Thurgood Marshall. My heart sank when I saw her the first day. She looked like a small child. She could not be the professor, I thought. But as soon as she opened her mouth, this tiny little person took command of the room. By the end of class, I knew that she was just as tough as any male professor. It was not until I studied feminist theory years later that I realized that I had let Rhode's physical appearance lead me into stereotyped thinking about her. She should have looked like an adult. Also, as a female, she should have been a soft and fuzzy nurturer, but she was not. Yet, I was insulted when whites or males had stereotyped impressions of me as a black female.

While Rhode was not warm and fuzzy, I did come to admire her greatly. Barbara Babcock was my other female prof, and she was a nurturer. I learned that you could not essentialize the entire female faculty. They varied as much as the males. I just wish that there had been more of them.

I was subsequently put on a committee that interviewed a potential female faculty member. She seemed wonderful to me with my limited knowledge of how things worked in the faculty hiring area. Clearly, the professors on the committee were not impressed with her scholarship in feminist legal theory. She was not quite up to snuff. Her name was Catharine MacKinnon. I later came to know and admire her work and was her colleague while I was a visiting professor at Michigan Law School many years later. In my view, it was a great loss for Stanford not to accept her into its ranks.

At first, it did not appear that there were any black faculty at Stanford, which was what I expected. Blacks, like women, were just breaking into the academy. I never had a black teacher in high school, but had loved several of my black professors at Princeton such as Mike Mitchell and Howard Taylor. They were my life lines and had become great mentors. Later, I came to find out that the olive-complected labor law expert, Bill Gould, was not Jewish. He was black. While some black students to this day do not realize that this emeritus professor was the first black faculty member at Stanford, I discovered him back then and he became my life line as well. He would become a mentor, and has even spoken at Iowa several times.

One of the worst experiences during my first year occurred in Constitutional Law. It was soon after the *Bakke* affirmative action decision, forbidding quotas at U.C. Davis Medical School, but permitting goals to achieve racial diversity.[166] The class discussion was highly charged. The few blacks

---

166. *See* Regents of Univ. of Cal. v. Bakke, 438 U.S. 265 (1978).

in the room felt under attack. One of the white students decried the *Bakke* result permitting affirmative action. He was upset by the fact that his white friend had not gotten into the NASA astronaut program because it had let in some black people—subtext—unworthy black people.

During my whole educational and professional life, I have taken great pride in conducting myself in a pleasant manner, maintaining my "cool" publicly despite provocations. This class was one time that I lost it. I broke my usual classroom silence. I said that I had no sympathy for my classmate's friend because the first black astronauts admitted by NASA were extraordinarily well qualified individuals by any standard. I remember that these pioneers included Dr. Guion Bluford, an Air Force pilot who had served in Vietnam. He held a Doctorate of Philosophy in Aerospace Engineering with a minor in laser physics.[167]

Another unspoken current in the room was that we blacks, who were the largest group in Stanford's history, were also unworthy. I remember being insulted. Ten of us were from the Ivy League or Stanford. Another black classmate, Betty Meshack, was the first from a black college, Spelman. Another one, Jaye Young, was a child prodigy, the youngest person in the class at age nineteen. Another classmate, Ronald Noble, was from the University of New Hampshire. He would go on to join the Law Review, become student bar and class president, clerk on the Third Circuit, become an N.Y.U. law professor, and is now the first American head of Interpol in Lyon, France. Yes, indeed, we were an inferior bunch!

At that moment in Con Law class, I felt I was alone defending the black race. Afterwards, there were some classmates who congratulated me for my bold words. Some wished that they had had the courage to speak up as well. There were others who felt I had gone beyond what was permissible in academic discourse. I was a rabble rouser, a bomb thrower, a crazy person—exactly what Stanford Law did not need.

Today, I don't remember which student made the point that set me off. I have thought about how that person might have felt when the first black female astronaut was named years later, Dr. Mae Jemison, a fellow Stanford alum. I wonder how does he feel that we have a black president of the United States? Does he think Barack Obama is one of those unqualified

---

167. *See* NASA, Biographical Data, Guion S. Bluford, Jr. (Colonel, USAF, Ret.), NASA Astronaut (Former), http://www.jsc.nasa.gov/Bios/htmlbios/bluford-gs.html.

blacks who took the rightful place of John McCain? Does he think Barack
Obama is an exception since he is half white and half African, not a black
American at all? Maybe he loves our new president. Does that section mate
even remember that class at all?

I needed intellectual assistance if I was to survive the 1L year. I found
a breath of fresh air when I attended one of the early conferences of Critical Legal Studies (CLS).[168] My Crim Law professor Mark Kelman was a
bigwig in the CLS movement. While it was very difficult as a 1L to understand the high theory jargon that the Critters were using, I knew that
they were on to something. The law was not neutral and objective as our
classes seemed to assume. The reasoning in the case holdings was not the
only reasoning possible. The law was mainly concerned with protecting
the rights of the descendants of our founding fathers—white rich men.
The law had no soul.

The day that the light began to click on was in Contracts with John
Barton. He was the kindest, sweetest instructor, yet I could not understand clearly what was happening until the day we covered the doctrine
of unconscionability in the *Williams v. Walker-Thomas Furniture Co.*
case.[169] Finally, there was something I could really grasp. I knew from the
fact pattern that the rights of a black person were involved. Washington,
D.C., resident Ora Lee Williams had all of her furniture repossessed by
the furniture company because of a provision that kept a balance due
open on all previously purchased items until all items were fully paid off.
My voice returned. I spoke up in support of the doctrine of unconscionability voiding such contracts. The professor said, "Yes, that's right!" I
glowed.

I re-read *One L* in preparation for writing this essay. I even had all of
my Iowa research assistants read it. What is shocking to me and to some of
them is how little legal education has changed in thirty years.

I now understand quite clearly all the things that disturbed me about
One L and the first year of law school, and the rest of legal education as
well. I fear that we are still preparing lawyers for the 19th or 20th century.
I have a few suggestions that might help haul us into the 21st century.

---

168. *See, e.g.*, MARK KELMAN, A GUIDE TO CRITICAL LEGAL STUDIES (1987).
169. Williams v. Walker-Thomas Furniture Co., 350 F.2d 445 (D.C. Cir. 1965).

First, I think that our instruction would benefit from exposure to educational theory and instruction in how to teach. While the MacCrate,[170] Stuckey,[171] and Carnegie[172] reports on legal education have raised questions and identified problems, nothing has penetrated into the curriculum from these reports the way that the Socratic dialogue first introduced in law schools in the 1870s has.[173] At Princeton, I had earned a high school teaching certificate to teach social studies. The process involved taking classes concerning learning theory as well as actual student teaching while under observation. We let smart young lawyers into classrooms with no required training at all. In law school, new profs can work on their class notes during the summer before starting, but no one will actually teach them how to teach or observe them teaching or teach them anything about how Generation X and Y think and learn before letting them loose on the students. Perhaps students would benefit from having clickers where everyone would answer certain questions raised by the professor on an anonymous basis. Perhaps they would learn more from doing presentations digging deeper into the backgrounds of the cases. Would they benefit pedagogically if they were evaluated by collaborative projects instead of three-hour closed book multiple choice exams?

To the extent that it still occurs, would eliminating intimidation or embarrassment enhance learning? I teach human rights, a field that did not exist in the 1870s when the case method and Socratic questioning were introduced. Would treating all 1Ls humanely enhance their learning? Could we maximize each student's potential in the most humane way possible by having them participate as adults worthy of respect, and not potential humiliation?

---

170. *See* AM. BAR ASS'N, MACCRATE REPORT, REPORT ON THE TASK FORCE ON LAW SCHOOLS AND THE PROFESSION (1992), https://www.americanbar.org/content/dam/aba/publications/misc/legal_education/2013_legal_education_and_professional_development_maccrate_report).authcheckdam.pdf.

171. *See* ROY STUCKEY, BEST PRACTICES FOR LEGAL EDUCATION (2007), http://clea-web.org/resources/bp.html.

172. *See* WILLIAM SULLIVAN ET AL., EDUCATING LAWYERS: PREPARATION FOR THE PROFESSION OF LAW (2007).

173. *See* ELIZABETH MERTZ, THE LANGUAGE OF LAW SCHOOL: LEARNING TO THINK LIKE A LAWYER 27 (2007).

Second, I think it would be very beneficial to infuse practical applications with theory in the 1L year. Curriculum B at Stanford enhanced the dry presentation of Civil Procedure by having us deal with a simulated case and its various components. I loved doing a deposition. I would have really enjoyed seeing an actual contract in the Contracts course. Imagine working through that contract and a master fact pattern throughout the semester to help understand the various doctrines.

I would expand the exposure to practical applications in the 1L and 2L years, and transform the third year into a mandatory clinical year, much as medical students are trained in their final two years. The clinical year could include client counseling, office management, and even discussions of how office politics operate. Mature lawyers know of many smart colleagues who failed to thrive because they never understood office politics.

As a matter of fact, all other countries mandate practical training for their future lawyers, sometimes during law school, and sometimes in clerkships that occur for up to two years after law school. We would never turn doctors lose upon the public without clinical training, so why do we continue to do so for our lawyers?

Third, I think that policy should be infused everywhere. Imagine an unconscionability discussion that would talk about race, class, and gender issues in contract formation and implementation. More generally, imagine exploring the politics, sociology, and economics behind decisions. Imagine if the 1L professor dared to say, "Many of us are hired guns who generally serve to keep the wealthy, very wealthy, and to resolve disputes in ways where money is god and justice has very little to do with it. Decisions often cannot be reconciled unless one understands the ideology of particular justices at particular historical points. There is nothing objective about this. You don't understand because certain things are not understandable unless you comprehend the politics involved. The decision changed because the justices changed—and they were not objective or neutral."

Justice is an issue that is often given short shrift in the 1L year. In an Introduction to Lawyering component, we could talk explicitly about justice. As a 1L, I would have craved that. On the international level, we could speak about the need for lawyers like South African former President Nelson Mandela who used his skills to fight for justice. We could mention Nobel Prize winning Iranian human rights lawyer Shirin Ebadi who continues to put her life and career on the line to challenge the denial of human rights for women. In Con Law, we could highlight the roles of NAACP lawyers Charles Hamilton Houston, and future justice Thurgood Marshall, who made legal arguments for justice for Negroes in *Brown v. Board of Education*.[174] We could talk about the young Asian American lawyers who got justice for their parents in the 1980s, who had been wrongfully interned during World War II.[175] For all these lawyers, law involved logic, but it also involved passion and channeling one's passion productively into legal arguments for justice.

An important extension of policy, passion, and justice is to instill the idea of service into 1Ls. We certainly did not have that during my first year. It would be my third year when I would become the eldest in a small group of Stanford students who created the East Palo Alto Community Law Project. It was later taken over by the Law School, which had no clinical offerings at that time. I am proud that Iowa has a Citizen Lawyer Program that has 1Ls involved in legal and non-legal service.

Fourth, I think that interweaving 1L courses could prepare students more effectively as well. Imagine a master fact pattern that could be applied in various ways throughout all the 1L courses the first semester. Imagine intersecting the Contracts unconscionability theory discussion with Con Law race discrimination. I would have benefitted greatly from such an approach.

As a professor, I have made an effort at interweaving courses. My colleague Steve Burton and I once co-taught a session with his Contracts class and my Race, Racism and American Law class. We discussed using state contracts law to pursue race discrimination claims based upon an article Steve had written.[176]

Fifth, as an international and comparative law specialist, I think it is essential to introduce global issues in the 1L year, and various schools have experimented in this regard. One small step is to have students choose an elective, and include international courses in the list of options. At Iowa, my human rights course is an elective for 1Ls. Those who have enrolled

---

174. Brown v. Board of Educ., 347 U.S. 483 (1954).

175. *See* JAPANESE AMERICANS: FROM RELOCATION TO REDRESS (Rogers Daniels et al. eds. 1986).

176. *See* Steven Burton, *Racial Discrimination in Contract Performance: Patterson and a State Law Alternative*, 25 HARV. C.R.–C.L. L. REV. 431 (1990).

in my course have told me that they were so grateful to be able to choose something they really cared about during the 1L year. I would have enjoyed this option as a student. Another step is to mandate a global course during the first year. When I visited at Michigan Law School, they had introduced Transnational Law for all 1Ls. I would have really treasured this course, and appreciated the message it sent to the whole class about the importance of global issues. A more difficult step is to discuss international issues in all the 1L courses. Some textbooks now have internationally oriented material in the notes. Yet, a professor with limited time and no background might easily skip this material.

One way to incorporate international issues for all students would be to mandate study abroad. Many universities are trying to enhance this possibility for students on all levels. Once again, I would have really appreciated this option as early as the 1L year. Imagine at winter break, winter term, spring break, or just after the spring semester ended, studying comparative contract law. Do other nations have the notion of unconscionability?

I have been the director of Iowa's summer program in Arcachon, France, for ten years. Most of the students who have attended have just finished the first year, and can really appreciate comparative constitutional law. During summer 2009, my colleague Angela Onwuachi-Willig exposed the abroad program students to affirmative action in various jurisdictions.

As I conclude the first draft of this essay, many of the books that surround me in this library appear little changed since 1979. Are they just for decoration? Do many law students actually borrow any of these books anymore? Aren't many things increasingly online? Shouldn't we aim to get everything online so it is accessible to everyone all the time?

I wonder if my grandson will face substantially the same law school training as I did in 1979, as my nephew did as a 1L in 2009?

The BLSA students I spoke to here look like those of forty years ago. The 1Ls still had the deer in the headlights look. The 2Ls and 3Ls appeared jaded. I had found the 1980 yearbook in the library that includes the BLSA photo from my 1L year. I looked so young, so innocent. I am standing next to a wise 3L, Clarence Otis. He turned out all right. He was the CEO of Darden Foods, owners of Olive Garden and Red Lobster. Today, BLSA is concerned with many of the same issues that we were, including financial aid and faculty hiring. While there are now more black male faculty than in 1979, there are no black female faculty. The students seem surprised to learn that we have four black female tenured full professors at Iowa.

I told the students that I was doing this essay. I was delighted that I had the time to reflect back, while I was at my alma mater. When they asked what I thought now about the 1L year, about law school in general, I said, "Despite the pain and agony, I would do it all again. I have learned that the law can have soul. The law can have heart. And I hope that in my teaching, I have shown generations of students that this *must* be so."